Teacher Research and Urban Literacy Education

Lessons and Conversations in a Feminist Key

Teacher Research and Urban Literacy Education

Lessons and Conversations in a Feminist Key

Sandra Hollingsworth

with

Anthony Cody
Jennifer Davis-Smallwood
Mary Dybdahl
Patricia Gallagher
Margaret Gallego
Theodora Maestre
Leslie Turner Minarik
Lisa Raffel
N. Suzanne Standerford
Karen Manheim Teel

Afterword by D. Jean Clandinin

Teachers College, Columbia University
New York and London

Published by Teachers College Press, 1234 Amsterdam Avenue, New York, N.Y. 10027

Grateful acknowledgment is made for permission to reprint the following:

"Close My Eyes" by Gloria Estefan. Copyright © 1990 Foreign Imported Productions & Publications Inc. (BMI). Used by permission of CPP/Belwin, Inc., Miami, FL. All Rights Reserved.
"From a Distance" by Julie Gold. Copyright © 1987 Wing and Wheel Music & Julie Gold Music (BMI). All Rights on behalf of Wing and Wheel Music administered by Irving Music, Inc. Used by permission of CPP/Belwin, Inc., Miami, FL. All Rights Reserved.
"The Perpetual Migration" from *The Moon Is Always Female* by Marge Piercy. Copyright © 1980 by Marge Piercy. Reprinted by permission of Alfred A. Knopf, Inc.
"Our Houses" reprinted from *Seeing Through the Sun,* by Linda Hogan (Amherst: University of Massachusetts Press, 1985), copyright © 1985 by Linda Hogan.
"Listen" by Linda Lancione Moyer. Reprinted with permission. Copyright © 1986 Christianity & Crisis, 537 W. 121st Street, New York, NY 10027.
"Here Comes the Sun" by George Harrison © 1969 Harrisongs Ltd. International Copyright Secured. All Rights Reserved.

Library of Congress Cataloging-in-Publication Data

Hollingsworth, Sandra.
    Teacher research and urban literacy education : lessons and
conversations in a feminist key / Sandra Hollingsworth with Anthony
Cody . . . [et al.] : afterword by D. Jean Clandinin.
        p.   cm.
    Includes bibliographical references (p.   ) and index
    ISBN 0-8077-3364-4 (alk. paper). — ISBN 0-8077-3363-6 (pbk. :
alk. paper)
    1. Language arts. 2. Education, Urban, 3. Action research in
education. 4. Feminism and education. 5. Teachers—Training of.
I. Cody, Anthony. II. Title.
LB1576.H627   1994
372.6—dc20   93-48148

ISBN 0-8077-3363-6 (paper)
ISBN 0-8077-3364-4 (cloth)

Printed on acid-free paper
Manufactured in the United States of America
01 00 99 98 97 96 95 94   8 7 6 5 4 3 2 1

Contents

Part II: Stories of Teacher Research

*Anthony Cody, Jennifer Davis-Smallwood, Mary Dybdahl, Margaret Gallego,
Sandra Hollingsworth, Leslie Turner Minarik, Lisa Raffel,
N. Suzanne Standerford, Karen Manheim Teel*

This book is dedicated to the spirit of

Miss Addie Maye Glover

a first teacher to four generations of kindergarteners in Texas—and to me.

PREFACE

If I could just close my eyes,
see just what I wanted to see,

it would be much easier to live this life
Thinkin' that it never really comes down to me . . . .

We could all close our eyes to all the things we know that are wrong
We could live selfishly protected lives
And never think about what we could have done.

Say it's not there, and maybe it will go away.
But the truth is it won't, down the line,
will be back again,

it will be back again . . . .

Gloria Estefan
"Close My Eyes"

How This Book Came to Be

This book begins with a narrative about a group of teachers and one of their teacher–educators who spent more than 6 years together learning to teach and conduct research on teaching. It ends with the transformation of the teacher–educator's research and practice as a result of our sustained conversations. Those of us who continued in the group until publication time of this book are named as authors on the cover: Anthony Cody, Mary Dybdahl, Sandra Hollingsworth, Leslie Turner Minarik, Lisa Raffel, Jennifer Davis-Smallwood, and Karen Manheim Teel. As is customary in a textual presentation, the narrative officially begins with chapter 1. However, as we met during a retreat to Karen Teel's cabin, in the Sierra Nevada mountains, to consolidate and summarize our stories, we thought it was important to create a preface to describe how the book came to be written.

In preparation for this volume, all of us (except Lisa) and some guests came together, at Karen's cabin, to look over our work, and weave together where we've been, with complex descriptions of where we are now. We took walks in the Douglas fir and cedar forests, enjoyed the company of Anthony Cody's partner, Kristin, and played with his baby, Alexander. We ate and talked and questioned. We read and reread and rewrote chapters of our story together, each using a different colored pen, each agreeing and disagreeing not only with the text of our earlier writings, which I (Sandra Hollingsworth, the teacher–educator) had compiled, but with each other's current comments and reactions as well. We have attempted to include all of our voices in this text with respect to our various standpoints and world views.

For example, we found that we were deeply connected by our passion and commitment to public urban education in schools characterized by ethnic diversity, limited economic resources, and locations in high crime areas. For various deeply personal reasons, we could not close our eyes to such situations. As we reflected on our common educational interest, we also realized that we had come to that commonality in various ways. I grew up a magnolia-white European American, in the deep south, with a keen sense of the inequalities between my outwardly privileged life and the internal (and secret) hell of my devalued self. I saw other such inequalities in the African-American children who, as sons and daughters of our family maids, were my close friends and playmates, but who were not allowed to come to my birthday parties, attend better-equipped schools, or swim in the public pools.

Leslie Turner Minarik originally came into urban school work—not from a sense of commitment—but because an urban district offered her the first contract. However, she still resides there. She has grown to love the challenges of working in urban settings, the passion and relationships she's developing with the variously experienced children, the personal sense of self that those challenges help her face. Leslie and Mary Dybdahl both dropped out of the corporate world to become midcareer teachers. Mary remembered the pain of her own discrimination as the child of working class parents and the difficulty she had in acquiring school literacy. She chose to work in urban areas to make some difference in that pattern both for others' sake as well as her own personal healing. Lisa came to teaching from a long association with the global peace movement. Jennifer Davis-Smallwood had lived through the personal discrimination of being African-American in a Caucasian public school setting, and had a lot to give, as well as to learn. Anthony, who had been active in organizing fellow teacher education candidates around issues of equity, brought his commitment to social justice to the classroom. Karen, through her years of teaching, reading, and world travel, had acquired a sense of mission and possibility for those less economically fortunate.

Because of our differing backgrounds, but also our common passions, we found issues about learning to teach in urban settings about which we could argue, laugh, research, and "resolve" over and over again across our continuing relationship. For example, while (I think) most of us converge at least in the spirit of feminist perspectives to our work, which I will expli-

cate in the text, two points are important to note: (1) we have jointly constructed these understandings through our experiences, research, and conversations; and (2) we come from different standpoints on the degree of
congruence with feminist epistemology in the way that I, as the story narrator, have explicated it in the text. Lisa, Leslie, Jennifer, and Mary have
come to basically agree with my position.* Karen is less comfortable with
the term "feminist." She does not want our choice of language to alienate
those in power that we might influence with this work. While we understand the political importance and caring stance of Karen's position, others of us worry less about upsetting others than providing a language that
will reach other women and teachers who have previously been alienated
from more socially polite texts. I also want to retain the spirit of our varying feminist views to both validate other teachers' experiences and celebrate the work of those pioneering women and men who want all experiences and occupations valued in this culture, and who are brave enough to
risk personal rejection to do so. Anthony identifies himself easily as a feminist, and is conscious of the role he plays as a white male teacher in a predominantly female profession. He often reminds us that feminist positions
readily transcend issues of gender.

Inside and outside of Karen's cabin, we dealt head-on with issues of
race, class, and gender. We spent a great deal of time talking about how to
characterize the differences between ourselves (as variously privileged individuals) and the urban public school environments in which we work and
study and learn to teach. As you'll read in chapter 3, everyone except me
vehemently rejected the descriptor of "lower class" to describe our school
communities. I wanted to speak clearly about the class differences that are
usually silenced in discussions of teacher education. The others felt the
term was nonfeminist, hierarchical, and discriminatory. As we talked, we
came to appreciate each other's points of view, and even shifted a little,
though we never found a common language to express our ideas. Most of
us consented to speak of ourselves as coming from "middle-classed" environments, and a few of us thought the school environments in which we
taught were variously "other-classed."**

---

* Mary explained: "I have identified myself as a feminist for most of my adult life.
Through this group, I have come to see the importance of articulating this way of thinking as a valid and important way to approach teaching."

** Jennifer wrote, "Yuck!" beside those phrases. Karen wrote: "I don't remember
deciding this. I still vote for middle class and poor." Mary clarified her position: "I
voted for working class, but Jennifer's comment is more accurate." Jennifer added:
"What we mean is that we are living fairly economically secure lives, and the students
with whom we worked were those with limited economic resources. The term "lower
class" describes the environments they live in, not the people themselves."

Jennifer and I felt that the children in these "other-classed and raced" communities were lucky. Not only did they avoid some of the pitfalls of being mainstream "middle-classed," they had a breadth of view from other-classed experiences that could not be eradicated by their schooling. These children see themselves as full and rich in many ways that others of us could not see. We suggested that perhaps middle-class children who do well at learning to work within the school system and to see the world primarily in rich/poor, good/bad dichotomies are not so lucky.*

In short, the discussion about class, race, privilege, and luck was an uncomfortable one. All the others in our group disagreed with Jennifer and me.** Mary, whose position in a year-round school required her to teach the day following this discussion, felt the need to withdraw from the intense conversation and return to something concrete. Finding our extended discussion both depressing and distracting from her business at hand, she folded laundry and made lesson plans, while the rest of us continued to talk about our varied understandings of the communities from which we came and in which we taught.

Though readers of this narrative will not find a restful order or consensus in our words, what is present is an attempt to include all of our perspectives, with all of their complexities and ambiguities. (Mostly,) we haven't worried about our lack of consensus or answers in our work. As our relationships developed, we became aware that "whenever a story appears unified or whole, something must have been suppressed in order to sustain the appearance of unity" (Flax, 1990, p. 37). Though we try to summarize what we have learned, readers will not find prescriptions for learning to teach or conducting classroom research in urban settings in this text, nor solutions for the struggle of teaching in a profession that (in this country) is one of the least respected and valued. However, readers should come to realize that we all learned to teach in relationship to each other as well as from other scholars, friends, and companions in our world, with and from students in the classroom. While my voice is admittedly too

---

* Lisa added: "I agree that poverty doesn't equal bad and wealth doesn't equal good (poor kids don't grow up seeing the world in such dichotomies), but, I fear this glosses over the tragedies of poverty." Jennifer responded to Lisa's comment: "But we're not talking strictly about poverty here. We're speaking of viewing the world through other than white, middle America's eyes."

** Leslie rethought her position after reading this text: "I remember our discussion there and the sense of being at odds, because the notion of 'lucky' in that context had not occurred to me. I change my mind now. As is often the case, Jennifer's words and the story she told then about a 'lucky' child to clarify her position has reverberated in my mind, and I have come to understand this position and to look at my students in a new way."

strong as the primary narrator of our journey, we have made genuine attempts to value all the colliding and shifting standpoints we all bring to this text. Mary, Jennifer, and Leslie have added notes to comfort teachers who will struggle with some of my academic language.

In any case, this book is clearly a labor of love, of friendship, of intimate conversation. We appreciate the support of our families, friends, and colleagues toward this increasingly widening conversation. We want to acknowledge the love and encouragement of Kristin, Woody, Skip, Liane, Katie, Deborah, George, Sarah, Ruth, Ellen, Chris, Gena, Jeff, Jose, Steve and Jim. We appreciate the care with which Patty Noell at Michigan State transcribed our tape recorded conversations for further reflection. We are grateful to Jan Knight at MSU for fearlessly tracking down permissions so that this text could be punctuated with music and poetry. We were fortunate to have the commitment of our editor, Brian Ellerbeck, to our project and to "the project" to educate all children. As readers, you may agree with us, find comfort or anger in our words and experiences, you may challenge us and/or extend our vision. We expect you will do all and more. In the spirit of optimism we feel about the potential for conversation (both literally and metaphorically) in the renewal of teacher education, and the vital importance in becoming aware of the variously configured opportunities for students in public school, we ask you to remember your own stories, and notice your own biases, emotions, and knowledges; then step away and move back into our conversations as openly as we have attempted to express them. We welcome your respectful critique.

Acknowledgments: Funding for this project came from several sources: The Office of Educational Research and Improvement Office (OERI) , Grant No. 6008720227; School-University Partnership for Educational Renewal, University of California, Berkeley; Center for the Learning and Teaching of Elementary Subjects, Institute for Research on Teaching, Michigan State University, OERI Cooperative Agreement No. G0087C0226; and the Learning to Teach Foundation, Lafayette, CA.

Sandra (Sam) Hollingsworth
Following a retreat at Karen's cabin
July 11–12, 1992

I

Introductory Conversation and Critique

1

Sustained Conversation

AN ALTERNATIVE APPROACH TO THE
STUDY AND PROCESS OF LEARNING TO TEACH

Once a month for more than 6 years, I met with five beginning elementary school teachers and two secondary teachers for dinner and conversation about learning to teach.[1] These teachers were part of a federally funded longitudinal study on learning to teach literacy that began with their preservice teacher education programs at a graduate school of education in 1986. They were asked to continue because they remained in the local area as they began their professional careers, and were roughly representative of the cultural, biographical, grade-level, and school-site differences of the full complement of 28 teachers across three cohorts and two programs. They did not join me because they wanted to conduct research or construct theory. They came because of genuine needs arising from their practices.

At graduation, most of these teachers from suburban backgrounds took jobs in unfamiliar environments of urban schools. Even those who took jobs in suburban settings were usually given the most difficult and diverse classes. In both cases, the new teachers found many variations from the middle-class school norms in which they were educated. They welcomed a chance to meet, exchange ideas, and get feedback on their work. They valued the opportunity to support each other through the upward spiral of learning to teach, with all the pain, confusion, regression, joy, and integration embedded in the process.

Part I of this book describes the collaborative and sustained conversation that began in our monthly meetings, with regard to the issues raised

3

about teaching literacy in urban environments—*and* the process of making sense of those issues.[2] Part II illustrates conversations about the teachers' research of those issues in their classrooms and the political implications of their research, while Part III details the changes in my role as a teacher–educator as a result of learning from the conversations. *My* intent in telling the story of our work together is threefold: (1) to contribute to an epistemological understanding of learning to teach in urban settings arising from problems of practice; (2) to suggest broadening the "curriculum" of teacher education in literacy; and (3) to raise questions about how teacher–educators can most appropriately facilitate and study beginning teachers' learning.

THE CONCEPT OF COLLABORATIVE CONVERSATION

The idea of simply talking together about the concerns of practice as both a method of longitudinal research and a means of support in learning to teach was inspired by these teachers' criticisms of the support structures offered through traditional teacher education formats such as course work and supervision. As one of their reading methods instructors, I had heard their critiques firsthand. I learned that, although they both appreciated and came to believe the academic theories on learning and literacy promoted by their programs, they also felt a lack of connection between formal teacher education settings, their personal beliefs about teaching, and their particular classroom problems. None of this is new information to students and schools of teacher education.

One aspect of that scenario may, however, be new or unfamiliar to many of us. The experiences of teaching practice in urban schools were also not unlike those of women in a world dominated by men and "male" ideology: These teachers were aware of a need to learn previously established rules for social and professional survival as educators, yet sensed that many of the "norms" they were expected to adopt both devalued their own knowledge and excluded their potential contributions (see Westkott, 1979). In short, most of these teachers perceived their teacher education programs as providing too many predetermined answers from theory that failed to include their experiences, and not enough questions.* Thus our group attempted a different approach—in the form of regular social meet-

---

* Karen Teel was an exception to this characterization. Commenting on a draft of this chapter, she wrote: "I never felt that way as a teacher. Maybe I was lucky—or an exception to the norm?"

ings where questions could be posed, and issues involved in learning to teach could be raised and investigated. The change was both methodological and philosophical: I hoped to better understand beginning teachers' learning while providing a supportive structure for its development through the difficult early years.

Politically, the move to the conversational format for support and research involved a shift in power from my previous role as these teachers' course instructor (see Foucault, 1980). I had to change my interactions so that I was no longer telling teachers what I knew (as the group's "expert" on the topic of literacy instruction) and checking to see if they learned my knowledge, to a process of working with them as a colearner and creator of evolving expertise through nonevaluative conversation. To accomplish that shift, I had to get still and listen; I also had to struggle publicly with what I was learning. In evaluating my success in facilitating their learning to teach, I could no longer only look at "them" and "their cognitive changes." Our change in relationship now required that I look at transformation in my own learning as a researcher and as a teacher–educator as equally important in determining the success of *teachers'* knowledge transformations. Thus, traditional assumptions about teaching and learning in college classrooms were challenged. Questions about "who teaches" and "who learns" as well as "what is taught" and "what is learned" had to be negotiated.

The conversational approach to learning to teach involved environmental aspects that supported the political and philosophical nature of our work. Similar to Freire's (1988) notion that education includes yet moves beyond the physical dimensions of schooling, the social context of our dinner meetings allowed all of us to take the floor as "experts" in special areas of interest and teaching. The safety of our continuing relationship provided many occasions for raising questions, for sharing the passion and frustration of what we were learning in our own voices, and for confronting our anger about our silence and lack of appropriate support in other settings. Since the ambiguity of our explorations was unsettling, I searched for literature that would place our group's ambiguity within a larger world view. I found some comfort, for example, in reading Jane Flax's descriptions of the uncertainty that accompanies the current or "postmodern" era:

> Western intellectuals cannot be immune from the profound shifts now taking place in contemporary social life. These transformations have deeply disrupted many philosophers' self-understanding and sense of certainty. One of the paradoxical consequences of this breakdown is that the more the fault lines in previously unproblematic ground become apparent, the more frightening it appears to be without

ground, the more we want to have some ways of understanding what is happening, and the less satisfactory the existing ways of thinking about experience become. All this results in a most uncomfortable form of intellectual vertigo to which appropriate responses are not clear. It is increasingly difficult even to begin to know how to comprehend what we are thinking and experiencing. (Flax, 1990, p. 6)

To work inside such postmodern dilemmas, we, like Flax, turned to conversation as a medium for understanding our experiences. Because of our ongoing relationship, the talk in our meetings did not usually take the form of *dialogue*—similar to the conversation in a play or novel, which appears to have two or more voices, but which actually comes from one author's perspective. Nor was it simply a *discussion* of prearranged topics and readings through a formal discourse structure. Rather the collaborative and sustained *conversation* became the exchange and reformulation of ideas, intimate talk, and reconstructive questions. Given the mutually informed agenda that developed through this process, the extended conversation both identified and helped us understand our common stories about learning to teach. Our vague, almost subconscious questioning and tentative knowing about teaching school was thus elevated, voiced, and connected.

Our method of using collaborative conversation both as a means of learning and support for learning is not new. It finds support not only in ancient methods of teaching and learning from the Greek era of education, but also in recent theoretical work which suggests that personally meaningful knowledge is socially constructed through shared understandings (Vygotsky, 1978); in cultural feminism which emphasizes a holistic and collective orientation to world and work experiences (Gilman, 1988); in feminist epistemology which values considered experience as knowledge (Belenky, Clinchy, Goldberger, & Tarule, 1986); in feminist therapeutic psychology which embraces emotion as a means of learning about self and relationships (Schaef, 1981); in the intersections of psychoanalysis, feminist theories, and postmodern philosophies (Flax, 1990); and in the critical and contextually relevant nature of the social use of knowledge (Lorde, 1984; Zeichner & Gore, 1990). Illustrations of these perspectives, as they help to illuminate our own stories, occur throughout the book.

A FEMINIST APPROACH

Unlike the modern apprenticeship approach to teacher education which basically values and measures cognitive/academic knowledge as it is transmitted from experts to novices (e.g., the stance I had initially taken as a beginning teacher–educator, described in chapter 11), ours became a process of articulating an emerging feminist consciousness. This process validated and encouraged both the cognition and the rationality traditionally and problematically associated with "male" or "normative" epistemic processes, as well as the emotion, intuitive leaps, and other less verbalized feelings linked (and thus devalued) with "women's" or "others'" learnings. Our process was also therapeutically and publicly supportive of the personal changes that accompanied the changes in our knowledge. The method of studying our learning, therefore, could not take on a rational, analytic stance, nor could it "bracket" (or hold in abeyance) our personal biases from influencing the learning process (Schultz, 1967). Our conversational approach thus became a means of facilitating

> continuous interaction between how we understand the world and who we are as people. It shows how our emotional responses to the world change as we conceptualize it differently and how our changing emotional responses then stimulate us to new insights. . . . [It demonstrates] how the reconstruction of knowledge is inseparable from the reconstruction of ourselves. (Jaggar, 1989, p. 148)

The approach we developed to facilitate, learn from, and articulate the collaborative conversation is thus an *example* of feminist research. When we began this journey, we really did not know that it was. What we were doing felt "correct," but we didn't know what to name our method. My wide reading outside the group helped. For example, I read Harding (1987), who told us that feminist research could be characterized by three features.

> 1. Feminist research recognizes the epistemological value of using women's experiences as resources for discovering new theory. Instead of simply validating or uncovering "scientific truths" about mainstream cultures, feminist research asks questions which lead to social changes in oppressed conditions—usually those of women, but which can equally apply to men and children in underpowered life roles.

The context of this research site, beginning school teachers' worlds—where their voices have little impact on the shape of their professional lives—seemed to problematically encompass the feature of "women's experiences" in the broader sense.

> 2. The second feature of feminist research involves inquiry aimed at women's needs and, therefore, is related to the first.

This feature, too, seemed to fit our process. Since most of us were female, but also included males (even more than Anthony in the beginning) who supported values traditionally and problematically labeled "feminine" (see Laird, 1988), the gender-associated needs and values of beginning teachers in gaining support for learning to teach were central to our method.

> 3. Equal vulnerability is the third feature of feminist research. That is, the researcher must be cast in as critical a perspective as the researched. The investigator is not an invisible, anonymous voice of authority, but appears as a real, historical individual whose beliefs and behaviors must be open to critical examination.

Because many feminist analyses include similar features, they (like ours) are often uncomfortable. They "unsettle traditional assumptions about knowledge as they challenge familiar beliefs about women, men and social life" (Harding, 1987, p. 189).

Using these features, the feminist approach we came to adopt for our conversational method became a process through which we could less than comfortably critique the "norms" of teaching previously claimed through established epistemologies and research paradigms, revision of our own gendered, classed, racial, and other-identified norms in inclusive terms, and reinterpret the process of our epistemic development.* The danger, of course, in such a process is that we will be pulled by habit into premature closure to avoid the existential stress that accompanies uncertainty and announce new "grand theories" to replace those we've rejected. We worked very hard to avoid that solution to our discomfort. We were not always successful, as you'll notice in reading across the stories, but we tried. I, in particular, found it difficult to overcome years of training of jumping on evidence and claiming theory to "prove" what I already believed. But I, and the others, want to do it differently—we want to know other ways by living them. The familiar ways we've been doing research and teaching clearly haven't worked to change the conditions and opportunities for many students with whom we relate. We realized that we could not change "them" and "their situations" without allowing ourselves to change in relationship to them. And part of the discomfort came

---

* The dilemma of what language to use in this text, reflecting our different readings and experiences, was a continuous feature of its writing. Karen responded to these words with others: "You lost me here." I wrote back to her: "'Epistemic development' refers to the processes through which we come to know and understand ourselves, others, and material phenomena in the world."

from not knowing in which directions we would change—and change again.

I learned that our willingness to take such risks and be changed by the research process itself was a continuous form of feminist praxis, "an encompassing of both reflection and action as a form of inquiry that promotes 'a better, fairer, more humane' world" (Miller, 1990, p. 13). The use of such an approach was justified not only by our experiences as teachers and the context of our work in urban schools and challenging classrooms, but also by its personal and social intent. Again, a primary goal of Part I of this book is to explicate our conversational processes, and demonstrate the many perspectives on how we made sense of our teaching and ourselves. The insights that emerge from such reconstructive readings should not only broaden our understanding but define an epistemology of learning to teach.

METHOD OF STUDY

As our method of study unfolded, the educational issues raised for discussion in our group and the collective processes we developed to learn about them were articulated or categorized in conversation through our collective sense of them. Part of my role was to synthesize various experiential examples presented by individual teachers and then check out those understandings with the group. Through this process, we noted that the issues that emerged were more organically connected than hierarchical, took root in everyday experience, and were consistent with many so-called "feminine" values and political aspirations (employing care, compassion, and critical questioning).

As we talked, we* decided to retain two empirical features of more traditional methodologies—documentation and systematic analysis of our conversations. I made these decisions for two reasons: One was to help us with the reflective development of our own knowledge through its documentation. The other was to have a means to make public and fuse what we were learning with the larger world of educational research which is still grounded in empiricist science (see Nielsen, 1990). Being taken seriously seemed an important prerequisite to acceptance of our alternative approach. To that end, we tape recorded our conversations and sent them (initially) to Lisa Anderson Thomas, a former research assistant with our

---

*Jennifer reminded me that the "we" of this decision was really "Sam." The sentence should read: "As we talked, Sam persuaded us to retain. . . ."

project, for transcription. Since 1990 Patty Noell, at Michigan State, has been providing us with the text of our conversations. Our research team (varying members across the years, but eventually just Karen Teel and me) also continued to visit each classroom an average of twice a month for the first 3 years, then once a month thereafter. Periodically, we videotaped classroom conversations, arranged for teachers to visit each other's classrooms, and then asked teachers to reflect upon their own and their students' lives and learning on audiotape and in writing.

Using the collectively articulated framework as a guide, I systematically reviewed the transcripts, thematically identifying common issues and the processes of making sense of them within a meeting day or across several days. The unit of analysis depended upon the length of time we discussed an issue. The analytic commitment was to a holistic sense of our learning across conversations, not with any given unit or topical category. To accomplish that purpose, we constructed and reconstructed the text. I initially summarized the findings by noting salient and shifting categories, then verified or amended the summaries with the group. Finally, we all composed narratives describing the issues we'd discovered together; we each contributed our own interpretations and words to the stories. Using an empirical narrative structure to represent our learning seemed to transform our experiences into a universal story form that was familiar and could be transferable (as it connected with and had meaning for others' experiences and stories) or useful to other teachers.

In short, we all contributed to this study as researchers, as is appropriate for a narrative inquiry, a methodology which also seemed to explain our conversational process. That approach to "re-storying" educational experience suggests that the researcher–practitioner relationship, in which each party has voice in the retelling, is as important as the data examined for synthesis and re-storying. From Michael Connelly and Jean Clandinin, I learned that

> narrative inquiry in the social sciences is a form of empirical narrative in which empirical data is central to the work. . . . A number of different methods of data collection are possible as the researcher and practitioner work together in a collaborative relationship. . . . In the process of living the narrative inquiry, the place and voice of researcher and teacher become less defined by role. Our concern is to have a place for the voice of each participant. The question of who is researcher and who is teacher becomes less important as we concern ourselves with questions of collaboration, trust, and relationship, and we live, story, and restory our collaborative research life. (Connelly & Clandinin, 1990, pp. 5, 10)

Narrative as a research device is not new to the field of education, although it is currently enjoying wider acceptance. Sylvia Ashton Warner's personal story of teaching (1963) has become a classic example of data supporting the current philosophical movement of "process" reading and writing. Vivian Paley (1979, 1990) and Robert Coles (1989) have also shown the importance of narrative as data not only in research, but in teaching and learning as well.

From almost 1,000 pages of data reflecting our conversations, we conducted many narrative analyses of emergent themes and issues. As Susan Florio-Ruane reminds us, "Conversation as a research method is very likely to yield stories as data" (1990, p. 240). An important method-ological feature that allowed us to hear and interpret the stories in uncharted forms was our willingness to be open and present to their tellings.* The stories told here thus stand as data for emergent grounded theories (Glaser & Strauss, 1967) which were constructed as they were ini-tially told, related to other stories and theories, and reinterpreted as our understanding of learning to teach evolved (see also Mishler, 1986, for responses as story).

Internal accuracy was determined by returning both the transcripts and narrative text of the stories representing categorical issues to the teachers for review and correction. External accuracy meant comparing these con-versational data with classroom observations and individual interviews col-lected during the same years. We assessed "validity" by confirming atten-tion to similar issues across the cohorts of preservice-to-beginning teachers. The believability or verisimilitude of these stories, moreover, becomes apparent through the multiple examples that form the narrative whole. The empathetic or corroborative response in readers with similar autobiograph-ical experiences is an example of their transferability and relative authentic-ity (see Van Maanen, 1988, for a discussion of alternative research criteria).

CAST OF CHARACTERS IN OUR COLLABORATIVE CONVERSATIONS

Before I begin the narrative, let me extend the informal references to our group made in the preface, and formally introduce my "dinner guests" and myself as we were when the conversations began. I, Sandra (Sam)

---

*Jennifer wanted to underscore how this open quality of our conversations was not just important, but central to the methodology.

Hollingsworth, as you know, serve as the narrator of these stories. An (often) outspoken feminist educator whose passion for this work was fueled through my own and my son's educational traumas, I contribute both personally and politically to the narrative interpretation. Two of my regular guests and costorytellers across the early years of this project were doctoral students and research assistants who worked collaboratively in the beginning teachers' classrooms. Mary-Lynn Lidstone was a school psychology doctoral student in her late 20s. Inspired (among other things) by her mother, a nursing administrator, to enter a helping profession, she was committed to principles of equity and relevance in education. Mary-Lynn's research partner, Karen Teel, was a doctoral student in teaching and curriculum. Karen differed from Mary-Lynn not only in her program of study and her age (early 40s), but also in that she was married and was mother to three children. Nevertheless, her preference for educational work in urban areas matched Mary-Lynn's, the other teachers, and my own. Mary-Lynn, Karen, and I shared primary responsibility for documenting the process of learning to teach during the first 3 years.

Five teachers joined us for the 1st year and continued into the 2nd. Four of them taught in urban schools. Lisa Raffel taught the fourth and fifth grades in such a setting, and made good use of her background in peace and conflict studies. A feminist in her late 20s, she also was brought up in a single-parent family who prized independence. Leslie Minarik and Mary Dybdahl came to teaching in their mid 30s with previous managerial experience in the business world. Leslie taught second grade in a school that lacked out-of-classroom supportive services for students. Thus she brought her talents as a mother, partner, and manager into the classroom. Mary taught a third–fourth combination class in a school that not only lacked sufficient materials and support personnel, but heating and cooling as well. Mary's calm and self-accepting nature, plus the support she received from her principal at school and her lifetime partner at home, helped her cope with the challenging teaching environment. Jennifer Davis-Smallwood, the only person of color in our group, was an African-American in her early 30s who came from a very supportive family background. She taught a second grade class populated by African-American children who lived in poverty. The fifth teacher in our group was Anne Weldon. In her mid 20s, she was the youngest of us, having just completed her Bachelor's degree in English before entering the graduate level credential program. After graduation she taught sixth grade in a suburban school where most of the children were Caucasian and came from middle class families. The contexts of our work gave life to other reports of the "savage inequalities" that exist, but are often not recognized, in the democracy of American education (see Kozol, 1991).

For reasons that will be explained in the narrative, Anne, Mary-Lynn, and Lisa left our group in its 3rd year, as did two preservice teachers in their late 20s, Marcia Cantrell and Lori Holmes. The last member to complete the group was Anthony Cody, an urban eighth grade life science teacher in his early 30s. Anthony, married with a new baby, joined us during the 2nd year, and remained with the group, as did Karen, Jennifer, Mary, Leslie, and I, through the 6th year.

Not only my life story, but my professional background as a historian, reading specialist, and public school teacher in rural, urban, and suburban settings, well connected me to this group. Having just completed my own doctoral program in my early 40s, I lived with my teen-aged daughter, Gena, in a predominantly working-class African-American neighborhood. In our stories told in this book, we have opted to take credit for our contributions by using our real names. I am using my nickname—Sam.

THE STORIES TO COME

The narratives that unfold across this volume are intended to reach a dual audience: Though primarily intended for *teacher–educators as teachers* who

Mother-daughter relations: Sam and Gena in Berkeley.

want to better impact their students' classroom practices, the stories told also will have meaning for *elementary and secondary classroom teachers as students* of education. Part I, Introductory Conversation and Critique, describes teachers raising, discussing, researching, and making sense of issues important to their learning to teach. Chapter 2 describes alternative curricular ideas about learning to teach literacy that emerged from our 1st year's conversations. Chapter 3 steps out of the narrative to look at the conversational process as both example of and method for locating educative contexts in which it becomes possible to learn to teach literacy in urban settings. Its purpose is to try to explicate the feminist praxis of this particular project. Chapter 4 illustrates Mary and Leslie's stories of praxis through "relational knowing" in urban reading classrooms.

Part II of the book describes these teachers' transitions from beginners to experienced professionals through their *stories of teacher research*. Chapters 5 and 6 will tell the stories of what Mary and Leslie learned about teaching elementary level African- and Mexican-American, Filipino, and other Pacific Island students to read and write and speak and listen. Chapter 7 shows Lisa's and Jennifer's personal inquiry styles into classroom management and their ensuing decisions to leave their classrooms. Chapter 8 recounts Anthony's story of his collaborating to teach urban, middle-school, life-science students, and includes Karen's and my stories of our return to the classroom to try to live out what we'd learned by integrating social studies and literacy in (separate) urban middle schools. Chapter 9 tells the story of Leslie's coming to voice and politics in order to teach. Part II ends with a conversation about the benefits and challenges of teacher research that is in chapter 10.

Part III of the book represents the next cycle of this work. It incorporates what I've learned from and with these beginning teachers into narratives of changes in my own work as a teacher/teacher and educator/researcher. It contains stories with *lessons on pedagogical re-vision,* intended for teacher–educators. Chapter 11 provides an example of myself as a teacher–researcher critiquing the pedagogical style I used in my literacy methods course, what I learned from the stories of teachers' research, and how I revised my course work to incorporate what I'd learned. It demonstrates, in particular, both the need and the process of moving beyond technical rationality and toward critically reflective practice in teacher education. The chapter also serves as an example of the critical reflection that might become part of a teacher–educator's role. Chapter 12 outlines the changes in a course on teacher research that grew out of my new understanding of feminist praxis in learning to teach literacy. It retells the stories of literacy teacher–educators—myself, and Pat Gallagher and Thea Maestre, doctoral students/teacher–educators who studied with me. That chapter also describes how we've learned to facilitate conversation around lessons developed in this book—both within the university class-room and without. Finally, our good friend and colleague Jean Clandinin responds to our conversations in an afterword.

INTENTIONS OF THIS BOOK

Some readers of this book may object that we have not cited very much of the extant literature on teaching and teacher education. Such a critique would be well-founded. Our intent is not to ignore the important work that has gone before us, but to use these pages to extend what we know about classroom instruction, literacy education, and learning to teach. For exam-ple, we know much about what experienced teachers do to support stu-dents' learning in elementary reading classrooms (Brophy & Good 1986; Clark & Peterson, 1986)[3], and what they know about their subject matter in secondary classrooms (Shulman, 1986). We also have a small but growing set of case studies on learning to teach (Clandinin, Davies, Hogan, & Ken-nard, 1993; Feiman-Nemser & Buchmann, 1985; Gitlin et al., 1992; Gross-man, 1990; Kennedy, 1990) and narratives of students' learning (Heath, 1983; Paley, 1990). The value of the work that has preceded ours is that it has (1) informed the educational research community of the importance of research on teaching; (2) moved the community of educational researchers from a position of knowing "about" teaching and learning from researchers' observations of teachers' and children's classroom behaviors (and using the "results" of good teaching as prescriptions for all teachers), to (3) cognitive explanations of understanding how they learn to teach and study (and an appreciation of the many personal and environmental factors which medi-ated—or influenced—thinking/learning and actual teaching behaviors), to finally (4) listening to the meaning that teachers and students ascribe to their own classroom activities. This book confirms and extends that line of research, and moves into how teacher–educators can learn to support new teachers to move beyond externally provided knowledge and construct their own instructional stories in relationship with students. It explicates the pro-cesses, content, and values that powerfully directed a small group of new teachers' learning and describes their own research.

This work also builds upon the rich literature into the sociocognitive and sociocultural nature of literacy instruction (Ahlquist, 1989; Au, 1980; Doyle & Carter, 1984; Grossman, 1990; Hilliard, 1974; Langer, 1987; Mehan, 1974; Mitchell & Weiler, 1991; Murray, 1992; Raphael & Englert, 1989) by incorporating stories about the culturally diverse stu-dents new teachers are typically assigned to teach. The text reinforces the importance of literacy for these students' school success. It also tells us that even beginning teachers, when supported as professional researchers, can precisely name and critique obstacles to teaching all students to become literate—and develop their own knowledge for overcoming those obstacles.*

Finally, the story about my own work as a teacher–educator suggests that we can't facilitate changes in the practices of others unless we reexamine and change our own (see Jersild, 1955). Our collective stories underscore a related and fundamental principle of teacher education reform—that learning to teach is a career-long process, requiring the support at all stages offered professionals in any field (see Nemser, 1983). The stories suggest conversational means by which such critical support might be incorporated into new professional structures.**

ENDNOTES

[1] Sam (Hollingsworth) serves as narrator to open every chapter.

[2] The chapters in Part I are reconceptualizations of three previously written articles: one was published as "Prior Beliefs and Cognitive Change in Learning to Teach" in the *American Educational Research Journal,* 1989, *26* (2), 169–189. The second, "Learning to Teach Through Collaborative Conversation: A Feminist Approach," appeared in the *American Educational Research Journal,* 1992, *29* (2), 373–404. The third was published in *Curriculum Inquiry,* 1993, *23* (1), 5–36. Its title is "By Chart and Chance and Passion: Learning to Teach in Urban Settings."

[3] See, also, the collection of articles that have been published as reports through the Elementary Subject Center, Institute for Research on Teaching, Michigan State University, East Lansing, MI, 48824.

---

*Anthony and others in our group helped me to avoid falling into the "new grand narrative" trap—which I do because of my training to report research "results"—by writing a question on the draft of this manuscript: "What if 'self-knowledge' or the experience of teaching is not enough to prepare teachers for a diverse setting? How does our approach deconstruct racism or middle-class bias?" Karen responded: "It isn't enough to just experience cultural diversity in the classroom to deconstruct racism. However, our conversational approach provides teachers with a forum for sharing experiences, confusions, misconceptions (bias), etc. In this way, new insights are acquired from one another and new perspectives emerge." Lisa added: "I absolutely agree that we need help in changing attitudes and skills."

**Leslie added a closing comment to this chapter: "It is unlikely that anyone would disagree. Rather sadly, they would agree that such support, in the form of 'in-services' exists for just such a purpose. Again, sadly, there has been little serious attempt to look at whether these forms are of any real support to teachers and, if not, what alternatives there are."

2

Rewriting the Conversation and Curriculum of Literacy Education

Very early on in our conversations, I saw that—for us to remain a group—
I would have to learn a different way, as a teacher–educator, to think epistemologically and act pedagogically. When we initially convened, I had
planned for and hoped that our after-dinner conversation would lead to
specific talk and research about learning to teach *reading and writing*. As
I mentioned in chapter 1, I had been a reading instructor in the teachers'
preservice programs, and had just completed a study of their cognitive
change in learning to teach reading within one program (see
Hollingsworth, 1989b). I knew that they had learned and could demonstrate adequate knowledge about reading theory and practice. I was now
interested in a follow-up study into how the teachers were applying what
they'd learned in their courses to their classrooms, and how I could continue to offer support for their efforts. Under the guise of "researcher" and
"helpful facilitator," I could still operate in an expert–novice mode, where
I assumed I knew what questions to ask about teaching literacy in urban
environments and how to evaluate the answers. However, these teachers
did not let me hide my questions or their responses behind my privilege as
"teacher–educator."

Because of the social environment for our continuous meetings, I
soon heard that these beginning teachers were concerned with many
things about schooling and teaching, but not specifically about literacy
instruction. As hard as I tried, I could not get the conversations to focus
on *my* interest in their subject-matter knowledge. The group, though, had
other goals in mind for our meetings. Lisa spoke for the group: "I like the
idea of finding out how we're doing in our classrooms. If we could start

with some larger problems, not necessarily reading. Reading doesn't necessarily jump into my mind."

Moving forward as a "good" teacher and researcher, and never forgetting my own goals (not to mention funding agency and academic publishing obligations), I tried encouraging them to *allow* reading and writing to jump into their minds: "Just keep reading in the back of your mind as you're talking. . . . there [may be] some things that come up that you can link with [that topic]. Then we'll see what happens. If nothing comes up around it, then we'll go with what does come up."

Nothing came up around reading during most of the 1st year of monthly meetings, not for the student teachers, or the 1st-year teachers, or even the 2nd-year teachers. Forcing attention to subject-related or curricular issues, in fact, became a primary complaint about the content of their preservice education programs. Lisa noted

> When I was in the [teacher education] program, before I knew what teaching was about . . . they just bombard you with curriculum and how you're supposed to be doing everything. I was so nervous about teaching the curriculum. I was inundated, and that was my focus. Now I realize the curriculum is not as big an issue. The reality is getting [students] to a point where you can teach them.

Jennifer suggested a reason for the attention to the material and instrumental concept of curriculum: "Well, *that was* the focus of the program!" Free from evaluative pressure to value and learn about curricular issues using predetermined views of curriculum and instruction, the group now wanted to broaden their learning—and their definitions of the curriculum or "what's worth knowing in schools." Leslie tried to keep her attention on textual curriculum during her 1st year of teaching, only to become disillusioned. She summarized the experiences of our conversational group in a paper presented to a national conference:

> For [several] years I have been involved in a teacher/researcher collaborative group. The focus topic for the group was to be *reading instruction* and often has been. The group's support and assistance in helping me explore and evaluate my way through language arts curriculum has been immeasurable. However, it was not infrequent that the teachers in the group could not *begin* by discussing reading. A wealth of "stuff" had to be unloaded, vented, cried about, and shared before we could discuss "our main topic"—the reading curriculum. Sam Hollingsworth, wisely, but with some frustration, listened and then tried to guide us back on track. I can picture many such evenings. (For more of Leslie's analysis, see Hollingsworth & Minarik, 1991.)

What Leslie and the others taught me was that they had been well educated in a philosophy of literacy acquisition that endorsed student choice of and involvement with meaningful text (Harste, 1990) and the process writing approach of the Bay Area Writing Project (Gray, 1988). These teachers had already learned from their teacher education programs how to evaluate the quality of a child's reading miscues, to select good children's literature, to avoid phonics instruction in isolation, and to integrate reading and writing instruction. What the teachers did not know was how to teach literacy to children who came to school too hungry or too tired to pay attention—except to invoke the rule of the method: Involve students more fully in a print-rich environment. They did not consciously know how to challenge institutional constraints—such as tracking systems, required texts, and mandatory testing programs—that limited opportunities for many children. Further, they did not know what to do with all the "real world" personal crises their urban children faced, because they had not been told. In short, they did not think they knew what to do with the difficult environments of urban schools. In actuality, they did or could know how to develop the relationships that would lead them to intuitive knowledge about teaching in urban environments, but such epistemological processes—being less verbal—were less available to draw upon for practice. Our open-ended conversational method of study became an occasion for articulating that knowledge.

The teachers' experiences were not atypical of either western teacher education or schooling in general. Impersonal knowledge of the disciplines is often an explicitly stated objective of formal education (Berscheid, 1985). These beginning teachers received praise for their logical analyses of children's reading behavior based on empirical evidence, yet their yearnings to employ *intuitive* measures of care and compassion through relations were sometimes disregarded as inappropriate. For example, supervisors in Leslie's program often counseled against developing a "friendly" style of classroom management and promoted a more "technical" or ordered style to create an appropriate academic atmosphere.

Mary's teacher education program emphasized the need for care, but only as grounded in the cognitive theory it supported (an interpretation about appropriate literacy instruction from developmental theory). If Mary had chosen an alternative, *cognitive* approach to literacy instruction (a deductive approach or direct instruction of phonics, for example, as a supplement to a patterned language or inductive approach to reading), her teaching might not have been viewed as caring.

Freed from program requirements and evaluations, these teachers spoke openly about such issues. Thus, it was out of necessity (because I no longer had evaluative power over the teachers to force them into my agenda) rather than from a commitment to a more inclusive, critical, and feminist approach that I suspended my original goal to continue looking at the cognitive aspect of learning to teach literacy. Because I could also *sense*, but not articulate, that there was something important to be learned from the teachers, I changed my role as facilitator/researcher to one whose primary role was that of a participant in a conversation and not the author of a dialogue. Though it was unclear to me at the outset of our meetings, I was beginning a journey that would lead me to see not only the critical importance of creating our own knowledge in feminist terms, but also the need to constantly critique our own and other's representations of what we knew about teaching. I came to agree with Giroux (1988), that teacher education should be cast as a "political project, as a cultural politics, that defines [beginning] teachers as intellectuals who will establish public spaces where students can debate, appropriate, and learn the knowledge and skills necessary to achieve . . . individual freedom and social justice" (p. 167). In fact, we all were moving toward that position by creating a space for ourselves in a know-in-conversational relationship. I explained the revised approach to our group.

> I'd like to tell you about the vision of this idea. I'm still interested in learning to teach reading. But I think we need to go further now. And what seems really appropriate to me now is to listen to you. Just flat out listen without any other agenda in mind but to understand better, from your own perspectives and own ways of being together, how you learn to teach. The one thing that seems to work [in learning to teach], here as everywhere, is [having an opportunity to talk] to each other. That's the most important vehicle.

Initially, the shift created some confusion about our purposes, particularly for Karen and Mary-Lynn who were not sure how we would "research" learning to teach within this ambiguous structure. The broadened agenda did help to establish a public space in which—eventually—every participant's current knowledge, needs, and roles were considered. In other words, because we continued to develop both social and professional relationships concurrently, we learned to articulate our positions, share our expertise, trust that we could disagree, and both give and receive constructive—and not-so-constructive—criticism. No longer denied the opportunity to learn from students, as happened when I dominated discussions with my disciplinary and cognitive expertise and my research agenda, I found each teacher focused their attention on personal, interrelated, and practically driven issues. I learned that the complexity of those issues could be articulated even by the preservice members of our group. Marcia, for example, illustrated the tangled nature of practice-situated attention as she summarized the differences between her graduate program and the on-line setting of the classroom.

> In my master's program I could think about anything I wanted to at any time and I could build on any topic and theoretically could do anything I wanted. And practically, in the classroom, [I'm] confined to thinking about what's going on with the kids in the classroom and trying to find the issues that fifth and fourth graders are dealing with. And trying to tap back into my theoretical knowledge about how I want to run classrooms and make it happen in the classroom, is really hard. Like I've got to get this fractions lesson in to [a program instructor] and I've got to watch out for the principal and [Billy] just wrote a story talking about sex and how can I—well, I am the authority—he can't write about it. It's what comes up in your situation that guides your thinking. It's a lot harder that way, but I think it's ultimately what everything's all about. I mean, theory doesn't mean anything unless you can act on it.

It was from a willingness to listen to open-ended and complex verbalized analyses such as Marcia's that I came to learn that such conversational processes could provide the context for supporting all of our goals—the

Conversational work: Lisa and Marcia.

research team's need to study learning to teach and the beginning teachers' need for support to learn about complex classroom issues. *I* learned what teaching issues were raised, why they surfaced, how the teachers worked through and made sense of them—and the results of their sensemaking. Consequently, I changed both my beliefs about the content and process of supporting teachers' learning, and my own pedagogical approach to teacher education course work.

All of us in the group had doubts about the degree to which we "should" be critical of the well-intentioned teacher education programs with which we were associated. While wanting neither to devalue the people involved nor their efforts, our group came to see that our critique was a form of fidelity. Nel Noddings helped some of us understand the obligation to be critical of our institutional experiences.

> It is this striving for the best in ourselves and in those with whom we interact that marks self-actualization, and a community that embraces this view of fidelity has a strong rationale for socialization, for it is not asking for fidelity to institutions as they are but as they might realistically be at their best. Further, fidelity is never given first to either self as individual or to institution, but to the others with whom we are in relation and to the relations by which we are defined. (Noddings, 1986, p. 501)

It was in the spirit of informing the well-intentioned programs with which we were associated—so that they could become even more effective in preparing new teachers to work in urban areas—that we could be open and honest in our analyses. After we settled into an agenda of letting our conversation become determined by our relations, our practices, and by our readings as they reflected our relations and our practices, we learned much. The curricular issues and challenges which we raised in the 1st year of our conversation are shown in Figure 2.1. They are listed clockwise in temporal sequence. In other words, the first important issue (that which dominated the conversation in our early meetings) was *classroom relationships*. Although the issue of relationships continued to surface across all years of our conversation, about the middle of the 1st year that issue no longer directed our talk. In the spring, we shifted the bulk of our attention to issues of *diversity in personal, school and community values,* then to *power and professional voice*. At the end of the year, prompted by mandated changes in the teachers' practices, we finally took up the issue of *reading instruction and curriculum*. Each issue became experiential background knowledge for the others and supported a deeper personally and politically relevant understanding of reading instruction. Each also led to the emergence of a feminist consciousness about our work.

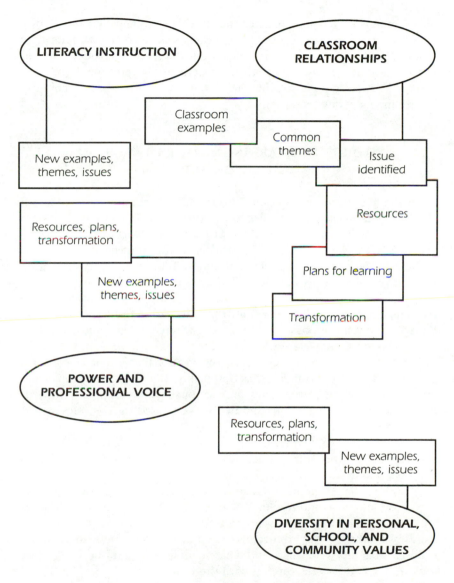

FIGURE 2-1
Issues raised through the conversational process.

Figure 2.1 also roughly illustrates the categorical processes of identifying and understanding the issues. Common themes initially surfaced as details or examples of real classroom problems, then were relocated within related but larger issues. Abstracting practical examples into theoretical or philosophical issues gave teachers perspectives from which to identify resources and formulate plans to learn more about the issues, and finally to report their transformational understandings back to the group. The stories that follow elaborate on both these general conversational processes and the curricular topics teachers felt were essential to their teaching in environmentally diverse settings.*

STORIES OF LEARNING ABOUT CLASSROOM RELATIONSHIPS

Every member of our group came into teaching because they cared about children. That sense was amplified as most teachers began to work in their classrooms with children from different backgrounds, cultures, and communities. Caring gave teachers the patience and interest needed to understand children's various interactional and communication styles. Caring provided the basis for forming a relationship with students, from which they could discern the possibilities and limitations of their teaching and students' learning much more readily than they could from reading decentralized communications of research on teaching and learning.** Therefore, although there were variations in their examples, most of the teachers' earliest attentional themes in our conversational group had to do with the social nature of learning to teach. Opening my agenda and thus making it ours brought forth stories on relationship development with students, parents, administrators, and peers. We treated those stories as curriculum for learning to teach.

In contrast with their teacher-education experiences, the teachers did not respond to experiential stories by giving each other concrete solutions or "answers" to their concerns, but by telling related stories. In that way they both validated the importance of the issue, and heard varying practice-based dilemmas and resolutions to incorporate into their own experiential understanding of the issue. Mary, teaching in a school where vandalism was a regular occurrence, where approximately one quarter of her children's parents were jailed, and where conflict was part of everyday life, took up the issue of relationships with this example:

---

* Jennifer commented on this section: "Reading this makes me think that teacher–educators should understand that reflection and conversation are key to good teaching."

** Our editor, Brian Ellerbeck, added: "The trick, as you know, is to avoid allowing the limitations to deny the possibilities."

I taught a lesson last week, with my arms around a kid for the whole 40 minutes. Can you imagine holding a fairly big, active third grader in your arms so he won't ruin the math class? I'm trying to be calm, "OK, next problem." The kid is going nuts and the class is watching the kid thrash around in your arms.

Mary's story—which her teacher education supervisors may have technically viewed simply as "problems with classroom management"— became personal and situational. It gave a whole new meaning to the concept of "time-on-task." Follow-up stories and questions in response to Mary's experiences grew out of our own related experiences.

The personal focus on relationship development in the classroom, particularly stories attesting to its difficulty and complexity, led the teachers to become patient with themselves during the process of internalizing the issue. Here's an example of Lisa's understanding of intimate relationships as a long range goal in her classroom.

So many master [or cooperating] teachers were so distant from the kids. There was no intimacy. I found myself in that role at times. Part of it is that there are so many things going on. I have so many responsibilities. I can't wait till I get over that part. I know that there will come a time when I've got my planning down, my long range and my short range. Till I know how to hand papers out so it doesn't take a year, and kids aren't shouting at me. But I know that will solve itself at some point.

Lisa's story of intimate relationships also shows how the conversational process helped her construct her own knowledge as she articulated it, and that she came to accept such knowledge as transitional. It also illustrates that she, as a "novice," could be critical of an "expert" with regard to this issue, based on differing beliefs. Her self-perception as both a learner and one who has learned from her own experience led Lisa to feel capable of supporting her own knowledge production and analysis—an epistemological position that has eluded many women and teachers. (This analysis of Lisa's experience—as well as similar stories from the rest of the group—will be further explicated as the narrative of our work continues.)

In addition to valuing the opportunity for ongoing practice-based conversation, the teachers identified other resources for their learning through the conversation. All of them mentioned the value of observing, then talking with peer teachers as a resource for learning. Jennifer's response to another teacher's statement about observation is an example.

I think that I have learned a lot about relationships from talking with other people and watching other teachers interact with kids. I pick up things. It's not like looking at a teacher supply store for helpful hints. It's like "Oh! I never thought I could say that to a child!" and I see a new vision of a relationship with students. I see the possibilities.

Once identified as a resource, the group members made plans to extend the conversation about relationships from our group into each other's classrooms. Most teachers asked for such support the 1st year. Leslie was the only teacher not convinced, early in our 1st year, that attention to relationships was as important as getting the materials and activities of her reading curriculum in place. She felt that other attentional emphases at that time would be overwhelming, but welcomed other visitors to her own room. So we secured some funding to pay for substitutes for the others, and asked all the teachers to talk and write about what they'd learned from each other on their visits.

The last step that surfaced in a "round" of conversation (see Figure 2.1) occurred when teachers talked about the transformative "results" of their evolving understanding with the group. Such results also included my learning outcomes. Unlike principled and objective findings resulting from traditional approaches to learning, our reports showed less cognitive or behavioral change as they did personal and connective "settling" or tacit understanding. That is, the threads of what we were learning seemed to gently fall into place in the fabric of our lives. I talked about my own transformation in understanding the relationship issue. Out of it had grown a new understanding and valuing of our common process in terms of "story" development—a connection of my personal preference for narrative voice and the professional need to show "products" from our conversational work.

I . . . think about [relationships] in terms of working in a group in our research team, and working in teacher education groups, and working in the university, and working with my daughter. The same things keep recurring. People make meaning together. I'm wondering if there's a way that we could somehow organize [the connections between] what we're doing and thinking about in terms of stories.

Probably because I listened to, learned from, and felt accepted by the teachers (through the realness of their listening to what I had to say, but also challenging my words without discarding me), I came to accept our process of evolving stories-in-relationship as both method of supporting learning to teach—and result, even though I knew that "storied" research results might make our work suspect to many of my peers who were grounded in traditional research.

And so, the stories poured forth. Jennifer reported how she'd given up on suggestions from her teacher education program and school curriculum supervisors for tight managerial control using preassigned groups for her African-American students. Instead, she trusted her intuition about relational learning structures that would better support students of her own race. She now encouraged a flexible form of self-selected grouping that seemed to promote cooperation and shared learning but looked much less orderly. Her story (detailed in chapter 7) included reference to the anguish of nonsupport in both her teacher education program and in her school for her culturally diverse and relational approach.

Many stories described how teachers better understood instructional issues involving classroom relationships, although much of the classroom-specific "problem" had not actually changed. For example, Lisa's stories about the relationship issue involved changes in herself. She told our group about changes in her standard "ideal" of a managerial relationship in her culturally varied classroom. "I was stuck in my work with these children. Applying standard rules for good behavior didn't work. I had to look at changes in myself and my relationship with them before we could both relax enough to move forward in new ways." A clarified understanding of classrooms as people in multiple relations led Lisa to change her expectation for children with many participation styles to conform to a single managerial norm. She came to accept their differences, and they, in turn, responded to her acceptance with more empathetic behavior (see chapter 7 for more of Lisa's story).

As the stories were told, we came to see that the development of relationships was not only important as a pedagogical tool, but as evidence of good teaching. Mary reported her pleasure when another teacher positively noted her personal interaction with students in a school not noted for easy student–teacher interaction.

> The best compliments that I've gotten all year were from the teacher right next door to me. We were walking out to get a key to lock up. Nobody likes to walk out alone because you come around the corner and you see about 60 kids, and they're all shouting. You don't want to be by yourself when they're all yelling at you, so you always wait for a buddy. So as we were walking out, she kind of got close to me and said, "You know, I know you're going to be a good teacher because I saw you talking to your kids." She just saw me interacting with my kids and she liked it. It made her feel comfortable. She's a person I really admire, so it made me feel good.

Through our conversational stories, we learned that the art and skill of forming relationships could no longer be left as an intuitive or tacit part of the literacy curriculum. We saw it as an important quality to nurture in learning to teach. (More stories on the importance of "relational knowing" follow in chapters 3 and 4.)

DIVERSITY IN PERSONAL, SCHOOL, AND COMMUNITY VALUES

Having the opportunity to both talk about and critique personal-relationship development raised broader examples of relationships between schools and communities. We talked about differences between acceptable values and behavior within the school community and contrasting out-of-school realities. We told stories about particular children who seemed to routinely find themselves in the principal's office for following the wrong rules.

> SAM: Let's begin with those two rules [just mentioned]: respect people and respect property. Those are school rules, but they are not "street" rules. So how do you deal with [the difference]? How does a teacher link those two worlds? Again we [find cases of] "student" separate from [out-of-school] "person."
>
> JENNIFER: Yeah, we had an incident at school the other day, the principal called two kids in for fighting and told them, "Even if the other person hits you, you don't hit back." And one of the kids said, "Well, my mom told me, if they hit you, you hit them back."
>
> SAM: Whose rules do you follow? And what are your own rules?
>
> JENNIFER: At school, respect is expected. In the street, it's earned. There's the rub.

Mary brought a story to our group that made us all think about appropriate support for many children's survival within school systems. She told us about a conversation about standardized test scores with one of her student's African-American grandmother. The story caused us all to think about the discrepancy between standardized evaluation systems representing school "rules" and alternative "rules" for evaluating students outside of school systems.

> [The] grandmother brought the point home to me. She took righteous exception to the "failing marks" I reported for her granddaugh-

ter. She said, "What does this say about my child—that she's a moron, she's stupid and slow? Does it say that I read to her every night? Does it say that her mother's in jail and her daddy died just last year? Does it tell you that she's getting her life together, slowly? Does it say that she's learning songs for Sunday school? Does it say she wants to be a doctor? What does this piece of paper say about my baby? I don't want it near her. She needs good things. She's had enough in her life telling her that she's no good. She doesn't need this and I won't have it. If your school can't come up with better ways to show what my child can really do, then I refuse to sign a piece of paper that says my child is no good."

Mary reflected on the grandmother's comments.

I wanted to give this wonderful loving grandmother a standing ovation. She spoke from her heart and her very sound mind. She expressed for me the misgivings I have about how we support the children in our schools.

Such reflective conversations eventually led Mary to understand "standard" concepts such as "assessment" and "parental involvement" in schools from a new direction: accepting parents' alternative values instead of demanding that parents comply with those of the school. As a result, although she was still required to evaluate students' academic performances, she began to develop more personally responsive strategies and measures. Locating caring and empathetic spaces to discuss and reflect upon competing values was important to her success in learning to teach in a school where diverse perspectives were common.

By spring, transformative stories about diverse values in self and others led us toward another issue and another level of discourse. Speaking about the overwhelming tasks new teachers face to learn about so many different kinds of children, Jennifer directly criticized the institutional norms that did not support her learning. Our emerging awareness of the complexity of learning to teach led us to redefine our social location and that of our children within a larger political system.

I just cannot live with [the failure of these children]. It's not my fault, it's not. It's the system. And I don't know about participating in a system that would send X number of resource kids to your room knowing that, no matter who the teacher is, you're going to have problems. The system is just not OK for the kids. And it's not OK for me.

STORIES OF POWER AND PROFESSIONAL VOICE

Evolving conversational patterns showed that developing understandings of (1) classroom relationships and (2) diversity in values, also increased the teachers' (3) critical awareness of power relationships inside and outside school. Influenced by their experiences and my own political views of their life's work—which also evolved as I gained a better understanding of the barriers they faced in learning to teach and broadened my reading to learn about overcoming those barriers—the teachers now wanted "to give those who live and move within [schools] a sense of affirmation and to provide the conditions for students and others to display an active voice and presence" (Giroux, 1988, p. 117; Gramsci, 1971).

The teachers in our group initially questioned their personal power to teach and learn from their own beliefs and experiences in a political climate that supported authoritative standards. Adopting a critical perspective about the social norms of that climate—and receiving the support to move through the emotional stress that accompanies such a perspective—was crucial to claiming their own professional voices within their schools—and attaining the personal and political freedom to reconstruct classrooms that supported diverse values and ways of being instead of restricting them.

In the next round of our conversation (which began about three quarters of the way through the 1st year and continued into the 2nd), the experiential examples discussed were those *imposed* on the teachers—such as testing requirements. Leslie gave an example of the school's emphasis on testing. "The [standardized tests are] usually in April but [district officials] moved them [to May] because they're trying desperately to get the highest scores." Such issues quickly moved from surface level examples to thematic clashes between personal ideology and the institutional system of American education.

> LISA: I guess I'm back in the space where it's not the details [of how to improve test scores] that matter. I'm just back to really questioning if what we're even doing works. It's partly because we're all just crunching what we didn't cover into their heads before there's a test. It's like, I don't *believe* in that, why am I doing it?

The issue became that of the struggle between power, personal beliefs, and professional voice. Teachers' plans to resolve that issue were both political and visionary in nature. Lisa continued:

> Jennifer and I started talking about this, what would we do if we were given a blank check and an empty building and told to

design a school, what would it be like? I'd like to do that. I'd like
to really think about what kids need every day, if I could design a
curriculum, what would I teach them? I think if we did that, then
next year we can say, "OK, that's what you'd *like* it to look like,
how can you make that as real as possible?"

JENNIFER: I really want, especially with [African-American] kids, to
teach them to have access to the system. I don't want to teach
them ways to be nonfunctional.

Such broad politically based plans required some structure. In order
to facilitate that structure and ground the issue in reality, I pushed for
written stories of their transformed understanding of the issue. Because
writing to clarify my learning was a technique *I* valued, and not all teachers shared that value, I did not always get the results I wanted. The results
I did receive were surprising and impressive, often reaching beyond the
boundaries of both our group and their schools and capturing the spirit of
transformation. The test of worthwhile knowledge for these politically
aware teachers with whom I was now working was not whether their
understandings would be considered "true" by objective standards (or
whether they could be verbalized, semipermanently attached to paper, and
published), but whether they could understand, encourage, and inspire
children to succeed both personally and academically in spite of institutional constraints. Lisa provided an example of such alternative "outcomes" to her teaching by talking about changes in her perceptions about
personal political power, her freedom to evaluate her own progress in her
working-class, teaching environment, alternative notions of students'
progress, and the acceptance of the emotion that comes from caring for
children and herself in relationship:

Many of my students are still at a fourth-grade level academically
[when they should be on the fifth], but *I don't think I've failed.* They
got to do things they've never done before. They had a good year, and
they feel better about themselves because how they feel about themselves was important to me. . . . Right now I feel like crying almost
everyday because I'm going to have to say good-bye to my kids soon.
They are some of the most important people in my life right now.

As we clarified and articulated our sense of power as teachers, our
group decided to take professional action and reach out beyond the classroom to share our developing expertise with other audiences. Such actions
resulted in many transformational stories. For example, Leslie talked to
our group about her new consciousness in relationship to an imposed

change in district policy. She rallied fellow teachers at her school to form a community voice and challenge policies that seemed to devalue teachers' knowledge or students' needs. (The complete story unfolds in chapter 9.)

For Leslie, the development of consciousness, power, and professional voice *did occur* interactionally with having something to say in writing. Leslie has now written and coauthored several stories about her transformation; she's presented some at national conferences, joining the conversation traditionally reserved for university researchers (see Hollingsworth & Minarik, 1991; Hollingsworth, Minarik, & Teel, 1990; Minarik, 1991). Leslie has also published some of her work (Hollingsworth, Dybdahl, & Minarik, 1993; Hollingsworth, Teel, & Minarik, 1992) and has been invited to talk about it at an international conference as an invited scholar (Minarik, 1992). Mary has also written papers for conference presentations about her learning to teach (see Dybdahl, 1990; Dybdahl & Hollingsworth, 1989); has published her work (Hollingsworth & Dybdahl, 1991; Hollingsworth, Dybdahl, & Minarik, 1993), and is joining a collaborative conversational group in her school to research alternative assessment methods for children at risk of school failure (see chapter 6 for more of Mary's story). Jennifer chose to speak at conferences, but not to write. Her words at an international conference on teacher research resonated so loudly that she was invited to speak at another.[1] One of Karen's "outcomes" of this work was to return to part-time teaching at an urban middle school where she organized a collaborative group the 1st year (see chapter 8). Another was to complete a doctorate researching her own teaching (Teel, 1993). Karen and Leslie have also written stories of learning to teach for national conferences (Teel & Minarik, 1990). Anthony wrote a critique of a university-sponsored inservice in his urban school, and started another featuring conversation among teachers (see chapter 8). He's been asked to speak about his work at a state-wide conference in California.

Some teachers' transformations also included, like Karen's, a change of classrooms in subsequent years. After a long history of unvalued efforts to impact the structure of her school from the inside, Jennifer resigned her public school position and is working on classroom education through alternative means. Lisa switched classrooms to take a job as a college instructor in New York, working in peace studies, and is now in graduate school on the west coast.* I changed classrooms (and universities) to work

---

* Lisa added: "It sounds as if I just switched classrooms, but the truth, as you know, is that I left because I saw the system as not working for my kids. I felt guilty about participating in reproducing inequality. The 10-year-old African-American males who began the year as nonreaders, ended the year in the same way."

in another setting, where collaborative research with teachers to challenge the many problems of schooling, is taken seriously.

Before we scattered for the summer, though, the topic of literacy instruction did eventually surface in our conversational group. It arose out of the teachers' practices near the end of our 1st year. I'll tell that story in chapter 4. Chapter 3 takes a slight detour from the narrative path of this book to investigate the process of our conversational learning.

ENDNOTE

[1] The first conference was the International Conference on Teacher Research, Stanford University, April, 1992. The second was the Classroom Action Research Network (CARN) Conference in Norwich, England.

3

Rereading the Conversation to Find New Ways and Spaces for Learning to Teach Literacy

Navigating by chart and chance and passion
I will know the shape of the mountains of freedom, I will know.
Marge Piercy
"The Perpetual Migration"

Let me begin this chapter not only with Marge Piercy's poetry which metaphorically describes what we are about, but with an assertion that might not have become clear in the last chapter. No different from other teachers and scholars interested in learning to teach, all of us in the group wanted to "know" what to do to teach children in urban classrooms. We all went to post baccalaureate teacher education programs hoping to receive charts for navigating those classrooms. We all quested (to varying degrees) for certainty in our lives and our work. Had the research findings and theories we had been taught in our graduate education been sufficient knowledge to successfully teach in urban environments, we would have been happy—and this group might have never come to be.

The reality was, though, that we didn't have enough or the right kinds of knowledge to teach all the children who came to us to learn. To perform our work, we needed to suspend many of the certainties provided to us through the "knowledge base" of teacher education and ask new questions. We had to risk a degree of "not knowing" in order to be able to recognize other ways and dimensions of knowing. Otherwise, what we "knew" (were certain of) could block us from noticing what we could come to know. Yet, it's also important to note that we didn't "decide" to suspend or question our knowledge. The processes of questioning what we knew, partially suspending knowledge that was "suspect," and reimagining ways of knowing to teach literacy in urban classrooms came through the living or doing of it. Those epistemic processes were made clear across our sustained conversations. In other words, while we actually learned to teach literacy through its practice and research in our classrooms, our conversations provided spaces or contexts for becoming aware of and naming both what we'd learned and how we'd learned it.

Stories depicting the results of this process are told throughout this book. For example, in chapter 6, you'll find a story about how Leslie had to partially break free of the certainty of some important theoretical knowledge promoted by her teacher education program, and which she had come to believe, in order to teach all of her children to read. In particular, she had to suspend the absolute "knowledge" that a print-emersion process of learning to read would work for every child to understand that it might not—and that she would need to try other "knowledges" of literacy instruction for some of her students. She was helped to put aside the "truth" of one-approach-for-all, and hear the voices and stories of nonreaders in her classroom by listening to similar stories of other children's nonreading behavior in our conversational group. From piecing together new stories and reading practices and conducting classroom research, Leslie transformed her knowledge and her practice. In chapter 8, you'll find a similar story of Anthony's learning that science teachers can also be literacy teachers. Chapter 11 tells a similar story of transformations in my practice as a teacher–educator.

So what made our conversational process work as a context for exploring the passion of teaching and taking the risk of becoming vulnerable and trying out uncharted knowledge in our classrooms? What made it different from just a place for pleasant and even informative chats, but not occasions for transformation? As I thought about those questions, three aspects of our work come to mind. The first is that our sustained conversations and our deepening relations became a context in which we could come to know (at least tentatively), and find the courage to talk about and act on our learning. The second factor was that the classroom/community contexts in which these teachers worked at the time, compelled them to find new ways of knowing and teaching. The third factor was the teachers themselves—and me and my relationship with them. Our common bond, as you remember, was a passion to learn to teach in urban areas. To do so, we had to take the risk of opening ourselves and learning primarily from ourselves in relation to others rather than from our relations to codified "knowledge" or ideas. Since learning-in-relation, the basis on which our stories came to be retold in this book, is such a complex epistemological notion, it is important to examine it further. Thus, this chapter steps slightly out of the chronological narrative which describes *what* we learned to clarify *how* our conversations became a space or context for knowing, *how* the teachers' school contexts served as motivational incentives to risk new ways of knowing, and *how* we came to recognize that our relational postures and attitudes were the means through which we could know.

CONVERSATION AS PRAXIS: A CONTEXT FOR CONTINUOUS INQUIRY INTO PRACTICE

I've already made clear, I hope, the immense importance of sustained conversation as a space for learning to teach. What I want to describe here are the particular features of the conversational process that emerged across the years of our work together, and seemed to transform a space for a social gathering into a context or opportunity for learning. That is, I want to articulate those features of the conversation that helped us both engage in reflection about our stored knowledges and current experiences, and to formulate plans where knowledge and experience could collide and reconstruct. You may notice that our conversational features encompass ways of living and learning that are traditionally (and problematically) associated with women—and that are usually omitted from traditional or "authorized" contexts for learning in schools and universities (but perhaps should not be).

Creating Opportunities for Good Food, Good Company, and Good Conversation

The development of ongoing relationships and the establishment of trust was the hallmark of our learning to teach in conversation. Thus, while I initially looked upon our regular meetings together in "social" settings, sharing pot-luck dinners, as an added benefit to our "academic" research on learning to teach, I discovered that food, company, and conversation were critical for creating a context where we could get to know each other well enough to carry out this important work.

The teachers also found this aspect of our collaborative work to be important—so important, in fact, that they created a presentation at an international conference by reenacting a dinner table conversation.[1]

This conversational setting afforded teachers more opportunities to formulate and explore questions from practice than did other environments for teacher learning where preestablished rules of discourse pre-

Dinner table conversations.
Left to right: Sam, Mary, Jennifer, Lisa, Karen, Anthony, Leslie.

vailed and personal critique was discouraged. I am reminded of Magda Lewis and Roger Simon's (1986) discussion of a university course where women's voices were silenced. Just as the female students in Simon's class found his emphasis on theoretical abstraction too distant from their experiences, the male and female teachers in our group complained that teacher education seminars were too curriculum-oriented, directed by topics that were primarily relevant to the course instructor. The less formal car-pool conversations became the contexts for really reflecting on and struggling with the practice and theory of learning to teach.

After graduation, similar conversational spaces were hard to find. Faculty meetings covered the procedural business of running a school. School-based, inservice conversations were planned around academic and/or administratively determined concerns, and rarely allowed much room for discussions of the broader issues surrounding teaching and learning in schools, or, for that matter, for day-to-day teacher concerns. It was as if these issues were to have been dealt with in preservice teacher education. If a teacher was to acknowledge that she had concerns or problems about which she didn't know what to do, she was considered ineffective. Thus teachers' voices that might have brought common concerns forward for public consideration and assistance were silenced. So they took away from school meetings new certainties or knowledges that an external "expert" or "authority" had given, tried to put that knowledge into practice in their classrooms, and felt like failures if the new knowledge didn't resolve their (unspoken) concerns. Informal conversations in faculty lounges were not much better. Limited to negative discussions of students or teaching conditions, they seemed to be places where the problems associated with urban teaching (i.e., the students, their parents, changes in society, public financing)—and the teachers' sense of helplessness at overcoming these problems—became pronounced.

Thus we "discovered" and noted the importance of having places for conversation about our specific teaching concerns situated in the larger world of education, without receiving feedback that would either negate our experiences or disempower our need to construct new ways of knowing. The continuous process of our social meetings was not extracurricular, but key to our learning to teach. Lisa explained how we found the continuity of our process more important than receiving authoritative solutions to our classroom concerns: "I think what's important is that we're meeting, listening, and understanding each other. That's more valuable than important tips."

Focusing Our Learning on Practice-Based Concerns, Rather Than on Disembodied Theory or Topics

Seeking tips, hints, or the certainty of "knowledge" through theoretical prescriptions was not what this group was about. You may remember an earlier comment of Lisa's from chapter 2 that "reading didn't necessarily jump" into her mind at my suggestion. In fact, the issues that dominated our conversation, and through which we wove our life stories, came from examining and reexamining our common experiences in practice, rather than from learning externally authorized topics or theory. After experiential examples were identified, one of us would abstract them into seemingly related theoretical frameworks, which we all critiqued. Although across our years of work together, the "one of us" who did the abstracting was usually me, these teachers encouraged me to risk theorizing differently from the way I had been taught. For example, initially content to use my framework of theories from cognitive psychology to analyze their knowledge of reading, these teachers challenged both the theoretical abstraction (cognitive psychology) and the experiential focus or concern (reading instruction) by insisting that they needed to develop knowledge of relationships in their urban teaching practices before they could attend to reading instruction. Later they taught me that differences in life experiences made it hard for their students to focus on theoretically neat settings and methods for reading instruction. So, when I theorized that their stories could be simply explained through a neo-Marxian emphasis on class differences, the teachers shattered my propensity to seamlessly and collectively theorize their varied experiences. Their experiences, and their trust in themselves and me, awakened my personal postmodern (or post-certain) era. Here's an example from a transcript of a conversation during which we're reviewing an earlier draft of this text in which I've explained the difficulty of putting into our lower-class teaching practice communities the theories we were taught in our middle-class schooling and teacher education programs.

KAREN [REFERRING TO THE DRAFT OF THIS TEXT]: So, this low income thing, now this is, this is pretty interesting.

LESLIE: What page?

MARY: I kept circling it, as I read. I didn't realize it was a major issue for a lot of people and so I just kept changing it to—

KAREN [READING]: "At graduation, most of these middle class teachers took jobs in the lower-class environments of urban schools."

MARY: I've thought about the term "middle class" for years, but haven't *really* thought about it in relation to myself until I saw it in the drafts of this book.

SAM: I guess my perspective has been colored not only by my neo-Marxian reading to try and make sense of your experiences, but by my own teaching across international settings. No matter where I go, no matter what culture I'm in, there are major, major class differences. . . . I think its interesting that here in this society, we don't say it, we don't talk about class. We have to decide how to say it.

JENNIFER: I don't like the term lower class.

ANTHONY: I don't think that we're going to convince anybody there's a class society by using the term "lower class," so I don't know whether its worth the confusion. I would say low income or something like that.

LESLIE: I would say, where I teach is economically depressed. The kids come from an economically depressed area.

SAM: I just don't think you can say . . . an economically depressed *area*.

JENNIFER: Why?

SAM: Because of varying economic classes within the same area. I've lived in an area which is probably labeled economically depressed (because of the low-rent apartments and the crack/cocaine houses), yet there were also professional families in the neighborhood.

MARY: The kids in my school community are poor. They are all poor. They don't have enough money.

LESLIE: Same with my kids.

KAREN: But no, wait . . . the point is . . . Why is it different, more difficult to teach a classroom full of black kids from low-income communities than it is white middle-class kids? Or is it? I mean what are we talking about here?

MARY: I have kids who come to school, honest to goodness . . . their mom tells them, "Tell the teacher to give you a Band Aid." They come in bleeding. . . . They don't have enough money for food, they don't have enough money for clothes, they don't have money for safe, decent housing. I say they're economically depressed. I say they're poor.

JENNIFER: Economically different.

MARY: No.

JENNIFER: I come from a neighborhood where, by the time we grew up, everybody said we lived in a poor neighborhood. And we didn't know we lived in a poor neighborhood. And if somebody would have told us we lived in a poor neighborhood, we would have all fought. There would have been a big war.

MARY: Right. Me too. If they would have said I was poor.

JENNIFER: I mean I don't want these kids to read this book and think. . . . Well I don't want them, you know, it's like the grandmother story. I don't want "lower class" on them.

LESLIE: Yeah. And lower class and poor speaks directly to the individual. It's like sticking a label on the person's body.

SAM: You've convinced me. I think we've sort of agreed on something.

JENNIFER [OUR HUMORIST]: And we always agree on everything!! The point, the reason, my understanding of the reason that Sam thinks of this as "class" is because, she has come to this understanding of class as an issue in schools. And she wants to make it clear. And she wants to just say it.

LESLIE: So we can't use lower class, we can use "other classed."

JENNIFER: We could use lower class, but we're going to have to define it for ourselves.

SAM: I think, here's one point—I think—we agree on, that we believe the kids that we teach are historically, socially disadvantaged because of their education. And that is unjust. And we don't even quite know how to right it. And that, no matter how we describe them, there are many experiences that our students have that we've never had.

JENNIFER: And the reason that it's hard for a middle-class teacher to come in and teach black, lower-income, economically deprived kids is because when a middle-class teacher looks at a kid who comes to school without food, they say, "Why did you? Your mom makes, uses crack, there's something wrong with your family." . . . Somehow, that kid takes on the responsibility, that family takes on the responsibility for the crack use and abuse, and the kid takes on the responsibility for not being fed. That's why it's hard for a middle-class teacher to teach a black, lower class.

LESLIE: "You didn't bring a note that explained why you were absent last week." And, it's a state law in California that you bring notes and stuff like that.

SAM: It's a middle-class expectation.

JENNIFER: We forget to look at the society, societal reasons for why this kid comes to school without being fed, or even without saying, "Well, hey, I've got some noodles in the closet, so eat and let's go on."

KAREN: But that has to come through in our book. We have to take the position, that, that it's these kids who are different from what the school expects. There's something that they're not doing, they're not following the rules, or they're, they're not prepared for—

MARY: They're not the group the curriculum is written for. So, then why don't we, why don't we label the *school* then, rather than label the people?

LESLIE: Well, why can't we say something like that? Why can't we make a paragraph where we say, teachers who came *from* an environment, came *to* an environment, which contrasted—

Conversational relations: Jennifer and Leslie.

SAM: However we do it, I think the point in addressing it here, even if it isn't clear or isn't comfortable, is that we need to pay more attention, somehow, to diversity . . . that a standard curriculum and standardized testing and standard ways of schooling, based on norms from middle class communities, are not appropriate for teaching in urban settings. That's all I'm trying to say. How can I say it? A categorical description obviously is not adequate.

KAREN: It's not that *we're* middle class. It's that the *curriculum* is middle class! Both are problematic.

SAM: In teacher education, the "curriculum" is often constructed by "white, middle-classed," educational experts, based on research that's been done with "white middle-classed" kids. Even when you get into the culturally diverse stuff in [specialized cultural studies] you can see that the class issue is often hidden. You know? The economic issue is hidden. The opportunity of privilege issues are hidden, so the authors talk about ethnicity, or language type, without talking about issues of power and privilege which seem to be critical to *your* teaching positions.

LESLIE: And the reason that we are successful is because we don't rely on middle-class curriculum and middle-class ways of being?

SAM: That seems to be part of it.

LESLIE: That we have . . . we have overcome the pitfalls of experience because of that.

SAM: Or, we're overcoming.

LESLIE: Overcoming the pitfalls of experience because—

KAREN: Working at overcoming.

Everybody talks at once.

Later.

SAM: Okay. Can we turn this tape recorder off? What did we decide about the "class" issue?

KAREN: Oh, yeah. What?

JENNIFER: Nothing.

Though we didn't reach consensus on the theoretical abstraction of "class" differences, I learned a valuable lesson—one that I would need to be reminded of over and over to remember and use. These teachers taught me the importance of working to overcome my habit, as a university researcher, to neatly theorize our experiences, and to work at constructing new and dynamic theoretical interpretations by paying close attention to the variations across our lives, values, and practices.

Discovering Our Biographical Connections and Differences

One reason that we were able to open ourselves to each other's viewpoints is that, because of the social nature of our conversation, we told stories of our lives, and came to understand that opinions and beliefs came from explicit biographical experiences.* As such, contrastive views were less threatening than others that seemed based on ideology alone. We didn't find spaces for telling the stories of our lives or for tolerance of different views based on our lives in many of our school settings. Here's an example where Lisa describes her worries about relational conflicts based on life styles and values, and wondered if she could survive as a teacher.

> I feel so uncomfortable at my school. I feel like the little young radical from Berkeley. I used to get razzed about my "Greenpeace" bumper stickers. There is this social camaraderie among [most of the other teachers there]. They talk about wallpaper and furniture stores and recipes, and they do all this joking around about teachers' short hours. I want to talk about the place of education to achieve world peace, but I can't at school.
>
> I went to this conference with one of these teachers and had a great time talking with her. We talked about our lives and our goals for education. She understood me. But it doesn't happen in the lunch room. Then, when I think about it professionally, it's even more depressing. There are no grade level meetings, no connection between other grade teachers. None. There's one woman who saves me. She's the resource teacher. She's brilliant and collaborative. She understands and validates who I am. I feel like she's saved me.

Lisa's confusion reflected her personal struggle to survive as a "Berkeley radical" without supportive relations with others inside a traditionally conservative school climate. Her story, and others like it, led us to hear and care for each other as extended family. Because we cared, we understood and valued our biographical differences, and could learn to teach from them (although not without the occasional arguments, conflicts, and reconciliations that come from caring across differences). This process—of listening to viewpoints situated in life stories, and letting those viewpoints interrupt our familiar perspectives and illusions of truths or certainties (or see another point of view)—was vital both to our learning to teach and to

---

* Karen emphasized: "Understanding the biographical reasons for our views and our actions is very important!"

the telling of our stories in this book. Even our discussion about the place of our biographies in print (and their importance to others outside our group) revealed differences that required respect.

> SAM: As we're struggling with what to include in the book, perhaps we should include biographical information. For example, Karen thinks for sure I should talk about how I came to see the world in the way that I do.
>
> MARY: I also would be interested in everybody's biographies.
>
> LESLIE: What do you mean by that?
>
> SAM: Well, like the question is, why are you teaching in inner city schools, and why are we—
>
> LESLIE: Where does that fit in? I don't understand why that.
>
> MARY: Yeah, is that appropriate to this book?
>
> KAREN: I sure think it is.
>
> JENNIFER: Yeah, because when you read most educational stuff, they don't even say they're men or women, they just say their names, and they are three people, and they teach in this class, and they do this and that and the other, and they have this and that opinion, and they treat the kids this way and that way. Who are they? Are they white, are they black, are they Chicano, are they—what? Are the kids bicultural, bilingual, who, what, are they urban, suburban? Is it a one-room school house? Is it in New York? You don't know anything about what they're talking about.
>
> SAM: And where and how they've lived certainly biases their schooling and what they've noticed about education and how they argue for or against points they raise. Although we've been educated differently, we've come to know through our experiences that text is *not* objective.
>
> LESLIE: Well, I agree, but there are some things about my life that I would feel comfortable sharing outside of this group; then there are others that I wouldn't. I guess it would depend on the purpose [gives examples].
>
> MARY: I understand. There are some things about my life I'd rather not disclose as well.

In fact, we all understood Leslie's statement—and Karen's, Jennifer's, and mine. Facing the prospect of placing ourselves in print was very different from talking through our lives in the safety of our group. The result of this discussion was that we agreed to treat the matter of biography in ways that would honor our individual preferences.

Leslie and Sarah.

Valuing Our Lived Experiences and Emotions as Knowledge

The support these teachers received, both inside this group, from their families, and often even from peers at school, was important to understanding why these teachers could take risks to learn to teach. In safe conversational spaces, we could be learners of biographical, emotional, relational, and political as well as academic knowledge. Another factor was that they had a place, in our group and at home, where they could explore the emotions that came with learning to teach. Because the atmosphere of this setting came to be nonevaluative and trusting, we could take the risk of questioning whether our experiences were educative, expose our mistakes, and learn from the emotion and confusion of facing difficult issues.

In safe conversational spaces we could clarify our own devalued beliefs—often expressed through emotions—and recognize we were not "wrong" for holding them. In other words, the conversational process allowed us to raise contextual, personal, and emotional concerns to a level of publicly examined knowledge, which, in turn, not only helped us all to see ourselves as knowledgeable, but led us to construct some across-experience theories. That was not always the case at school. Here's a story Mary told to illustrate that point.

> I was talking about this child that—today was the day I gave her a report card. Two seconds later she had taken it out, she had her pencil out, she was changing every one of her grades. I mean, it became this horrible scene. It was awful. I was in tears, she was in tears. So I'm sitting here in the teacher's room crying a little, and I'm talking to this person and I can see in her face: "Who the hell are you to be talking to me about this? We don't talk about that. We talk about P.E., the kids that were in my class last year, and. . . ." I was inappropriate. It was really funny. So I just sort of picked myself up and found somebody who looked appropriate to talk to.

Articulating Professional Feminist Voices in Narrative Form

As we've demonstrated, our group was a safe place to talk about the emotional, political, and academic work of learning to teach, and discover our ways of knowing were both legitimate and interconnected to the work and lives of teachers. It was also important to get some perspective on our experiences by reflecting on them out of the classroom. Pulling back from the immediacy of our professional lives, we could explore the difficulties of our work, and see its passion and promise. Coming to see ourselves as knowledgeable allowed us to unapologetically critique structures and content that were inappropriate as support for our own learning and that of our students. As newcomers into the world of teaching and feminist thought, it was important to both raise our consciousness about our undervalued knowledge, and then act upon and revise it as we critically incorporated our experiential theories into the *established* socialized systems where we were employed as teachers—and where so-called "women's" concerns were devalued.

Tracing these teachers' transformations from first notions of self from their teacher education programs through their 4th and 5th years of teaching, I clearly saw the development of voice from a perspective of feminist epistemology. During this time together, we moved from a compliant position of received knowledge (applying others' knowledge to survive in an evaluative system of schooling) to another position of self-constructed knowledge (Belenky et al., 1986). Additionally, my own evolving sense of self as a feminist teacher education scholar developed dialectically in response to the teachers' emerging consciousness. It was because I learned that their different knowledges and experiences were devalued *at the same time* that I was coming to realize that similar experiences had occurred to me throughout my life and my experiences, that I began to seek the comfort in feminist analyses of knowledges and experiences (see chapter 11 for more of my story). In other words, being in relationship to this group helped me not only notice their development, but helped me take the risk to step outside my own education and critique it. I realized that, by doing so, I would also risk rejection by others in my field.[2] The continuous support of this group and their fidelity to this work gave me courage to do so. And, the risk seemed necessary for my own personal growth, if I was to come to imagine the world of teacher education differently. Through the gentle voices of these friends, I learned that transformations stimulated by and identified through the collaborative conversations don't need to be loud or frightening—just clear, narratively structured, and action-oriented.

Moving Toward Praxis

The feminist perspectives we developed and debated through our conversational method took on a perspective of *praxis*. In other words, engaging in continuous cycles of critique, knowledge construction, and social action were both method and result. Fortunately, we also learned from our experiences that we didn't have to know everything about teaching immediately. The evolutionary nature of the conversation led us to an awareness that learning to teach is a life-long process. Even as beginners, these teachers did not hold an expectation of immediate expertise that their schools and programs seemed to demand. In that sense, this group was privileged in their opportunities to learn to teach. I knew many other beginning teachers outside this group—learning to teach in the traditional individualistic, isolated, "sink or swim" manner—who were afraid to follow their hearts and beliefs in contrast to school policies (because they stated, as novices, they thought they should trust the guidance of those with more experience/authority). In contrast, I often found the teachers in our group consciously putting aside school-mandated curricula for others they felt were more appropriate for their students. When I asked Mary what she would say if called on that practice by an administrator, she told our group, "Why, I'd say 'I didn't know I was supposed to use those materials. I'm just a beginning teacher!'" More than gaining specific guidance for immediate concerns, the conversations seemed to provide the intellectual stimulation and social interaction needed to create, act upon, and analyze our own broader knowledges about teaching. (Chapters 4–10 contain examples of the teachers' actions resulting from the conversations.)

From the strength of our personal convictions about our work and the support of our group as a learning community, we came to know that we could take action to transform our professional worlds, and that we had already begun that process with ourselves. Moving across uncharted ground in this work, the language for telling our stories has not always come easy, nor is it always clear. Actually, there were pioneers of feminist praxis who had gone before us and whose stories might have helped us understand and articulate our own, but they had not been provided for our education. So we often had to rely on dim memories or imaginings of those who had gone before us. Sometimes we discovered similar stories of transformation-in-practice through women's poetry, novels, and other "unauthorized" text. Finding support in our own memories and those of other feminists helped us keep our senses open and "see" that our transformational work was valid. We could accept our intuitive sense of our own development as appropriate, even though others had rejected it most of our lives. Now in our 30s and 40s, it was not only validating, but a relief, to find stories of similar experience. Linda Lancione Moyer's poem, for example, speaks to our sense of the nonlinear but critical connection between our work, our biographies and our growth.

> Standing in the garden,
> left hand laden
> with ripe strawberries. The sun
>
> beams off the glassy backs of flies. Three
> birds in the birch tree.
>
> They must have been there all year.
>
> My mother, my grandmother
> stood like this
> in their gardens,
>
> I am 43.
> This year I have planted my feet
> on this ground
>
> And am practicing
> growing up out of my legs
> like a tree.
>
> *Linda Lancione Moyer, "Listen"*

As difficult as they are to describe, our transformational stories present a feminist challenge to traditional conceptions of learning to teach.

THE IMPORTANCE OF CLASSROOMS/COMMUNITIES AS CONTEXTS FOR LITERACY INSTRUCTION

The need for Leslie, Mary, and the other teachers to construct their own ways of knowing and teaching became clear in their descriptions of their classrooms.

> MARY: Our students have to deal with so much stress in their lives that sometimes I'd rather show them some love than make them struggle through another reading assignment.
>
> LESLIE: Several of my children live in households with relatives instead of their parents. In one home, there are seven children in the household—three from one family and four from another. . . . Chirna [3] is in a foster home again with a working mother. There's no father there, and the working mother has three of her own daughters. Chirna has had a lot of problems because she's been in foster homes and sometimes has had to steal to survive. When she comes home, she's not getting the attention that she needs either. When problems occur in the home, the family blames them on her.

Leslie and Mary, white American women, teach in multiethnic schools where standardized scores on literacy examinations are traditionally low. The schools themselves are set in communities where there were no "standardized" family units with the freedom, the economic security, and the motivation to encourage further study after school. In Mary's class, as we've already noted, many children had a parent in jail. Leslie's teaching day was frequently interrupted with children being pulled from school because their families had to move away to find work. Some children in both schools were homeless. The discrepancy between the children's personal reality and the real expectations of school left much of the "authorized" school curriculum with little meaning for either the students or their teachers. Too often the children had other, more important issues on their minds, such as their personal safety while getting to school. Here's an example of a discussion that I had with Mary's children. We were probing the personal sense they had made of a literature unit on Rosa Parks (an African-American woman whose refusal to give up her seat on the bus to a white person in 1955 became a precipitating event in the American Civil Rights movement).

> PARNEL: Some of the kids [at this school] act like gangsters. Some of them jumped me on the way home because I was wearing a red hat. They took it.
>
> KEENA: They was Bloods!

ANGELICA: Yeah, from the Blood Gang. You can't wear a red hat! You
  have to cover it up with something else.
KEENA: I don't care! I got red on!
ANGELICA: Sometimes, they don't want you to walk around or anything. Like my brother, Fred, you know, he's white. He's afraid
  to walk down the street to the bus stop.
SAM: Sounds like you've got a little civil rights work to do in this community.
KEVIN: My cousin, she said that the [North Side Gang] is starting to
  come over here to fight after school.
SAM: Why do they fight?
KEVIN: I don't know. I think because they don't like white people or
  they don't like people coming into the parts that they live in. And
  on the sidewalk, it has ["North Side Gang"] written big.
PARNEL: Yeah, they're bad!!
KEVIN: One time my brother, he went to a party. And then some people came into where the party was and they had guns. One hit my
  brother in the, uh, jaw with a gun and he had to go to the hospi-
  tal and his jaw was like real big, like this big. And he had to have
  his teeth wired shut, and he couldn't talk no more.
SAM: How did that make you feel?
KEVIN: Mad. Sad.

Understandably, many of Mary's and Leslie's children lacked the
secure sense of personal safety needed to sit quietly focused in a classroom
and work together. The contexts of their broader learning communities
sometimes made focusing on reading lessons seem trivial. Others, *fully a
third in each classroom,* had such poor literacy skills that performing academic work of any nature was difficult. Their attention was turned more
toward coping with the demands of literacy tasks rather than acquiring literacy. Therefore, the children's teachers not only faced the enormous
challenge of teaching them to read and write, but learning to know their
children well enough to provide appropriate emotional support. Unfortunately, external support was not consistently available from school psy-
chologists. Even the presence of such support would not have helped the
teachers personally know and relate to their children. Thus they spent part
of their teaching time getting to know the children's stories so that they
could appropriately respond relationally as well as academically to them.
Here's an example of Mary's coming to know her student, Angelica, and
the effect of that knowing on their instructional relationship. Angelica's
story, told orally, transcribed, and then edited by Mary, is somewhat
lengthy, but worth the effort.

Angelica is a fourth grade girl—an African-American. She has one brother, an older brother, so she's kind of the baby of the family.

Angelica has been raised by her father since her mother's death about a year and a half ago. She died of cancer and Angelica has had a very, very difficult time dealing with life since then. She probably had a difficult time dealing with life when her mom was still living just because her mother was sick. She kept her emotions under wrap more at the beginning of the year, and I did not see the pain that she was going through as much. As she began to trust me more and I began to challenge her more, she was able to show me her emotions and her pain. That's been very hard because of the position I'm in as her teacher. She's a very bright little girl. She has really good skills, she gets some support from home, not so much from her dad, although he is there for her on some important levels, but from her grandmother and from an auntie. She's just having such a hard time focusing and I can't blame her. It's got to be a painful thing going through as a child, having lost your mother.

As a consequence, she has been declining in her productivity. Actually, I don't think it's really been declining, I think that I've been able to see the fact that she is not focused. I've been able to see in her work the lack of attention. When I can get her attention, some things work really well for her. The Rosa Parks project was a really, really strong connection for her. She was able to pull a lot from her family and from her own personal history, from her connection with the church and bring all that together to keep her enthusiastic and interested in that project. But when we got to the next reading unit, the free-choice reading program, there was not that connection for her . . . there wasn't a circle of strength for her. It was a real solo thing and I don't think she has a lot of personal strength available for school.

Throughout the year something would be . . . hard or emotionally painful for Angelica. For example, I wanted to read a poem from Eloise Greenfield's book, *Nathaniel's Talking*. A character in the book talks about how he feels about his mother dying. It took me 2 days before I could read that poem out loud because I knew that Angelica and I would both be having a hard time with it. And sure enough, when I did get around to reading it, she and I both fell apart. Her mother's death was really painful—and painful reminders were all around her, even at school.

I digress, I'm talking more about Angelica and myself than I am about the reading program . . . but, I've had a hard time assessing Angelica based on any of the work that we've been doing because of the backdrop of her life, or the substance of her life that hasn't to do with school. I don't think that she's made a whole lot of progress in developing her literacy this year and I don't know that that's such a horrible thing. From a teacher's point of view, I think it's horrible. I want her to enjoy books. I want her to find solace for her pain and her fears by reading about other people but she's not ready to do that. I want her to not lose years of her academic growth because she lost her mother. I don't want her to find herself in ninth grade and having all the pains of being a ninth grader and not having any basic math, for instance, so that she can go on and take algebra and be able to choose to become a doctor or whatever. . . . I know that that's a leap to project Angelica out into her life like that, but it's what happens. . . . I think about my responsibilities and what it is I need to do in the classroom but then . . . when I read a poem and Angelica starts crying and I know exactly why, it's real hard for me to say "You need to write in your journal today. You didn't do your math this morning. You didn't do this, and you haven't done your homework and your reading log's not coming in and—." The nature of my responsibility is not always clear and it is often conflicting. It's a dilemma that I'm not going to solve today or tomorrow or maybe anytime.*

Mary didn't solve the problem of the conflict between students' out-of-school worlds and their in-school performances in the more than 7 years I've known her. But neither did she just close her eyes and ignore or trivialize those differences. In fact, through careful attention to such tensions, she learned to critique, not the children or their communities, but the normative events of school—such as standards for goals and objectives, academic work and assessment—and enact the curriculum through her own and her students' lives.[4] The importance of community and life on her curriculum, instruction, and evaluative choices became part of her knowledge of teaching literacy.

PERSONAL CHOICES THAT FOSTERED LEARNING-IN-RELATIONSHIP

It became clear in our conversations that Mary, Leslie, and the rest of us not only cognitively "knew" that we should set up classrooms that would

---

* Leslie added: "This is wonderful insight on Mary's part. It is because she understands that her 'job' changes as the children change that enables her to be such a good teacher and an excellent learner–model. Teaching is often more learning than teaching." Mary also added a postscript to this story. "Angela's father recently married a woman from his church. Angela has 3 new sisters and a wonderful new mother!"

allow us to learn about their students' lives, but that we also personally *preferred* relational or cooperative classroom structures to more competitive or authoritarian designs. Leslie, for example, talked to us one evening about her belief against a traditionally competitive classroom. She, like Mary, saw that standard, competitive, and "objective" evaluation systems—like testing and grading—went against the varying needs for compassion her students showed.

> I have always tried in my classroom to downplay competition, for some very strong, personal reasons. My motto has been that "the important thing is to try." Learning by working together became so normal in the class that helping your friends to write or read was just what we did. As competition and comparing decreased, the classroom became a more equitable environment for all students. Those who had trouble reading or writing could always be involved in a project because they were supported and helped by their friends.

Mary also disliked having students read without the support of a group. She talked to a member of our research team about her rationale.

> I rarely have the kids read aloud. The acoustics in the room are so bad that it is hard for kids to hear. I don't like to do it. The kids who enjoy reading out loud aren't necessarily the kids who do the best job at it. . . . It's not effective. My kids don't listen to each other. They complain: "I couldn't hear!" "She reads too fast!" The story just gets ripped to pieces. By the time that we've gotten two pages done I've had to interrupt them 15 times and ask somebody to speak up and ask somebody to slow down. And I will not let them correct each other, not out loud. If someone is sitting next to someone and they help them in a whisper then that's fine. But I don't want five kids jumping on poor Jamika. She just can't stand to be corrected. She gets furious and embarrassed. She's real sensitive about her reading.

Mary's instructional choices fostered an atmosphere of safety and trust in her classroom. She promoted student choice in both instructional grouping arrangements and curricular selections, which demonstrated her trust in students.

> Kids weren't really restricted to any of the books that I chose. They could choose books that they brought in or that they got off of our classroom library shelf. In one case I took a girl into our school library to see if we could find a book that she wanted to read. So, it was self-selected material that they were reading, skewed by the fact that I did

bring in books and made suggestions of books that they should read. They self-selected their partner or partners or they could choose to work alone. Now, they were not making a commitment to stay with the partner the entire 9 week period. They could change partners when they finished a book. As a matter of fact, I really didn't hold anyone to making a commitment to another person. (For more on Mary's "friendship pairs," see chapter 6.)

Mary's acceptance of children's choices led them to trust themselves as capable of and responsible for their own relational and academic learning. Another point is worth mentioning here that becomes the basis for the stories of teacher research presented in Part II of this book. Mary didn't just organize her class for her *students'* knowing-through-relationship. Encouraging them to take control of their instructional environment freed up her time so that she could learn from observing their interactions. Here's an example where she wonders if her structure is helping with social development as well as the cognitive work of learning to read.

Keena did one book report with Celeste. This is interesting. They did a reconciliatory book report on the *Grandfather Stories from Mexico*. It was a reconciliation considering that, days earlier, Celeste and Keena were ready to kill one another. When I look at the dynamics of their relationship, I see this whole process as being so social, yet I did not [consciously] build this factor into my literacy program. Nowhere did I say I want you to work with X number of people, and I want you to work with the person you've been having the most problems with on the playground—or, I want you to work with the person that is your best friend. Of course I was never saying any of that, but I think what had happened, is that, by allowing that flexibility, it allowed them to use that academic program to facilitate some of their relationship problems. . . . Anyway it's an interesting idea and it would be a whole different study to figure out the social ramifications of any kind of a reading program and whether it helped with social development, whether it had anything to do with emotional development as well as cognitive development.

Consistent attention to her students' relations led Mary to appreciate the simultaneous development of personal and academic achievement. Here's a story of Keena in another cooperative relationship with Wanda.

I can't hide my absolute thrill at how those two girls worked together. It made Keena see herself as a serious student. Wanda has always been

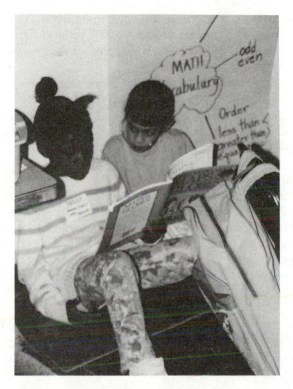

Two friends in Mary's classroom.

a serious student. What happened for Keena was that she saw herself as an achiever, as a productive, serious person, not just the girl that is totally boy crazy, not just the girl who maybe can get by, but she was a serious intelligent student. . . . Wanda was one of those perfect little students. She finished everything she started. She did a really wonderful job, but was not particularly creative. She was a fairly good tutor if I put her with younger kids but she was never what I thought of as a leader. I wanted her to be a leader real badly. And so I kept putting her in positions like that and it just never worked out. But one on one with Keena what happened was she was able to experiment a little bit with creativity rather than just the rote work. Wanda would produce the perfect sentences, the perfect everything. It was boring. As she worked with Keena, she loosened up, she became more creative, I mean even with their writing forms. They would switch the colored pens back and forth to create a rainbow of sentences. For Wanda that was real progress. She was trying something new. They decided to write each other's biographies, instead of writing their own. It was a creative, sensitive way to express the success of their partnership.

Yet cooperation was not the rule if students needed other approaches.

MARY: I frequently worry about a few kids who would prefer just very strict routine. On a daily basis they'd read for 20 minutes then they'd do a worksheet and have a spelling test. I think a lot of kids would be happy with that.

SAM: Like—

MARY: Kevin, Celeste, the kids who said to you, "Why are you asking what we're doing?" They are the kids who are the most uncomfortable with my free-flowing, noncompetitive activities. And I did accommodate them. They're the ones I gave contracts to. They felt good about that and they did, as much as I didn't like their impersonal conclusions about the books that they read, they did feel like they were successful.

Mary's acceptance of herself as an explorer of human and curricular relationships also allowed her to try on *my* perception of a case where the emphasis on cooperation might be relaxed. She later reflected on the effect of that conversation.

Micky had . . . tried so hard, remember at the beginning of the year? I didn't want him to be a "loner," so I was forcing him to work with a partner and I kept making him, making him, making him. And finally, you know, you said "Wait a minute! You need to look at this child differently." I was having such a hard time with him. And I realized that I needed to back off and let him choose his own way and in that [free-choice] reading program, he was able to do that. He was able to float in and out so that he might just really, really work hard by himself on *The Great Cheese Conspiracy,* and then entice others into his isolated corner, and then come out of it with them. I mean . . . I loved that! There was this dance of my little "loner student," in and out of these social relationships based on his incredible retelling skills, and his artistic skills, and his attempts at being asocial without the threat of forced cooperation.

Telling Our Stories Outside of Our Conversational Group

At the end of each set of stories across chapters 3 and 4, I want to step out of the narrative to connect our stories with others in the world of education research—to show how other's theories of experiences have helped me understand our own. At the end of chapter 4, I will then weave the strands together to create a theoretical tapestry of our learning to teach.

THEORIES OF THE SOCIAL CONSTRUCTION OF KNOWLEDGE. It is probably clear that these sets of stories described in this chapter show an allegiance to what has been often called "a social constructivist view of learning." Some readers might suggest that Mary and Leslie were operating out of such *cognitive knowledge* when they designed their literacy programs. It is correct to say that they would have heard not only Lev Vygotsky's (1978) research on learning which suggested that personally meaningful knowledge is socially constructed through shared understandings, they would have also read John Dewey's (cited in Bruner, 1962) writings on education as a social process and the school as a form of community life. The social life of the classroom "gives the unconscious unity and background of all [the child's] efforts and all his attainments. . . . The true center . . . is not science, nor literature, nor history, nor geography, but the child's own social activities" (p. 116).

So it is probably accurate to say that Mary and Leslie (and the rest of us) were significantly influenced by the cognitive knowledge acquired in our teacher education programs (for example, that socially constructive learning is theoretically "good"). However, the teachers' classroom actions and performances also appear to have come from ways of knowing about children's learning that were less prescriptive and perhaps not entirely cognitive. Their sense of care for these children, and their apparent desire to be in relationship with them—not just to foster the children's learning, but their own as well—is a common example.

OTHER WAYS OF KNOWING

The combination of the compelling need to learn about the contexts in which they were teaching, the safety of the collaborative conversation, and the strength of their own personal convictions about relational learning gave Mary and Leslie a motivation, a context, and a means to come to learn what they needed to begin to develop more-successful-than-not literacy lessons for urban students. Similar circumstances were found in Jennifer's, Lisa's, and Anthony's classrooms, as well as mine and Karen's public school classrooms.

As my relationship with them grew and I listened to their stories, I came to understand that learning to teach in urban classrooms is a personal and emotional process, perhaps as much as it is a cognitive and rational affair.* I will say more about their learning to teach in cognitive and other ways as we create a theoretical tapestry of their experiences in the chapters to come. The stories that follow in chapter 4, for example, will not only further illustrate the passion involved in learning to teach, but will also argue for personal and relational development as a primary way of knowing about teaching.

ENDNOTES

[1] The presentation was at the International Conference on Teacher Research, Stanford University, April, 1992.

[2] As academics in teacher education, we feel comfortable in critiquing teachers' knowledge and pedagogy, yet we are less comfortable in critiquing our own. In the most recent volume of the *Handbook for Research on Teaching* (Wittrock, 1986), for example, there are no studies reported of teacher–educators' knowledge and pedagogy—yet it is surely relevant to teachers' knowledge. My reading in feminist research methodology suggests that researching the "other" without researching the "self" lacks a sense of ethics. Fortunately, that situation is changing now. There is even a Special Interest Group beginning within the American Educational Research Association which looks at teacher–educators' own practices. For an excellent example, see Zeichner, in press.

[3] All students are referred to by pseudonyms.

[4] For an excellent discussion on the concept of curriculum enactment, see Doyle, 1990.

---

* Concurring with this text, Leslie added: "I don't believe it's possible to teach well without employing an emotional, intuitive process."

4

Stories of Relational Knowing in Learning to Teach Literacy

At the end of the 1st year in our conversational group, feeling successful about our broadened understanding of the complex concerns and issues we had raised, we were now ready to directly take up the issue of literacy instruction. As with other issues, our conversational redirection was grounded in practice. Late in the spring of our 1st year, most of the urban schools in which these teachers taught mandated a switch from literacy programs based on individually selected pieces of literature to basal programs (which contained graded literature-based text selections). Teachers' attention to reading was thus influenced by school requirements to attend inservice workshops on the new commercial reading program that had been adopted by their districts. As a group, the teachers felt that issues of diverse values, interpersonal relationships, and personal power were at stake in complying with the new mandate. Mary talked to our group about her concerns.

> Who *is* the audience for this reading series? I have heard that over 75% of the school districts statewide have adopted this popular text. I can't believe that the state population is that homogeneous. Take my class for example: 72% of my students are black, 24% are Filipino, and 4% are white. This is a very different population from my student-teaching experience in Berkeley. It is a very different population than some other parts of Vallejo. Given this diversity, it is hard to believe that 75% of the elementary school children could be well served by the same reading series.

Beginning with those district mandates, the teachers chose to spend our 2nd year (and eventually our 3rd, 4th, and 5th) working on the issue of personally and contextually appropriate literacy curriculum and instruction. Initially, they each chose literacy instruction methods that were working well in their classrooms and shared what they were learning, how the students were changing, and how they were changing as teachers. Their reports took the form of "showcasing" their knowledge as the teachers became peer instructors for the group. The others asked questions and took back new ideas for their own classrooms. Eventually, they brought instructional situations to the group that were *not* going so well, and received encouraging feedback.

The ongoing group conversation allowed them to get specific support from teachers with "specialized knowledges" in a way that they could not from me alone as a reading course teacher, from distant and often inapplicable reading research, from many of their field supervisors who knew little about reading, nor from generic inservice programs. You will also notice that not only reading and writing, but the speaking/listening aspects of literacy (so often left out of classroom instruction, partly because they are difficult features to assess), became a central part of our own process of learning to teach in the conversational group—and often an important part of these teachers' literacy curricula. As we have seen in chapter 3, conversations about literacy instruction were supported not only by the cognitive knowledge acquired by their preservice programs, but by their learnings about the less-well understood relational and social issues underlying their work in challenging classrooms.

RELATIONAL KNOWING

The importance of relations in learning to teach, in fact, continued to surface in conversational examples of classroom reading practice across the years. As I examined stories for patterns in their learning to teach literacy, in order to report to a funding agency who had supported a portion of this work, the relational stories stood out. The theoretical explanations for the stories came from the examples of practice. That is, my watching, listening, and learning from these teachers in conversation, noticing, but not fully understanding their practices in terms of the traditional educational literature, led me to look for other experiences—often summarized as theory—that supported the practices. It was a figure-ground problem, similar to learning to weave—an art that was part of my life before graduate school. In traditional educational research, I learned that we "weave" practice to theory where the warp (or framework) is the existing theory and the weft (or patterns) is data explained (or made possible because of) the warp.

Because of the messiness of the conversation, the complexity of the individuals with whom I was collaborating, and my intention not to directly manipulate these teachers' thoughts and actions (except for my undeniable power—as the one who initiated and would report our conversations—in telling *my* stories and pointing out *my* views in conversation), trying to make sense of these teachers learning to teach left me somewhat theory-less. I found that the data or stories revealed patterns that did not exactly fit existing knowledge theory in which I was educated (except for the sociocognitive theories described in chapter 3),[1] and I had to reposition the stories as warp or framework through which strands of theory served as weft. I had to read in new fields, and try out and recommend other theories as figure for the grounded stories. In the end, we had to construct our own theoretical interpretations of our experiences as a group. I'll try to give examples of such analyses as I tell the stories, by periodically stepping out of the narrative.

Details of what these teachers learned about literacy instruction through conversations about their practices and their active research are addressed in chapters 4–10 of this book, each chapter featuring specific teachers. This chapter contains accounts of Mary's and Leslie's learning to teach literacy in relationship with their students. The stories, organized as narrative sets, will show that both women display a passionate belief in themselves and their children as knowledge creators and evaluators, a willingness to honor the diverse styles and skills of their students, an ability to create innovative approaches to literacy instruction that respected students' needs, and a propensity to look critically at both their children and themselves in relationship to evaluate the results.[2] The theme of "relational knowing" will become clear in the clusters of stories that follow.

In case the stories told in Part I are mistakenly read as cheerful and seamless progress toward an easy freedom,* it is important to note that other stories that describe their struggles in learning to teach are reported in the chapters to follow in Part II. However, to offer some hope in a prevailing sense of hopelessness across stories of urban education (e.g., Fine, 1990; Kozol, 1991; Rose, 1989), we thought it important to select stories early on in our text that demonstrate the potential for success in urban settings. These stories are organized in sets to describe Mary and Leslie's

---

*Karen asked: "What does this mean?" Leslie responded: "That the whole process of learning to teach has been difficult because we essentially had to find our way along, but may appear easy in the retelling."

learning to teach literacy in relation to curriculum, self, and pedagogy, and the politics of literacy education. They are interspersed with theoretical discussions that connect them to related stories outside of those told here.

Stories About Curricular Relationships

Leslie, as you may remember from chapter 2, originally was concerned with curriculum as the "course of study, as product, as text to be covered, and ends to be achieved and measured." She withdrew, for a while, from the conversational group in order to focus on such issues. But, as we've noted, she found there was more than academic curricular knowledge in learning to teach, and returned to the group in its 2nd year.

With the passion of newcomers in careers of choice, both Mary and Leslie believed themselves and their children to be capable of working on the tension between personal sensitivity and academic progress together. To meet the challenge, they engaged in many types of learning relationships that helped them rewrite the "standard" or instrumental concept of curriculum (i.e., facts and ideas as text) to that of curriculum as life. They learned from their students, sought support from other adults for their dilemmas, and broke away from the boundaries of traditional curricular programs to follow their own interested relationships to the tasks. Leslie wrote about the relational support she received to move away from isolated subject instruction, and integrate the disciplines through reading, discussing, and responding.[3] She began to see the subjects of curriculum as lived instead of learned. What excited her about experiencing the interconnections between life and school, she found, also excited the children.

> During one spring [in my 3rd year of teaching], a friend, who was also the other second grade teacher, and I began sharing our frustration with science. We found ourselves in conversations along the lines of, "What are you thinking of doing for science this week? I've got a rock collection." Both of us felt extremely unhappy with such a disconnected, piecemeal approach, and neither of us felt that it could make much sense to our students. It did not tap their interests nor help them make meaningful connections. There was a district science text, but following it was again a disconnected approach unrelated generally to any other curriculum covered during the year. The conversations increased and ideas began to flow. By the end of the year we had committed ourselves to the idea of doing "themes" the following year that would integrate science and social studies for the first time into our language arts program.
>
> The integration of science and social studies opened up our cre-

ativity and enthusiasm. We turned out to be excellent role models for
our second graders because we were learning as they were learning.
We encouraged them to teach us. We all became "scientists" or
"researchers," who, by the way, needed to read to gather information,
write to record or transform what we had learned into stories, poems,
letters, etc. We created art projects because, for example, it was a good
way to learn how the Navajo Indians wove. We learned songs, we saw
videos, we took walks and used the environment in our projects, we
did plays and performed them. With the focus being the theme and
not the text, anything was a source. We found ourselves much more
creative than we had been when we had taught second grade curriculum from a more traditional approach in which the district-mandated
textbooks run the curriculum. This, in turn, allowed the students to
be more creative.*

Mary wrote about the new unit on Rosa Parks in her Civil Rights literature theme developed outside of the traditional curriculum in her 3rd
classroom year. Though her curricular choices differed from Leslie's, the
goals were similar, as were the means—a personal relationship between
teacher, the curriculum, and the children. Mary was hesitant to include her
personal needs and interests in a discussion of curricular goals in the discussion. Yet they were clearly as important to the selection of the materials as were her children's needs and interests.

I set several goals for myself and for my students for this particular
unit on Rosa Parks. First, research skills: I wanted the children to
develop research skills so that they would have the power within
themselves to find out about any topic they wanted. The next were
the basic language art skills of reading and writing, listening, and discussing. I wanted them to learn to generate their own questions about
a particular topic, to write about it, talk and listen to others, and to
find new ideas and information from the songs and stories we were
reading together. I wanted them, of course, as I always do, to become
better cooperative learners, and an overwhelming goal was for them
to be successful.
    There was another overriding goal as well, however, and I think
that motivates me more than anything, if I'm going to be honest

---

* Leslie added a footnote to this story: "Taking control to write curriculum which
I thought to be more relevant to the children also gave me encouragement to do the
follow-up teacher research on the effects of such an approach for students."

about the goals that I set for myself and my class. I wanted the students to be really enthusiastic about Rosa Parks. She was a person that I have always had a great deal of respect for and . . . as a symbol to me, she epitomized a regular person who takes a lot of risks, who seizes a certain amount of personal power in becoming politically active. I wanted the children to see that as a way to empower themselves in a world that very frequently takes power away from people. I also wanted the kids to cooperate. Although I don't think I taught that directly in this particular project, I wanted them to look beyond what Rosa Parks stood for. I wanted them to look beyond the Civil Rights movement, and I wanted them to look at what all of that stood for as far as people being able to get along—whether with a racial issue or from an organizational point of view. And somehow I wanted them to experience that. Those were the overriding goals.

Mary changed specific strategies and curricular materials several times during the unit to achieve those goals. Her fidelity to curriculum that had personal meaning both for herself and her students, and her close attention to students' responses—rather than a focus on curricular principles or popular pedagogical strategies—guided her instruction. Pleased by the enthusiasm of her African-American children about the Rosa Parks unit, but troubled by the minimal response from Filipino children, for example, Mary then brought in the *Grandfather's Stories from the Philippines.*

I don't think I had a single Filipino student in my class that did not read those. . . . At first, there was a certain amount of embarrassment about the book, that it had to do with the Philippines and self-consciousness, but it was one of those things that I really pumped up. . . . I wanted those kids to feel really comfortable about having that book in the classroom and that we all need to know about other cultures and we all need to know about our own cultures that we've left behind and in some ways that we have brought with us. After making this big public statement about it and sharing the book and looking at it, I got a lot more book reports from the Filipino students. . . . They recognized things that they'd either been told about or had seen in their own lives.

For Mary, curriculum was not only a vehicle for learning literacy and content knowledge, but a means for developing relationships between life and school—and for developing friendships across the various cultural ways in her classroom.

Stories of the Self in Pedagogical Style

> A teacher in search of his/her own freedom may be the only kind of
> teacher who can arouse young persons to go in search of their own.
> (Greene, 1988, p. 14)

Neither Mary nor Leslie was concerned about the fact that they did not
have permanently formulated literacy programs—even at the beginning of
their 4th years. Remember Mary's solid ring of self-acceptance in response
to my probe about the fear of administrative critique of her innovative
reading program in chapter 3? She intended that her children feel just as
secure in their progress. As a result of their continuous questing (further
described in chapters 5, 6, and 9), Mary and Leslie came to firmly believe
that they could design programs that honored and respected their children's lives, that validated their dawning senses of self, and built this on a
developing core of trust. They designed programs where children could
see themselves as capable of literacy in school as well as in their lives. Mary
summarized her views about eclectic reading programs to foster success
that demonstrated fidelity to children as individuals rather than to a particular theoretical perspective.

> Using a single approach hadn't worked. Because the kids are so dif-
> ferent and at such different levels of skills, and different levels of inter-
> est. . . . What I tried to do was to make the program itself have so
> many different parts so that kids could be successful at some place in
> that program. Maybe they were really good writers or were really
> good drawers, or maybe they were able to do an oral report compared
> to doing a written report; these options were available. They could
> tape record themselves reading instead of working publicly. I wanted
> kids to see someplace in this program that they could be successful.
> They could look forward to some activity, at some point, either dur-
> ing the day or during the week where they could be successful.

Mary's compassion for children who were struggling with literacy was
grounded in her own memory of herself learning to read.

> I think my own struggle with learning to read is something that I
> share very readily with kids and with parents in my school. Because I
> think there is an assumption that if you don't get it you're lost, it's all
> over with, and I can't stand that. I can't stand that notion that people
> will think that it's too late. I didn't have anybody come to my rescue.
> My ability to read came of its own free will when it needed to. There

was also the expectation that I would read, and I can't stand that people will remove that expectation [for these children] and in fact will replace it with sort of a condemnation: "You won't read!"

Mary's own story was clearly background for her conviction that she would find a way for her third and fourth grade students to become literate. Leslie has a similar story of turning questions she had about her own schooling (which often surfaced in our conversational group) into instructional lessons for her students.

> As I became more engaged in the integrated/thematic approach and more analytical about the value of this approach in reference to my own education, I couldn't help but return to the basic question, "What is learning?" And so I engaged the children in this question. There were discussions on what learning was, why we did it, how we applied it, where it happened and who did it. . . . By the end of the year I was a very happy teacher who gazed out on a room of 8-year-olds who had transformed themselves from "students" to "researchers, teachers, and scientists." Students were more conscious of nature/science programs on television and of gathering information from them, as many sharing times in class demonstrated. . . . There were more discussions in class about what they had seen or noticed on the way home. Children discovered new sections in the library and books around their homes that they brought in to use as teaching sources.

Connecting personal life stories to the curriculum was a common theme for both teachers and students in these classrooms. However, while noting similarity in their commitments, their connections, and their interests in program variety, it is also important to note that Mary's and Leslie's particular teaching styles reflected their unique ways of being in the world. Though their goals were similar, their enactment of curriculum and pedagogy was very different, reflecting differences in their personalities, energies, and senses of order. Listen to Mary's conversation with me about differences between herself and Leslie.

> MARY: Leslie's reading approach is much more organized than mine. I can't hold my interest that long. I can't, not even for daily journal or free writing. It doesn't fit my temperament. So my teaching has to change. It has to have movement. And that's one way that I'm real different from Leslie.
>
> What Leslie does that I really appreciate is within her struc-

ture she provides choice. I think she can do that because she's a calmer person than I am. Her energy is directed in a different way. Her energy is directed more emotionally. She's just a lot calmer in her presentation and in her approach. She's . . . I don't know what it is. One of my colleagues, Meisha, and I were talking about this. Our style is more hyperactive. We are the people in our classrooms who generate the most free-floating anxiety and energy. That we're the ones that set the pace. That we're the ones who cause the kids to be out of their seats, who cause the kids to sharpen their pencils when they shouldn't, that it's somehow or other the kind of energy that we bring. We interrupt ourselves in the middle of a lesson to say excitedly, "You know what we should do!" We'll get kids off task because we see something so incredible we can't stop ourselves from saying "Look! Look what Kanisha did."*

SAM: Sort of a spontaneity.

MARY: Yeah. We've talked about how our energy produces a different kind of interaction with kids. We can't learn a management style that's not part of our way of relating with kids in groups. Even if other people think we should. It's not just that we've learned, "Oh, that's not what you do if you really want to have good classroom management." We didn't . . . we're not going to have that, we're carrying our own styles into the classroom Leslie didn't have to learn [an artificial managerial style] either. She's had a sense of herself in a different way in the classroom from the beginning.

Mary's understanding of the importance of self in learning carried over to her expectations of children's responses to text. In giving performance feedback to her students, she often asked that they involve themselves.

I asked the kids to research Rosa Parks and that phase of the Civil Rights movement by coming up with questions that were important to them. One interesting thing that happened in this particular activity was the ways that students formed their questions. Some students addressed their question as if it would be answered by Rosa Parks herself, for instance, "Do you still live in Montgomery?" Other students

---

* Karen's response to this passage: "This reminds me so much of myself!"

addressed their question to sort of a broader audience, such as "What was it like in Vallejo back in those days?" "How old would Martin Luther King, Jr. be today if he was still alive?" . . . . One of the places that the questions came from involved homework assignments where I asked them to go home and ask questions about Rosa Parks. . . . I think what happened with that particular activity was that it localized the issue for students. . . . They were grappling with the concept of historical perspective and what they were trying to do, it seems to me, was to ground it in something that was closer to home. Something that was a lot nearer to them than Montgomery, Alabama. There was also a real marked difference between some Filipino students and some African-American students in the questions that they generated. For some Filipino students, it wasn't as personal, while I felt that the whole issue of the Civil Rights movement became significant to most of the African-American students. [See Figure 4-1.]

Telling Our Stories Outside of Our Conversational Group

THEORIES OF SELF/OTHER RELATIONS. Stepping outside these stories for a moment, I should note that because of my sense of their universal nature—and because of a perceived need to relate our experiences to preconstructed theory (to be taken seriously as a professor; see Rich, 1985)—I continued my search for other stories and theories that would help me better understand ours, and moreover, help us link our experiences in the group with others in the larger world. I searched for similar patterns in others' experiences to weave into the tapestry of our stories. My reading was also personally rewarding. I discovered many educators who suggested (as I had sensed from listening to the stories) that teachers require a dynamic understanding of self in relationship to both self and others across multiple contexts! Our group was surely providing a context for self/other relationship development. I found that much good theoretical work had already been done in this area, including that of Michael Connelly and Jean Clandinin (1986), Maxine Greene (1979), Arthur Jersild (1955), Jennifer Nias (1989), Nel Noddings (1984), and Max Van Maanen (1990). The heart of those works, for the purposes of the current argument, is that knowing through relationship to self and others is central to teaching the child. I'll share some of those alternative arguments for knowing differently here, in case others don't know them, and to help illuminate our own experiences and stories.

While the value of relational knowing is emphasized in the stories told across these books, it seems important to draw attention to it outside of the stories, in order to make clear that there are other important ways of

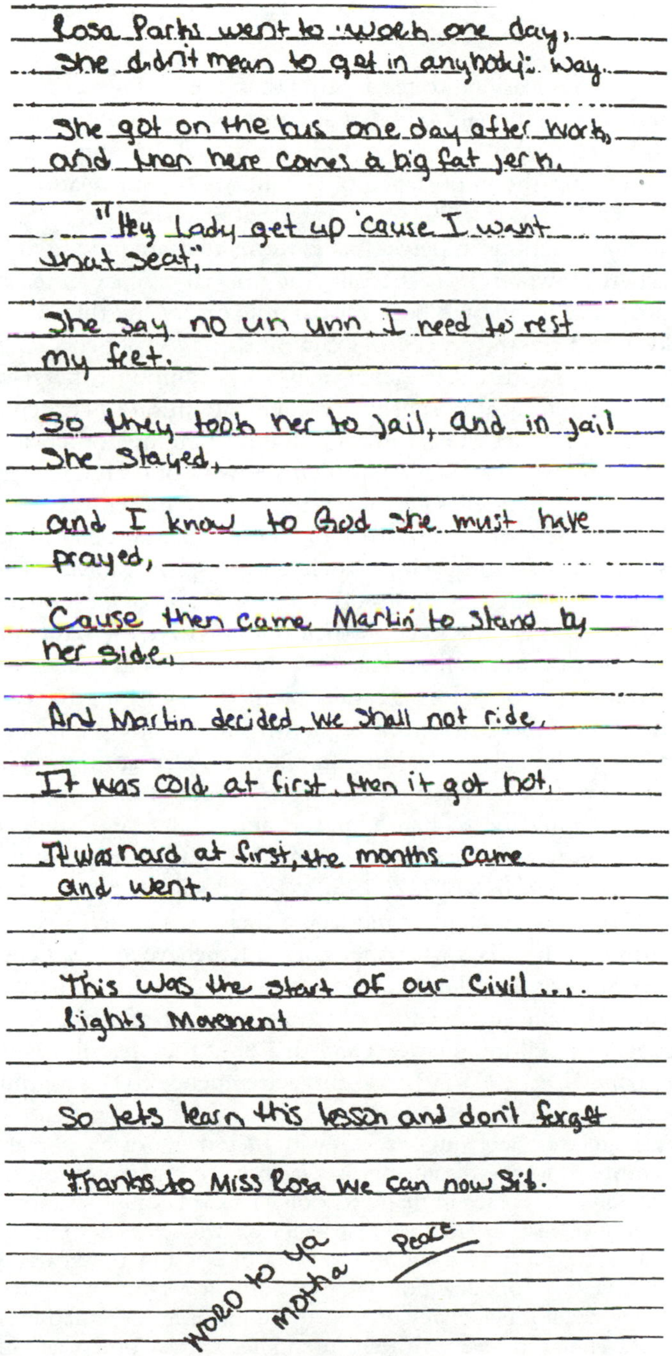

Rosa Parks went to work one day,
She didn't mean to get in anybody's way.

She got on the bus one day after work,
and then here comes a big fat jerk.

"Hey lady get up 'cause I want
that seat."

She say no un unn, I need to rest
my feet.

So they took her to jail, and in jail
she stayed,

and I know to God she must have
prayed,

'Cause then came Martin to stand by
her side,

And Martin decided, we shall not ride,

It was cold at first, then it got hot,

It was hard at first, the months came
and went,

This was the start of our civil....
rights Movement

So lets learn this lesson and don't forget

Thanks to Miss Rosa we can now sit.

WORD TO YA
motha   peace

FIGURE 4-1
Student's rap on Rosa Parks.

knowing about learning to teach other than the traditional cognitive, individualistic, and rational views that are promoted in teacher education programs. Moreover, even the best cognitive models become suspect without acknowledging the importance of self-knowledge in relationship to students. Jennifer Nias (1989) reminds us that teachers interpret their pupils' actions and reactions in perceptual patterns that are unique to the person of teacher. However, it has become the normal practice in teacher education programs to sidestep both the painful anxiety and the complexity that would come from the process of examining one's experiences of self in various relational settings. Teacher–educators (among others) with good intentions often turn prospective teachers' attention to curriculum, pedagogical tasks and activities, and even to understanding others in a rational, dispassionate manner. Accomplishing the work of such knowledge acquisition at a pace that defies personal reflection is another way that educators avoid the anxiety of coming to know either central beliefs about themselves, or the meaning behind their chosen profession as teacher. The result can be technically "correct" but less than compassionate teaching because teachers are not freed by their training to develop the potential for compassion that comes from knowing themselves and others well.

Yet knowing ourselves is a valuable part of learning to teach. Arthur Jersild, in an important but infrequently cited study published in 1955, speaks to the difficulty of learning to teach in social settings, since teachers do not *know themselves* in relationship. He argues that a major purpose of education should be to help children and adults know themselves and develop healthy attitudes of self-acceptance—in the midst of others. Following Karen Horney (1937, 1950), Jersild suggests that teachers must begin the process of naming and facing their own anxieties resulting from discontinuities between what they currently believe about themselves and what they must pretend to believe to gain acceptance by others. Only then can teachers claim the freedom of attention to relate to the self-conscious anxieties their children may feel and that limit their learning.

Maxine Greene (1979) gives further credence to this argument.

> Alienated teachers, out of touch with their own existential reality, may contribute to the distancing and even to the manipulating that presumably takes place in many schools. This is because, estranged from themselves as they are, they may well treat whatever they imagine to be selfhood as a kind of commodity, a possession they carry within, impervious to organizational demand and impervious to control. Such people are not personally present to others or in the situations of their lives. They can, even without intending it, treat others as objects or things. (1979, p. 29)

The teachers in our group certainly were "personally present" to themselves, others, and the situations in their lives. That seemed to be a key factor in understanding why they could "see" their experiences through a self/other relational lens. These teachers' practices also show us that the development and articulation of favorable relationships can be understood through *an ethic of care*. Again, they not only demonstrated a caring for self and other, but a capacity for learning to teach through caring relationships. Their stories remind us of Nel Nodding's work on moral relations in education (1984, 1992). Interestingly, the teachers didn't read about moral relationships or an ethic of caring in their teacher education programs, nor were they coached in caring after they began their jobs. However, their stories clearly show the care in their teaching. And, though they haven't all read Noddings, even yet, their practices support her words, as she suggests organizing education around centers of care:

> For self, for intimate others, for distant others, for nonhuman animals, for plants and the physical environment, for the humane-made world of objects and ideas. . . . At the present time, the curriculum is organized almost entirely around the last center, ideas, but it is so poorly put together that ideas are swamped by facts and skills. Even those students who might find a genuine center of care in some arena of ideas, say mathematics or literature, are sorely disappointed. In trying to teach everyone what we once taught only a few, we have wound up teaching everyone inadequately. Further, we have not bothered to ask whether the traditional education so highly treasured was ever the best education for everyone. (p. xviii)

The personal senses of care that Mary, Leslie, and the other teachers in our group displayed became a major theoretical pattern across our stories. It led them not only to reconstruct the concepts of "curriculum" and "instruction" within their classrooms, but also to reconstruct the social position of teaching—in their own voices—in the political conversation that is education.

Stories About the Personal as Political, and the Political as Personal

Let's begin this concluding story set with one more example, to bring full circle Leslie's stories of her initial teaching attention to recommended curriculum, then to her relationship with children, then to the broader context in which learning to teach is situated. The words came from her presentation at a national conference.[4]

Five and one-half years with this conversational group has had a profound effect on my teaching and my views on education. More profound than I probably know because they have been with me my whole teaching career. I don't know what it would be like without them. . . . I remember supportive visits to my class, gentle questions and suggestions, hours of being able to unload my frustrations and fears without fear of judgment. Ironically, the biggest impact my conversational group had on me was pushing me out of the classroom. I began teaching 5 years ago, having come from a business career. I was well aware of the shortcomings of working within a bureaucracy. I was very clear on one point when I began teaching, if not on others. Focus on your work in the class. Don't worry about what happens around you. . . .

By my 3rd year, a number of our group were invited to deliver papers at the American Educational Research Association. This was a group of educators who work mainly in universities on educational issues. It was a thrill to sit in on so many seminars. Real teachers rarely attended and seemed to be a novelty. The [university folk] seemed interested to meet me. But as time passed I began to get irritated and by the final day I was angry. These were people who changed the course of education and affected curriculum and practice. I had known nothing about them nor what they did. I had not known of their size nor their impact [on educational policy]. In spite of their power, few seemed to collaborate with teachers. Few seemed to have a true picture of what happens in a classroom, the impact of family life, of the diversity of the classroom, and the challenges it presents. The picture I was presented in teacher training based on their research rarely matched the picture and critical issues I had found in the classroom. I couldn't sit there any longer. I clearly had been wrong about hibernating in the class. The push outside my room made me find my voice. It made me realize that I had made a commitment as an educator which meant that I had also made a commitment to many larger issues such as policy issues, curriculum issues, expenditure of funds, etc., which affect my students. It was a dramatic awakening.

The distanced and different stance of those who held power over Leslie's work was too threatening—once she became aware of it. From initially thinking that she only had power over the curriculum inside her classroom, to having that view challenged by the power she held in our conversational group, she then discovered her power in the outside world. From a realization that those who might even know less about the day-to-day enactment of teaching in urban classrooms were given power over her, she developed a sense of responsibility for educational relationships beyond the classroom. The sense of power she was constructing through her learning to teach gave her the authority to carry out that responsibility. (Leslie's story continues in chapter 9.)

Telling Our Stories Outside of Our Conversational Group

THEORIES OF FEMINIST EPISTEMOLOGIES. As I realized that the relational, personal, caring, connecting, and political patterns in these stories related to new ways of knowing about learning to teach that I was never taught, I continued my search to interpret them theoretically within the world outside our conversational group. In our conversations, as I've pointed out, I noted how teachers' positions were not valued. They talked of how their own lower social and political status in relation to administrators and university researchers, where logical analyses carry more status, led to a rejection of their own multifaceted values and experiences. I wondered why. I found much help, solace, and insight in my reading of feminist theory. I learned that feminist perspectives involve an existential level of awareness and consciousness of "one's social location and its relation to one's lived experience" (Nielsen, 1990, p. 24).

As I talked about these ideas with my colleagues as potential illumination for these stories, many suggested that feminist theory was not useful because (1) it was not politically popular in the academic ranks, and thus my association with it could damage my career; and (2) other theorists—social reconstructionists, critical theorists, postmodernists, pragmatists, and so forth—had already established the tentative and social nature of knowledge, and we didn't need another related theory. However informative the critical theories are, I found them lacking in addressing the point of this text—the gendered nature of opportunities for knowing in the profession of teaching—so I persisted. I found support for my hypothesis that we did need another theory for understanding learning to teach in the United States where the more distant one's occupational position from children, the more prestige it held. And a devalued position understandably leads teachers to want to be shown precise techniques or strategies that were discovered by someone personally, politically, and epistemologically distant from the classroom. It also seemed important to pay attention to the feminist critique in national debates and discussions about the need to improve (read: increase) teachers' knowledge. I wondered if perhaps reconstructing teachers' opportunities to claim and capitalize on what they already knew would be more appropriate. Belenky, Clinchy, Goldberger, and Tarule's work (1986) on feminist epistemologies helped me understand the importance of claiming personal theory and experience as valid ways of knowing. They demonstrated how some women, secure in their own interpretation of reality, create their own knowledge as well as critically examine others'. The women in Belenky et al.'s study who were most distant from personal knowledge interpretations had to rely solely on others' objective observations as truth. It occurred to me that some teachers without feminist perspectives may behave similarly.

Belenky et al.'s study (for all of its omissions in knowledges it failed to describe) made sense in light of our collaborative group's experiences. It seemed that perhaps *we* had undergone such a process while describing our learning to teach in conversation. After abandoning a quest for "the truth," or master narrative about teaching and researching literacy begun in our teacher "training" programs, we learned to understand our instructional dilemmas by assuming critical stances, retaining important objective or empirical findings that seemed epistemologically compatible, while allowing alternative ways of knowing with others to stand out in our reconstructed narratives. I thought it was important to retell our stories of finding and knowing the shapes of pedagogical and relational freedom to educational scholars who had not been part of our group. Weaving our stories with theories of social constructivism, self/other relations, and feminist epistemologies could result in a more complete and complex understanding of learning to teach.

I brought my musings about such theorizing, particularly regarding feminist epistemologies, to the group. The response was varied. At one end of the response continuum, I heard Leslie, whose experiences were further given voice and credence by my reading.

SAM: Leslie, when you said that for the last week you've been thinking a lot of things and then it sort of clicked when you read this stuff. What did you mean by that?

LESLIE: Oh, well, this whole thing about being devalued. You know? Of not ever feeling valued for what I now understand is a feminist whatever you call it. That's the way I felt for a long time of my life. Do we have a label for this so I can be more clear about this in the future?

SAM: A feminist stance.

LESLIE: My feminist stance, my way of viewing life, hasn't ever been actually valued. And, it wasn't until recently that I worked out the tension I had always felt. And then, I read this paper and I realized oh, that's the way I've been thinking, and it has a name, and there are other people who actually, you know, have studied this and analyzed this and that it's okay and it's good.

Jennifer had a similar but different reaction to my reading of feminist theory. Like the experiences of many other African-Americans, it was reminiscent of her life, but differed in the language.

> JENNIFER: When I hear you talking I think about myself trying to say something about myself, and not being able to, and feeling like I'm not able to because it's not, I don't have this logical lockstep way of doing it. It's just like, it just starts coming out and this is who I am and it's not, it doesn't have a natural progression and I don't have the right, language . . . to talk about it correctly so that everybody can understand it, and so I don't want to do it. I just want to sit there and not say anything, you know, it's more comfortable.*

As our conversation continued, Jennifer articulated the fear of speaking for ourselves.

> JENNIFER: Yet, when I hear you talk. I hear you talking about me . . . because . . . my father was raised this way or wasn't raised this way, that I should turn out that way. You know? . . . It's my intuitive sense of who I am. And that's not, that's not okay. It's not validated. And that's what I hear you saying. That you know a sort of intuitive self. It's like, you start thinking about things and they just start kind of making sense . . . but if nobody has written this before, or said it before or done it before, so it's kind of not as valuable as if it were. And when what you think is going to be published, it's scary to . . . even think about it, to even acknowledge that, that there might be some value in, in who you are as a person and how you came to be there, no matter how you came to be there. And, you know, and saying it out loud, and never mind putting it in print, I mean to me that's really oooh.**

---

* Lisa responded: "I feel like Jennifer is speaking to my experience of being in graduate school—feeling dumb, afraid of speaking up in class, distrusting my original ideas."

** As Patty was transcribing this tape, she wrote to us: "Some of Jennifer's comments specifically made me feel better about the way I've decided to live my life . . . and made me realize that it's okay to do what I want to do, not what "society" thinks I should do. . . . My priorities are different. Now I can feel good about my decisions!"

Karen and Anthony had still other reactions to the idea of linking our experiences to feminist theory. Karen, as you'll remember, did not understand her experiences as a woman or a teacher in feminist terms. She was the most uncomfortable member of our group with my attachment to feminist theory.

KAREN: I just don't see how my perspective fits into this book at this point.

ANTHONY: I don't know if I agree that it doesn't fit in. I think there are kind of two different levels of analyses going on. I think Sam is taking more of a . . . a sociohistorical analysis that, it kind of provides an explanation for some of the disempowerment that we discovered. And I think our experience is more about playing out what that means in the classroom, what that means at the school. If, you really disagree with her to the point that you don't want to be an example, that you don't want your . . . experiences interpreted in that light, then, then I don't think your perspective should be in it. You know? But on the other hand, I think your experiences are . . . valid and do fit. And so, I think, you need to figure out how, you know, if there's a way to inject your own . . . sociohistorical perspective so that it's distinct, so that it's clear, you have your own editorial comment, or whatever, that distinguishes you from Sam's . . . You know what I mean?

KAREN: I'm not sure.

SAM: Well, I think it's important that you do the latter, to distinguish yourself at your place . . . I mean. . . . It's the same thing we've faced across our years of collaborative writing. Do we have to be associated with the majority view? I think it's almost critical at this point that we have some contrasting views.

KAREN: Well, I'll have to read, I need to read it again just to see how it's kind of all laid out. I mean I don't want to weaken it . . . don't want to in any way.

SAM: I think you'd strengthen the argument. There are many people who are going to read it who will not agree with the feminist point of view that helps explain our majority position. That point was raised over and over in our conversations, remember? Your experience provides a contrasting perspective that will be comforting to many and make the book more legitimate. Do you see?

KAREN: Um hum.

ANTHONY: There could be a way where you could say . . . that you, accept this, and this and this, yet you have concerns about this and that because of your own experiences.

KAREN: I kind of like that. The challenge for me is to really think through what it is I agree with, what things I'm comfortable with and what things I feel uncomfortable with and why. That'd be a real, interesting commentary.

Karen's concerns about having her experiences shoehorned into a theoretical framework that didn't fit them not only provided another example of a feminist critique against silencing minority experiences, it became powerful feedback that transformed the shape of our stories retold here. Karen reminded me, once again, that as narrator of our stories, I should be sensitive to individual variations in experiences, and that I should critique my own learned practice of speaking for the group as a researcher.

RELATIONAL KNOWING: THE COMPLETE TAPESTRY

The stories told here not only illustrate the passion involved in learning to teach, but also argue for personal and relational development as a primary way of knowing about teaching. Here, I will again step away from the stories to summarize the intersection of theories of socially constructed learning described in chapter 3, theories of self/other relationships (including the ethic of care), and theories of feminist epistemology. The intersection of the three theoretical positions results in what I have come to understand as relational knowing.

Relational knowing, as it has unfolded across chapters 3 and 4, obviously differs from the single concept of a cognitive or "known" base of externally authorized information that is learned through canonized curriculum—relatively independent of the people and communities who will be using it—and "banked" or stored as "pedagogical currency" for future use (see Giroux, 1988; Tierney, 1991).* It also differs from Donald Schon's (1983) concept of knowledge-in-use, or the thoughtful reflection of what's known as it is applied, because of the lack of a notion of the relational influences on that reflection. As we saw in the teachers' stories, while their learning to teach began with cognitive knowledge—such as theories of learning and literacy—it was enacted through a sense of care for self and others. The concept of knowing through relationship, or relational knowing, involves both the recall of prior knowledge and the reflection on what knowledge is perceived or present in social and political set-

---

* Jennifer adds: "A familiar feeling when it comes to doing 'school.'"

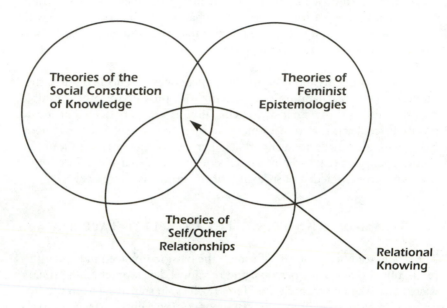

FIGURE 4-2
Theoretical framework for the study of relational knowing.

tings. It is similar to Clandinin and Connelly's notion of personal practical knowledge that is narrative knowing, embodied in persons, embracing moral, emotional, and aesthetic senses, and enacted in situations. Relational knowing is also similar to Max Van Maanen's writings on knowledge as lived experience and the pedagogical relations. Leslie and Mary's stories in this chapter of establishing (different and changing) curricula that were true to social constructivist theories, but were also true to what they knew about themselves and what they were learning in relationship, within and without the classroom, are examples.

In some of the stories we've read, and particularly in stories to come, we find that relational knowing does not rest in contemplation but becomes clarified in action. It took on, therefore, both a "nested"[5] character of reweaving knowledge (or certainties that were authorized and cognitively learned or known), with knowing (or what is coming to be known and that partially challenges the known) and intuition (or what is felt or sensed through relations more than is known). Intuitive modes are characterized by four major features: involvement of the senses, commitment and receptivity, a quest for understanding or empathy, and a productive tension between subjective certainty and objective uncertainty (Noddings and Shore, 1984). Mary and Leslie's stories clearly show the interweaving of knowledge (e.g., the social construction of literacy), knowing (e.g., the generation and articulation of different ways to literacy), and intuition (e. g., the care for and learning from students as well as authorized text).

Because of the fluid and present character of such ways of understanding, it would seem problematic to label what they came to know as "relational *knowledge.*" Even the grammar is problematic. The solidarity of the noun "knowledge" can be relaxed and unbounded by its conversion to the present verb participle "knowing." The narrative discourse that is displayed in Mary and Leslie's coming to know in relationship suggests the characters' slippery representations of the world, which, kaleidoscope-like, change form as the scenes and settings change (see Nespor & Barylske, 1991).* Stories of learning to teach like Mary's and Leslie's show that selves who come to know in relationship often enter a hermeneutic circle as conversational participants, or "persons whose paths through life have fallen together" (Rorty, 1979) rather than simply leading their lives as those who have learned about, practiced, and entered a clearly articulated epistemological framework to reach some fixed, consensual goal. Though the goals were clearly present and directed their learning to teach, their paths to those goals were often full of surprises. The ideal conversational situations for relational knowing, therefore, were those that provided opportunities for a renewed sense of questioning received wisdom through hermeneutic dialogue—conversation that contains a space for wonder, mystery, uncertainty, and the barely knowable (Beyer, 1988). Although points and perspectives will be temporarily held, such conversation would rarely yield rigid conceptions of truth and knowledge or master narrative.** As listeners and readers, these teachers' conversational stories that illustrate their relational knowing help us understand possible new results of urban children's learning to become literate.

---

* Karen asked for simplification in language. I replied: "Telling stories in the present about relationships as they evolve, rather than reporting an old (and cognitively filed or "indexed") or known story, shows more of their complexities and colors and shifts." Does that help?

** Leslie gave the reader an example: "Clearly, in terms of discipline, what works for one student doesn't for another. It's only through developing a relationship that I can make a decision about what to do."

Extending Relational Knowing

This chapter has been an attempt to highlight the spirals of relational knowing that were an important part of Leslie's and Mary's learning to teach literacy in urban classrooms. It was intended to describe their learning through the support of ongoing conversation, a passionate belief in themselves and their children as knowledge creators and evaluators, a willingness to honor the diverse styles and skills of their students, an ability to create innovative approaches to literacy instruction that respects students' needs, and a propensity to look critically at both their children and themselves in relationship to evaluate the results. This focus was not intended to diminish the additional importance of their cognitive/logical knowledge of teaching and learning.* Its purpose was to dramatically show how their own successes, and those of their children, rested, to a large degree, on their relationships. When they found the disciplinary knowledge from their teacher education program important but insufficient for reaching the urban children they were charged to teach, Mary and Leslie reached out for relational support and knowing. They discovered, by doing so, their freeing capacities for empirical knowledge creation and critique. Their own philosophical commitment to teach and succeed in this difficult environment, and their passion for these children, were both personal and political. Our stories that show the importance of relational knowing, then, have both an epistemological and a political purpose.

We are sensitive to the thought that some readers of this chapter might have trouble locating themselves here. Clearly there are multiple ways of relating to teaching that we have not addressed. Our intention was focal rather than exclusionary. It was to validate the reality of these teachers' experiences—and others like them. There may also be charges of gender-specificity against this text. The point of telling the story from the perspective of Leslie and Mary, and to highlight relational knowing, which is traditionally and problematically associated with women, was not to isolate it there. Anthony, remember, was also a member of our conversational group who shared similar personal and political values. The ultimate goal of a feminist agenda is the degenderizing of every aspect of social life, so that traditionally genderized values can be claimed by women and men. Before that can occur, though, traditionally cast (and often devalued) women's values and interests must receive an equal public recognition

---

* Jennifer adds: "I now believe that to stop at the cognitive/logical knowledge level of teaching is not to know what teaching truly is. It is to have stopped before you have really begun to learn what you must know."

(Ferguson, 1989). The personal, situational, political, and epistemological importance of such values must be acknowledged.* Employed in the fields of teacher preparation and teacher learning, the concept of relational knowing could provide a space to help resolve the tension between acquiring knowledge of what schooling presently is and what it should or might be (the lived world and the theoretical world).

ENDNOTES

[1]It was interesting to me why, in my graduate education, I had not already encountered theory to help interpret these experiences. It made me doubt the "truth" of the theory and wonder what experiences had been left out. It made me reflect on how much I probably hadn't been "educated" in my undergraduate and high schooling—perhaps even my elementary schooling—although I couldn't remember it as clearly. I began to wonder whether it was possible to come to "know" relevant theory in institutionalized settings. Then I saw it clearly: The theories that counted as my "education" were personally, socially, and historically selected by people with particular biases as "canon" for my education. Others were *not* selected for the same reason. How many other theoretical interpretations of experience—which might have validated mine—had not even been articulated? In honoring and requiring only authorized "canon," what sort of education was I shaping for my students in relation to me? These stories opened up a whole new world—and became a definite marker for changes in my own learning to teach and research and live.

> Little darlin', I feel like ice is slowly melting
> Little darlin', I feel like years since its been clear.
> Here comes the sun.
> Here comes the sun.
> And I say
> It's all right.
>
> *George Harrison*
> *"Here Comes the Sun"*

[2] Mary and Leslie's stories are used only as focused examples here to pull in somewhat from the larger group and help clarify this complex notion. Rela-

---

* Karen's passionate response to the conclusion of this chapter: "Does our book ever really address this critical aspect of our 'agenda'? Do we make recommendations for specific changes in teacher education programs or in the day-to-day restrictive schedules that teachers must contend with? How can we concentrate on and try to promote relationships with and among our students when the demands on our time are so overbearing already? Reflecting on what we need is not enough in my opinion. We have got to suggest realistic changes and work toward them!"

tional knowing, as a construct in learning to teach, was also important to the others of us in the group. Incidentally, devoting chapter 4 and most of chapter 3 to Mary and Leslie's stories was not intended to privilege them over the others. As it happened, during 3 years of our work together, our funding sponsor requested that we focus on two teachers only. Mary and Leslie volunteered.

[3] See Drake, 1992; Heidi Jacobs, 1989; and Walmsley & Walp, 1990, for more on interdisciplinary themes.

[4] The conference was the American Educational Research Association, Boston, April, 1990.

[5] See Lyons, 1990, for a complete discussion of "nested knowledge."

II

Stories of
Teacher
Research

5

Mary's Research

MARY: I want to know . . . what [my students] think [as they read].
I have to figure out how I can structure a lesson to find that out—
or a discussion. I prefer to set it up and then see if I get any reactions to it. Otherwise, I'm doing all of the thinking and I'm doing
all of the talking and am pushing my point.

Mary, Leslie, and the other teachers found it was not only knowing about
teaching and learning that led to their success with children's literacy, but
their continuing questioning into the process of their actions as literacy
instructors. The chapters in Part II report teachers' investigations into the
issues raised in our conversational group through praxis or research-in-
and-on-action. The work thus exemplifies not only learning to teach, but
the international movement toward "teacher research" across all of its
three interrelated stances or standpoints: curriculum improvement, professional critique, and epistemological/societal reforms. A derivative of
action research, teacher research from a *curriculum improvement* stance
seeks to improve practice in social settings by trying out curricular ideas as
both a means of increasing knowledge of the situation and improving it.
Teacher research from the standpoint of *professional critique* intends to
learn about and improve the structures and social conditions of practice.
The focus of teachers as researchers relative to *societal reform* is on how
schools and teaching are shaped in society and what epistemological views
are important for their transformation.

As we noted in Part I, knowledge constructed through teacher's own research can be understood in feminist terms. Instead of practicing blind obedience to administrative authority, acting as researchers gives teachers personal and professional power through which they feel free to make significant changes for their students, and defend those changes to administrative challenge. While engaging in this work, female and male teachers "come to trust their own ability to construct knowledge, to be meaning-makers, and to improve their practice. Buoyed by trust in themselves, they gather confidence to take new risks. The impact expands like concentric circles around the stone thrown in water" (Glesne, 1991, p. 11). The cumulative effect of the teacher research movement has been to influence the manner in which teachers are perceived as professional curriculum developers and agents of social change. It has also influenced current collaborative research models, staff development programs, and school restructuring plans that emphasize "teacher empowerment." Finally, the concept of teachers as researchers is at the center of reform across the educational enterprise: research, teaching, the profession, its moral purpose, its impact on societies.[1]

In this book, the stories of teacher research are presented not only as they inform research for social change, but the epistemological process of learning to teach. Examples in this and subsequent chapters in this section of Part II will illustrate the value of teacher research as an integral part of literacy education for urban students.

LOOKING FOR LEARNING IN THE LITERACY CLASSROOM

Mary Dybdahl teaches in an urban elementary school in the North Bay of the San Francisco area. Though you wouldn't recognize its urban-ness if you encountered it in the early morning sunshine of the golden hills of California, it is situated in an economically depressed community. You'd have to look closely to see that the windows on the school were barred, that the graffiti has been painted over, that the heating and cooling facilities were so poor that the teachers had to take legal action to cool the rooms to less than 100 degrees in the summer and warm them to more than 50 degrees in the winter.

The ranch-style brick school, situated near the California coast, really doesn't "look like" a semi-neutral space in a gang war zone. Though not far from the school we can see evidence of poverty and crime in the streets and neighborhoods, it is hard to see the suffering going on inside, as teachers like Mary try to make a difference in the lives of the urban poor. As we go to press, those teachers are technically "on strike" because of the distrust and misunderstanding by local authorities. However, the teachers are still in class—though the bulletin boards are bare and the stress is as thick as the coastal fog—for the sake of the children.

Another feature that disguises the personal struggles that occur in and around the school is the "progressive" nature of the curriculum. Since Mary joined the school staff in 1988, the school has endorsed a literature-based, process-writing approach as the material and philosophic bases of its literacy program. "Literature" for student choice usually took the form of trade books but also meant patterned language stories by well-known authors—especially in the primary grades (see California State Department of Education, 1987).

Mary, and all the elementary teachers in our conversational group, had become familiar with process approaches to literacy in their teacher education programs, with me as one of their instructors. They had also studied the relationship between classroom tasks and students' cognitive and social responses (Doyle, 1983). They were surprised to discover that task formats for whole-class, literature-based instruction, as popularized in the urban schools they joined after graduation, often limited their students' opportunities for meaningful social and personal responses to text; that is, the teachers noticed that their students' responses to literature tasks (or their spoken, read, and written reactions) were sometimes either nonexistent, because they couldn't read well, or were "school-bound" and artificial. They had reported to our conversational group that students' responses in literature discussions often replicated question-and-answer task format patterns to ensure correct responses, and their written responses were dependent upon mechanical features such as spelling and heavy teacher feedback to check "correctness." Many children's responses, in effect, resembled tests intended to measure their abilities better than their own true communication skills—which demonstrated greater creativity and insight. Moreover, their responses didn't show their lives. Except to copy or mimic their better praised peers, they rarely interacted with each other when responding. Children were less likely to give the rich and varied responses to literature—or "multiple literacies"—that they exhibited in their play, casual conversation, and other social interactions. Such interactions revealed their community and personal literacies as well as standard or school literacies.

The academic literature contains many examples of this phenomenon across the United States. Shirley Brice Heath's classic work, *Ways with Words* (1983), documents the differential effect of community language patterns and school success. Many others show that the language used in homes can limit the success minority students realize in school (e.g., Au, 1980; Au & Jordan, 1981; Bloome, 1989; Collins & Michaels, 1981; Cook-Gumperz, Gumperz, & Simon, 1981; Gilmore, 1987; Gumperz &

Tannen, 1979). Still other work speaks to the differences in languages across economic, cultural, and class communities (e.g., Ogbu, 1979; Scollon & Scollon, 1981). The feminist literature speaks to difference in personal literacies (when one's sense of self as a communicator does not match the community norms for communication: see Belenky, et al., 1986; Gillian, 1982; Lewis & Simon, 1986). My own work in urban areas with this group in California and another in Michigan (see chapter 8) has led my colleague, Margie Gallego, and me to think about the pedagogical relationship between school, community, and personal literacies as "multiple literacies" (Gallego & Hollingsworth, 1992).

Community literacies can be thought of as the appreciation, understanding, and/or use of interpretive and communicative traditions of culture and community. Mary heard it as the polite respect of authority of the Filipino-American community and in the rap song and slang of the African-American community. *Personal literacies* are ways of knowing and beliefs about self and personal communication norms arising from historical or experiential and gender-specific backgrounds. In Mary's classroom personal literacies were particularly exemplified in the strong voices of the African-American women. Finally, *school literacies* are the interpretive and communicative processes needed to adapt socially to school settings, maintain a good sense of self, and gain a conceptual understanding of school subjects. Mary's work was to try to encourage and develop school literacies, without devaluing community and personal literacies.

Mary was teaching against the grain (see Simon, 1992). When children failed to become standard or "school" literate, the popular response was to fault the children, not the literacy approach. Mary rejected this response—both in principle and action. Though educated, like most teachers, to apply standard methods with her class, she had claimed the right to construct her own standards—and that right had been validated as part of her learning to teach in our conversational group. Her sense of herself as one who was as knowledgeable as the educational leaders who had authorized the standards, allowed her to enact different standards in relation to her students—varying standards that not only taught them, but validated them. Because she researched her methods, her confidence that she could demonstrate the "effectiveness" of the approaches she used if called upon by school administrators or parents, also allowed her to take necessary risks to learn to teach urban students. Her confident stance gained her approval from the building principal. Some of Mary's research to transform her classroom into a place where she could challenge the "norms" that urban children would fail in literacy and in school is documented here. It is an example of her personal attempts at social change on an immediate level.

For example, instead of faulting the children in her class or their families for their poor performances in standard literacies, she simply rolled up her sleeves and got to work to find new approaches. Encouraged by examples of others in our conversational group, she learned to hear and value the many ways they were intelligent that standard measures didn't recognize: their strength of convictions, their oral abilities, their feelings, their arts, and their physical energies. Through her research, she broadened both the traditional measures of literacy success—word recognition and comprehension—and the traditional means of assessing it (standard questions and responses) to value and honor the multiple ways children were comprehensively literate. Her measures of standard or school literacy included both community and personal literacies. She looked at whether a child could (1) demonstrate an understanding of the author's meaning of text by responding through art, movement, story, and writing; (2) show the relevance of the textual message to their own lives—or "own" the text; (3) and cooperate with others to understand the textual message not only through the intellect, but through the senses. To meet the evaluative requirements of her school, she still assigned "grades" to these measures, but she dramatically expanded opportunities for these urban children to earn "good" grades. For example, in her unit on Rosa Parks, Mary obtained a sense of the depth of children's comprehension by looking at how well they cooperated to complete group research reports and internalized the authors' messages about the power of cooperation into their lives outside of school. She talked to our group about those measures:

> One of the ways that I have been measuring cooperation is by the stability of the groups. . . . Whether kids stay together to finish a particular literacy project on Rosa Parks . . . I question that now, but it was one of the measurements that I felt I could use. I determined whether a group of students was developing better cooperation skills by looking at the stability of the group.
>
> Then I began to measure cooperation by looking to see if they were able to move from the topic of Rosa Parks into our own lives. Are they able to see the significance of political activity? Are they able to see the power of the individual in the bigger picture? Are they able to see how important cooperation is in something like the Montgomery bus boycott, so that children can see that's a skill, that's not just a school skill, but it's a life skill? Those are all ways that I would measure whether or not we were successful.

From assessing comprehension by noticing whether a group of children could talk through the issues concerning Rosa Parks well enough to sustain their interests to finish the project together—to recognizing and talking/writing about the importance of the concept of cooperation in their lives, Mary's evaluative measures reflected both her growing understanding of her students' learning in relation to them, and their need for varying assessment measures to demonstrate success. Here's another instance of Mary's assessing comprehension of the Rosa Parks unit through Keena's emotional response to the historical character of Rosa Parks, through a demonstrated acknowledgment of the relevance of the text's subject—racism—to her life, and through articulating a supportive connection between the text and her own family.

> Keena came closest of anyone to coming out of this project with the kinds of feelings and questions that I had hoped that we would all come to. She was struggling with issues of racism in her life and in our classroom. And I think that she was able to do that because of the support that she was getting at home. I wish that I had been more keyed into that to begin with because I may have been able to figure out a way to bring more of that into the classroom.

Such measures of comprehension—researched by watching and listening to children, as well as by analyzing their academic work—not only validated her students' multiple literacies, but accomplished her goals for their literacy comprehension in a way that teacher-directed comprehension questions (even using the popular "knowledge-to-evaluation" questioning scale or taxonomy)[2] never could. When children did not achieve the intended literacy goals, Mary did not only question specific behaviors or understandings, she also investigated their emotional relationships to the topic—and to her own emotions to children's responses as their teacher.

> Celeste had real resistance to the whole project and I speculated about that with her. I asked her whether it made her uncomfortable. She said no, she thought that Rosa Parks was boring, she was more interested in Dr. Martin Luther King. . . . I suggested to her perhaps that I was the one that chose the topic and that she was much more interested in choosing her own topic. She said yeah, that was it but . . . I doubt that because she really didn't have a replacement. And I wonder if the issues of the racial tension were such that it was hard for her. She was one of the kids who persisted in coming back to the issue of Martin Luther King's relationship with white people. It was of interest to her, it was a challenge to her, and I think she saw [resisting the study of Rosa Parks] as a challenge to me. "Classroom

resister" is an important function she plays in the classroom. I think that may have been part of it. Very complicated.

Another example of this line of inquiry involved a rather complex relational analysis into the quality of children's questions about the text. Mary hypothesized that their comprehension of the text could be measured by the degree of "ownership" in the questions students asked about a text when working in cooperative groups. Those demonstrating comprehension could maintain individual interests rather than succumb to group pressure and ask questions that were more "popular" but that had less personal interest. She discovered that the degree of ownership had to do with the children's emotional interest in the topic and their history with the topic, as well as the availability of written materials that could answer their questions.

However intriguing and sophisticated as Mary's research into children's literacy comprehension was, and as important as it was to her learning to teach, such investigation alone could not resolve her instructional dilemmas with urban children's literacy. Mary told our group about a serious problem in her fourth grade classroom to which she could not close her eyes and hope it would go away—or be resolved by some other teacher. In spite of the fact that the students could "comprehend" the materials that she read to them and/or were discussed in a group, at least a third of her students could not read the text well enough to comprehend it independently. In other words, they could comprehend literature through conversations with others, but still had trouble with word recognition. She brought the dilemma of her beginning readers to our group.

By the end of my 1st year of teaching, I was devoted to the concept that children need to learn to read, preferably before they reach the fourth grade. I had managed to avoid first grade but I hadn't avoided beginning readers. It was painfully obvious that I didn't have the tools to teach these kids. Maybe this was a failing from my own elementary school education. Maybe it was a failing of my credential program. By the end of the year I even blamed my school district.

It is important to emphasize, however, that Mary *did not* blame the children's abilities, intelligences, or efforts for their inabilities to read independently. Having learned to hold a deep respect for their courage in the face of so many difficult odds inside and outside school, she faulted the educational system that had allowed them to get to fourth grade without a knowledge of word recognition. She was determined that they would not be denied such basic literacy instruction—literacy skills they would need to succeed in school and in their lives—even though it was politically incorrect to engage in "skill" work.* As is evident in her story, she took her responsibility as their teacher and as an agent for social change seriously. But there were so many students who couldn't read independently! And she felt she lacked the knowledge to teach beginning reading.

Mary knew that she would find some support for this dilemma through her belief in a literature-based, process-writing approach to literacy—an approach, you'll remember, that she learned in her teacher education program. However, she found that she needed something more.[3] Thus, relying on herself in relation to her students to learn from them, she attempted, researched, and reconstructed other approaches to literacy through her close attention to children's responses to those approaches. In short, Mary conducted routine classroom research on her own instruction, and used students' enjoyment of literature—and their ability to read words and comprehend them in narrative and expository text in groups and independently—as evidence of her own success in learning to teach literacy.

MARY'S RESEARCH INTO GROUPING FOR INSTRUCTION

Realizing that the beginning reading students, in particular, would need the support of a group to successfully read and comprehend, but not totally certain how to group them for instruction, Mary systematically looked at her attempts to structure literacy tasks, noted children's responses, revised her lesson structures, and then analyzed the changes. She criticized the whole-class lesson format that was standard practice at her school: "The whole-class lesson did not work for my poor readers. Their responses were limited. They did not tune into the whole-class lesson and they did not benefit from others as reading models."

Following a method that had worked well for Leslie in her classroom, Mary's first change from a whole-class format was to employ an in-class, pull-out group for beginning readers. She reflected on her early attempts in a presentation to the California Reading Association. "We would read together, then each student would reread the passage aloud, taking turns. This worked for less than a month. Every time I tried to work with [that] group, the rest of the class would go wild."

---

* Mary told us about a new teacher who had joined her school faculty, and, without knowing the politics of literacy instruction, admitted aloud in the faculty lounge that she taught phonics. We asked what happened. "Many of us secretly sent our struggling readers to her!"

Later, at the suggestion of a veteran teacher, Mary tried round-robin style reading, direct vocabulary instruction, and partnered responses. She structured the response groups by pairing "good and poor" readers, according to their standardized test scores. A few pairs, however, were "natural" good and poor reading groups, and the pairings were primarily based on friendship. Alan and Mitchell, two Filipino boys who often chose to work together, were an example. "Mitchell and Alan . . . asked to work together. I agreed with their choice. I was sure that Mitchell would benefit from Alan's superior abilities." In the fall I observed a lesson where Mary collected data on her new approaches. Here are excerpts from my field notes:

Mary reviews a little of the story *(Warton and the King of the Skies),* points out new vocabulary, and talks about internal word structure (suffixes and compound words). The children press her to go on with the actual reading. She has given them each part of the text on numbered papers. They assemble themselves in order, sit in a circle, and read. [Though the format is new, children's responses are similar to those of basal reading groups, e.g., attending to text only when it is one's turn to read.] At Mary's request, I pay particular attention to Alan and Mitchell. They are sitting next to each other. Alan reads, then looks at Mitchell to prompt him. Mitchell looks up at him, "Me?" "Yes," replies Alan. Alan looks on while Mitchell reads. He helps Mitchell with words he doesn't know.

After all the children have read, Mary questions them to see if they've understood important points in the story. She finds that the disjointed reading left them confused and asks their help in how they might read so that they have better understanding. She responds to their suggestions by rereading the text to them with some expression. Then she asks them to work in pairs, interpreting the story by discussing a central point, then writing and illustrating their response. [Kids scatter themselves around the room, under desks, in the rocker, and on carpet squares.]

I watch Alan and Mitchell at this task. They begin to formulate a summary-like response orally, then collaboratively write and illustrate. Both actually write on the same paper, occasionally erasing and rewriting each other's work. As Alan writes, Mitchell reads each word. When he leaves something out, Alan fills in. Alan reflects on the story. "He had a washtub and rope and . . ." (asks Mitchell: "What else?") Mitchell: "a needle." Then Mitchell continues: "put in—'he saw lots of birds.'" Alan writes that, then adds "and bees."

When their written response to the story is complete, they begin to discuss and work on the drawing. Mitchell: "We should draw the toad. We need the book." (Goes to his desk to get it.) Alan draws the toad in the basket. . . . Mitchell tried to draw the balloon. Alan erased it. Mitchell says, "I know how now." He then retraces Alan's lines, with some deviation.

Mitchell and Alan displayed many of the comprehension competencies that Mary wished to see: responding to text through oral storying, writing, and art and cooperation. Mitchell was far more attentive and engaged in the partnership work than he was in the round-robin style session. Though Alan was clearly the better reader and served as a peer teacher to Mitchell, Mitchell also helped Alan to formulate a different response than he would have had on his own. From the expressions on their faces as they worked together and the quality of their final product, it was evident that there was a sense of equality in this friendship-based partnership. I shared my observations with Mary. On the basis of Mitchell and Alan's and other children's responses to her new structures, she decided to drop the round-robin reading but keep the partnered response format.

Mary found the data on her classroom that the research assistants, other teachers, and I collected quite useful for her own instructional analyses. In addition to taking notes and/or recording the students' responses to the text during the reading and writing phases, we also videotaped lessons. As with all of our data, we gave tapes and transcripts back to her. Later we left a tape recorder, tapes, and microphone for her use. She listened to the children's talk while she was driving to school. By reviewing data that would be hard for her to collect while she taught, Mary continued to critique and fine-tune the partner format, and became even more firmly committed to the structure for rereading, conversation, writing about and illustrating the story, and sharing cooperatively authored stories. Mary's careful observations of students led to changing her response structures. As the partners worked together, she evaluated their responses:

> I walk around with a notebook. And I go through and I write down—
> I have a section for every kid—I walk around and look at Abraham,
> Paul, and make note . . . Abraham wasn't reading. . . . He
> depends on the other kids to do the reading. . . . Alan does a lot of
> the reading but he gives Mitchell a chance. And when Mitchell's read-
> ing he assists him with decoding words. I make notes like that.[4]

Sometimes her observations helped Mary pick up misconceptions which guided her task designs. She talked to our group about an example:

Later in the story of *Charlotte's Web,* Wilbur the pig is entered into a contest. In preparation for the big event, Wilbur is washed in buttermilk. Neither Alan nor Mitchell knew what buttermilk was but Alan figured out how to make sense of the events in the story. He decided buttermilk was somehow related to butterfingers or butterscotch, something sweet and good smelling. He extended this to make the contest be one based on the winner being the best-smelling pig. Mitchell thought his was a reasonable explanation and it fit the story perfectly.

With such observed responses as a guide, Mary had students first reread texts to use the context better to make sense of unknown words, and then make notes of those they still did not know and look them up in the dictionary. Watching the partners gave her further feedback on her choice of dictionary work to improve their responses to text:

In our study of desert ecology and desert cultures, we read a beautiful book called *Desert Giant,* a story about the life cycle of the saguaro cactus. One reading period I asked the students to read and reread the first part of the book. I asked them to make a list of all the words they

An example of Mary's classroom groups.

didn't know (either how to pronounce them or the word meanings). . . . Mitchell and Alan are good at this kind of activity. As
they read they stop and write words down. . . . [As a follow-up
activity], I asked them to use the dictionary to find word definitions,
and they were to illustrate one of the words. Alan did the writing,
Mitchell used the dictionary, and Mitchell did the drawing. The word
they chose was accordion. Although the word was used in the story to
describe a characteristic of the saguaro, Mitchell drew a picture of a
person playing the accordion. Alan seemed pleased with the end
product.

From collecting and analyzing similar data, Mary decided to (1) continue direct vocabulary instruction and (2) use the Mitchell/Alan friendship model for reading pairs. Her close observations had shown her the
value of social relations and compatibility in pairing. She noticed that
some pairs, grouped solely on good/poor matches were not socially
appropriate: "When I had Mattie and Jamelia work together, it would
always end in a fight and fit of tears."

Continuing to observe Alan and Mitchell eventually even led her to
question the objectively based distinction that ranked their literacy skills as
"strong" and "poor." Her teacher-research analysis of the equity in their
relationship proved much more comprehensive than mine, as an occasional visitor to her classroom.

After carefully watching them and documenting their progress, I have
come to understand that Mitchell and Alan have an equal partnership. . . . When [they] work together they prefer turning in one
written piece between them. Mitchell admits that he hates to write.
The physical action of writing is tedious and aggravating to him. On
the other hand Alan enjoys writing. He does beautiful printing and
cursive. His spelling and punctuation are well developed. What Alan
dislikes is thinking about the story. His comprehension only extends
to literal information and sometimes he misses that. This is where
Mitchell steps in. He obviously has been forming ideas and making
connections as he reads or is read to. He may not be interested in writing his ideas, but he can express them orally. He refers back to the text
or he recalls some detail to support his thinking. Alan sometimes
questions Mitchell's point of view, but generally he is convinced by
Mitchell's arguments.

Mary then questioned the other "strong and weak" pairs she had
arranged:

Cita is a fine reader but she has a deep, muffled voice. She could not project her voice to her partner, Mingo; he couldn't follow along, especially because she reads too fast. When they tried echo reading, in which the slow reader follows along after the better reader, it sounded like total babble.

Mary's continued investigations also led her to see that pairing children even on the basis of similar reading abilities did not necessarily improve their responses:

Nina and Nicole were well matched academically. Nina is fluent and expressive. She likes to read aloud. She is also competitive. Nicole is a fluent reader, but she lacks self-confidence. Nina berated Nicole for every error and hesitation. Neither student benefited from the partnership.

Mary concluded that:

The planned pairs did not work. In general students were not attentive to their partners' reading; they were not helpful and all too frequently they were frustrated and angry. The results were not much better than my whole-class lessons. I went back to Mitchell and Alan as my models. What worked here was not necessarily the fact that they were correctly matched academically; more to the point was their choice to work together, a fact that I noticed but had not valued. The strength of the partnership was built on friendship, mutual interest, and trust.

Mary changed her literacy structure once again. And she kept researching the process:

Students are now encouraged to work with a partner or partners of their choice. Children's responses to the "friendship–partnerships" as a group still vary as much as before, but now the responses are more uniformly positive. I've collected samples of their individual and paired written responses for assessment. I found that children are doing more reading in self-selected pairs and were more actively responding to stories. The amount of discussion and collaborative writing has increased significantly.

When I visited her classroom in the spring, I saw the results of her research in action. Using *Amigo* by Byrd Baylor, Mary had children choose partner groups (some worked alone, some in pairs, up to four in a group) and reread the story, discuss the story using the pictures, then write about their discussion. Here's an excerpt from my field notes:

> I watched and wrote down [partner] conversations. . . . I noticed variations in the process. For example, some talked about the task itself: Bart asked Kaleb "What does it mean to discuss?" Some referred to the text when they lost the gist of the story or had a point to debate about the meaning of the story. Others had organized turns for talk-ing, writing, drawing; others were more integrative, inserting new ideas into their cooperative text, even taking the pencil from the other, or erasing and rewriting.

Near the end of the hour, Mary asked the partners to read their inter-pretive responses to the class. Bart and Kaleb read theirs together. They had changed the scenario of the original text to a lighthearted fantasy about a Nintendo. Mary praised them for their inventiveness. When it was Mitchell and Alan's turn, Mitchell began, then Alan finished reading. Though their response to the text was fairly standard, the improvement in Mitchell's reading was dramatic.

Other beginning readers not only showed similar improvement in reading ability, but greater evidence of their lives in the responses—an indi-cation of ownership. Jay and Parnell made up a new ending, reflecting their favorite television programs. Latoya and Jamaica read their response chorally, retaining the "rap" beat of their retelling. Most students listened to their peers in quiet attention. Some, like Alan, added to their stories on the basis of what they had heard reported by other groups (see Figure 5-1).

Mary's research to improve students' interpretive responses through various social groupings is ongoing. Satisfied that a partnered grouping structure, based on friendship, helped her beginning urban readers to overcome their predicted failure in school and life, she has turned toward further investigations into patterns of relations in groups. For example, she became curious about socially varied responses to text—including her own:

> There are undoubtedly patterns in all of these groupings. It is note-worthy that each year I have had a pair of Filipino boys form a strong bond. It is also noteworthy that girls change partners more frequently than boys do. High readers don't necessarily make good partners for low readers, but they do seem to make good tutors. But that is not the point of my study. The point is to respond to my students whenever I

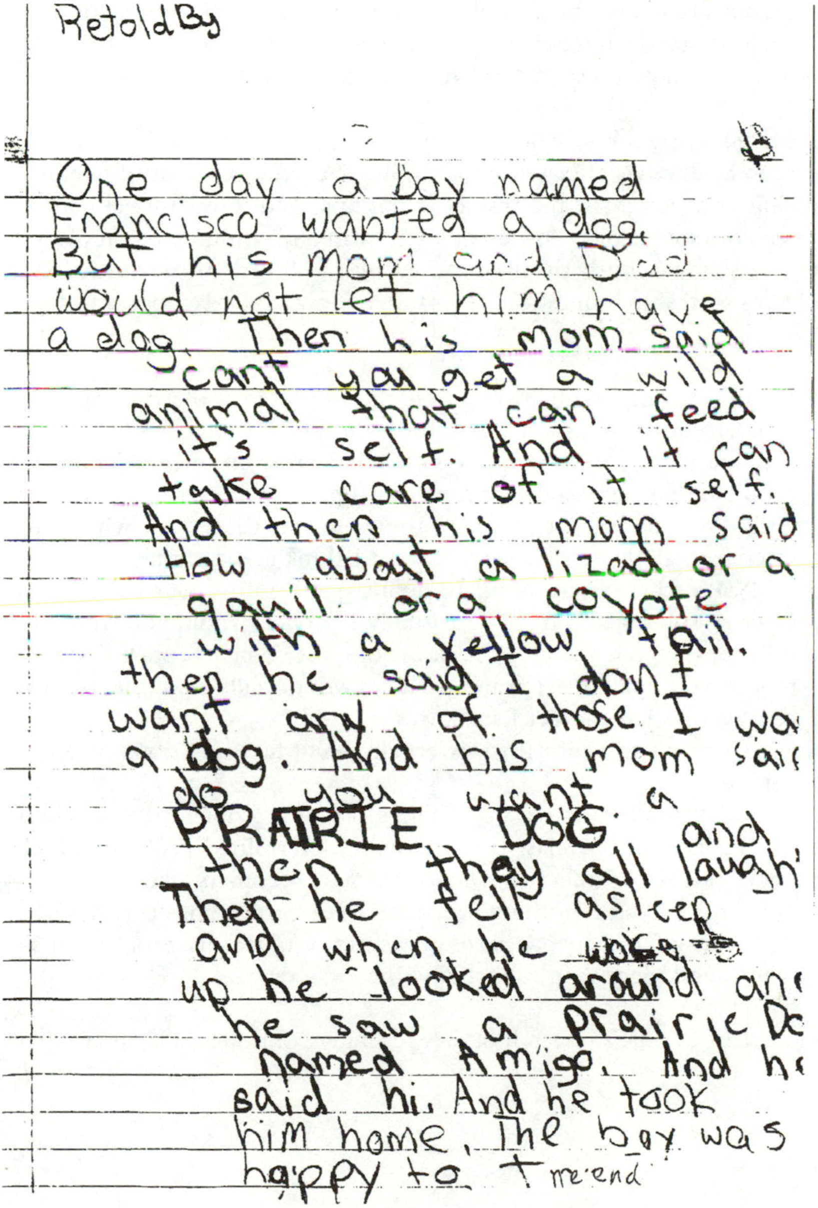

Retold By

One day a boy named
Francisco wanted a dog.
But his mom and Dad
would not let him have
a dog. Then his mom said
cant you get a wild
animal that can feed
it's self. And it can
take care of it self.
And then his mom said
How about a lizard or a
qauil. or a coyote
with a yellow tail.
then he said I dont
want any of those I wa
a dog. And his mom said
do you want a
PRAIRIE DOG and
then they all laugh.
Then he fell asleep
and when he woke
up he looked around and
he saw a prairie Do
named Amigo. And he
said hi. And he took
him home. The boy was
happy to. the end

FIGURE 5-1
Mitchel and Alan's work.

design a task or set up a whole program. Because, while it is important to understand why students think and act the way they do, what really matters is how I respond to what their thoughts and actions tell me.

Mary's stories underscore the importance of coming to view teaching as research. She has also written and published the research of her own teaching and presented the results at national and international conferences mentioned earlier. As Leslie heard, read and commented on Mary's research, she saw clearly the need for teachers to "own" their instructional problems or research questions—as students own their responses to text. She wrote:

> I think it's important to mention the importance of "owning" the problem or the question. The observation of the students in my case and Mary's and everyone else's (maybe) arose from our defining a problem that was important to us (grounded in an observation). It is critical for the teacher to define the issue. That is exactly why many inservices fail. Here's a model of what I think is happening:
>   (a) teacher observation; (b) define question for yourself; (c) seek external solutions from those (usually teachers) whom you trust; (d) do your own research in your classroom; (e) come to conclusions; (f) modify your methods; (g) and (maybe) wonderfully continue the process again when another issue arises.
>   Contrast this model to externally identified questions or problems.
>   (a) district or university decides issue or problem; (b) teachers attend inservice or class on externally determined problem which might not be a significant issue for them; (c) teachers take notes dutifully or doodle; (d) nothing happens; (e) district or university despairs at teachers; (f) teachers despair at district or university people, but sit quietly and silently; (g) unhappily, the cycle repeats.*

Stories of Leslie's research on her teaching continues in chapter 6.

---

* Comments on this chapter—Karen: "Fabulous chapter! Such powerful examples!" Jennifer: "I liked this chapter. It really highlights the idea of teaching and teacher–researcher as a dynamic (as opposed to static) undertaking." Mary: "I only wish the readers could see the faces of these students. Most of them are graduating this year. Reading this has reminded me of how much they have grown."

ENDNOTES

[1] For a current discussion of this movement, see Hollingsworth and Sockett, 1994.

[2] See Anderson & Sosniak, in press.

[3] Many of our colleagues have suggested that the children could not read well because the teachers were not adhering to the principles of a "whole language" philosophy closely enough. While that point could be argued, our point is that these teachers felt the need to critique the literature-based approaches they found popularized in their schools to teach the children. Their risk in challenging instructional "norms" is what foregrounds the story here, not the particular approach to literacy.

[4] Mary wanted to drop this quote as unimportant, but her peers overruled her—pointing at the need to describe the way in which she made observations. (OK, Mary?)

6

Leslie and Aaron

DEVELOPING CONFIDENCE IN BEGINNING READERS
THROUGH CURRICULUM RESEARCH

I remember first seeing Aaron on a bright, fall morning visit to Leslie's classroom.[1] His body movements while he worked attracted my attention. With his right cheek resting on a crumpled piece of writing paper atop his desk, he gripped the stub of his pencil between two fingers of his left hand, and poised it slightly above the three illegible letters he had printed a few minutes before. Suddenly he stood up, reversed the pencil and, his whole body arching over the paper, began rubbing out the letters (and the paper) until the desk was visible below. With a frown, an audible sigh, and a dropping of his 8-year-old shoulders, this handsome African-American boy pushed his first draft inside his desk, ran to Leslie, his teacher, and asked for another sheet of paper. Then Aaron began again. By the time my visit ended, he had added three new paper wads to his inner-desk collection.

The next time I visited Aaron's second grade classroom, I noticed his participation in a choral reading of a class-composed story. The text was based on a familiar piece of children's literature and punctuated with a predictable refrain. Leslie used many such patterned activities in her language lessons. While other children were joining in the increasingly familiar chorus, Aaron was mouthing different and disjointed words, eyes fixed on the ceiling, but face knowingly directed toward the chart. If my attention had not been drawn to him in my previous visit, I might have mistaken his behavior for reading. I shared my concern with Leslie.

On my third visit, Leslie asked me to sit and observe Aaron even more closely. His deep brown eyes questioned my presence at first, but soon we shared smiles and stories. I noted his vast oral knowledge on the Christmas theme the class was discussing through literature. I also noted his skillful search for "Christmas" words listed both randomly and in sentences on hanging charts. He wanted to copy some of these words and "make a story." "I need *reindeer,*" he said thoughtfully, standing by his chair for a better view as he scanned the walls. "Is that it?" His outstretched arm and fingers pointed toward *candy.* I answered his question with a cueing probe. "What's the first sound of [the word] *reindeer?*" Aaron shrugged his T-shirted shoulders. "D?" he guessed hesitantly. I gave him a hug (as one new friend to another) and helped him finish his work.

Although this instance occurred in her 3rd year of teaching, Leslie was still having serious concerns about her ability to teach Aaron to read and write despite her efforts to engage him in a rich and full literature-based, process-writing classroom environment. In fact, she was worried about a dozen children like Aaron in her classroom—males for the most part, but including some females—from various ethnic groups: African-American, Caucasian, Hispanic, and Filipino. Leslie sensed that she needed to diversify her present curricular program to teach these students. The holistic philosophy of literacy she endorsed required more than just the integration of reading, writing, speaking, and listening. The approach was essentially "a theory of voice that operates on the premise that all students must be heard" (Harste, 1990, p. 245). Aaron's voice—although he was working with familiar language in a collaborative classroom setting, chanting along to familiar rhymes, and "reading" his own words to classroom partners—was not clear and strong. To understand how Leslie critiqued, researched, and restructured the curricular approach to amplify Aaron's voice, it is necessary to look across her own story of learning to teach and how Karen and I recorded it.[2] The story takes us from her student teaching experiences through her 5th year of teaching.

LESLIE'S SOCIALIZATION TO LITERACY: ENDORSING A CURRICULAR APPROACH

Leslie, as you will remember, had entered the graduate-level credential program in which I taught from a business background because she wanted to do work that would benefit people instead of products. She wanted to diminish the need to invoke the competitive sense of herself required by the business world, and amplify the relational world of the elementary school classroom. Her desire to teach by knowing her children well, however, was interpreted negatively by the teacher–educator who interviewed her as a credential candidate. "It's not clear that teaching kids is what would best suit her needs—she might like counseling kids." Five points were deducted from her interview score. For a while, Leslie's relational understandings went underground as she put her faith in the teacher education program's emphasis on cognitively based teaching. After a period of retreat within the boundaries of her classroom to try and apply the approaches she was taught, she recalled "other" ways of knowing which she used to critique the more distanced teaching and learning stances promoted by her program.

As Karen and I watched her socialization into literacy instruction, we noticed that Leslie modified loosely formed, preprogram beliefs in a *cumulative skills approach* to literacy (reflecting her own experiences as a student in public school) and came to value a more *holistic curricular approach* in which whole-class literature discussions and experientially based process writing became a motivational means to literacy skills and subject matter knowledge. The change was easy for her, because it fit the philosophy she had for children's learning, not just the methods by which she was taught. Our records show that her student teaching practice settings and the curricular emphases of her early teaching experiences were socializing influences on her endorsement of this popular approach.

Leslie and her fellow student teachers were assigned to classrooms where children were reading fairly well, not only to see positive holistic, inductive literacy models, but to lessen the managerial complexity involved in teaching less enthusiastic readers, so that the new teachers' attention could center on learning the curricular approach.* The concurrent course work and student teaching requirements in the 9-month, graduate level program forced Leslie to give the bulk of her attention to managing and developing curricular activities. Even when students in the assigned classrooms were culturally diverse, the all-consuming curricular development effort left little time to reflect upon or modify activities to meet the needs of specific children. The normative examples Leslie saw and experienced in her program socialized her to fully endorse a literature-based, process writing approach to literacy. (For more on the topic of socialization in learning to teach, see Zeichner and Gore, 1990.)

MODIFYING EXISTING PROGRAMS TO DEVELOP HER OWN CURRICULAR APPROACH

As Leslie completed her student teaching and started a new career in her own classroom, she moved beyond a socialized endorsement of the pop-

---

* Lisa amends this general statement: "All kids weren't reading well in the sixth grade class where I student taught. However, everyone at the school endorsed the inductive approach, stating that, eventually, kids would learn to read."

ular curricular approach to modify and develop her own. In addition to the general development of relational knowing, described in chapter 4, three subthemes emerged from the data as supportive of her learning: curricular modification as a critical strategy, peer support, and children's responses.

Curricular Modification as a Critical Strategy

One of Leslie's student teaching experiences had run counter to the curricular endorsement model described above and stimulated her critically reflective nature. The experience became the foundation for her *future* development of an instructional program for children who could *not* read and write well within a standard program. Even though most children in the sixth-grade classroom where she spent the last months of her credential program year had few difficulties with literacy (compared with her own urban classroom), Leslie had an opportunity to modify the existing literacy model even as a student teacher. The cooperating teacher with whom she worked employed an individualized contract approach without whole class discussion. Leslie's critical perspective about learning to teach, her belief in the interactive requirement of a holistic approach to literacy, and supportive materials from the teacher education program gave her tools to critique what she saw. "In light of what I'm reading, I wonder if more discussion is not necessary [with the students] during the week."

Supported by good relationships with both her cooperating teacher and her university supervisor, Leslie was encouraged to try and modify much of the preexisting program. Though her modifications took her more fully toward the popular whole class discussion model of the literature-based approach used by most of the other cooperating teachers, the success Leslie experienced in the change encouraged her to see curricular modification as part of her teaching role.

During the summer following graduation from her credential program, Leslie prepared for her first teaching assignment in fifth grade. She assembled literature and expository texts and created lessons from the text selections to extend the focus on material curriculum development required of her as a student teacher. However, she was forced to make new plans at the last minute. Leslie wrote about her 1st year.

> I found out the week before school started that I was now to teach second grade [and not fifth]. . . . They handed me a key and pointed me towards the room. The previous teacher had left all her materials in the room in disorder. I spent the first 3 days cleaning out cupboards and scrubbing. I eventually got the room squared away.

Then I began to look for books. I realized I had no idea what the second grade curriculum was. . . . What I found were basal readers, grammar books, and spelling books. There seemed to be no other books on which to build my print-rich environment. There were no literature books to use for my reading program.

Despite my feelings about basals, there was pressure to use them as they were the district-adopted program and there didn't seem to be anything else readily available. One advantage to the basal, in the beginning, was that the teacher's manual did outline the skills that second graders were to cover. It was a start.

Soon the basal became noticeably boring for the children and for me. The stories seemed unrelated to the children's natural interests or backgrounds. . . . At this point, about halfway through the year, I decided to take a step in developing my own reading curriculum [in place of] the district's.

Peer Support

Because the basal program was boring and controlling, Leslie rejected it in favor of the literature approach she'd learned as a student teacher. Beyond her firm belief about the curricular approach which *would* motivate children and a propensity to look at recommended programs critically, she found that she needed the collaborative support of other teachers at her school to actually make the necessary modifications.

So several of us have been trying to pretty much use [literature books] as a basis for our reading and language arts program. I've done it probably 75% of the time. . . . One help is that we can get "big books" through the ESL programs. I've been borrowing those to use in our regular classrooms.

Leslie talked to Karen about the importance of peer support in developing her program.

I feel extremely fortunate that I teach at [this school]. I am not sure how such a tremendous staff came to be here, but [they are] a valuable source of information for all curriculum questions. They are willing to share information, loan you books, lessons, materials, help your class, help you teach if necessary, and—above all—listen with a concerned ear and give out hugs when needed.

Children's Responses

Leslie's critique and modification of the required curricular program was partially based on its appropriateness for her class. She was beginning a change that would eventually lead her to choose curricular materials and instructional strategies based on her research into the responses of her children to the materials.

> My critique [of the recommended basal curriculum] comes from a personal feeling that the kids can do quite a lot and yet the goal of a teacher should not always be to have all that control and do every-thing for them. If teachers always think for them, they'll never learn to think for themselves. . . . My main goal is to get the kids to the point where they'll teach themselves, which will be more exciting for them because they are more actively involved. Learning has just got to be fun.

Leslie continued to use both her personal convictions, her peers' opinions, and her children's responses to modify her literacy curriculum in her 2nd year, when she incorporated writing into her literacy program. She explained the instructional changes to Karen:

> I was trying to decide whether to do journals or not. I wanted to [incorporate them into my writing program], but for some reason I didn't know whether these [particular children] could handle them.[3] And then [at an inservice workshop], I talked to another second grade teacher in the school who wrote a curriculum on writing, and she was really enthusiastic about journal writing. So I thought I should try.

The children responded positively to journal writing. Thus, by the middle of her 2nd year, Leslie had a curricular program in place that inte-grated familiar songs, sign language, drama, and poetry into the reading and writing experiences. She included time and structure for individually listening to taped books, writing with partners in journals, participating in variously composed readers' theaters, conducting small-group research projects, and composing class books. Leslie was basically satisfied with her literacy program:

> I was feeling confident that my search had ended. I had found the "best way" to teach reading. Next year I would expand my material and refine my skills. I felt happy that my new discovery appealed to my

holistic view of how one should teach skills and that it supported the reading model mentioned in the teacher education program. It felt good to me. Obviously, my assessment of skills at this point was rather weak. If the children were on task, in other words, engaged in reading and seeming happy, it felt comfortable.

REFINING THE CURRICULUM FOR SPECIFIC CHILDREN: A CHANGE IN FOCUS

Once her own program was confidently in place, Leslie talked less about curricular concerns and more about children. Here she began to critique the dissonance between her own curricular program and children's various performances within it. In this part of Leslie's story, several themes emerged that led to a change in focus in her learning to teach literacy: the role of attention, the importance of caring for diverse children, changes in curricular materials, and the support of collaborative inquiry.

The Role of Attention

As mentioned earlier, while Leslie's primary energy still focused on developing material for literacy curriculum and activities, her attention to *individual* students' performances within those activities necessarily lessened. Because of the complexity and multiple demands of learning to teach, not only Leslie, but all of her credential program peers that I taught, had to initially focus on the global aspects of classroom management and curricular routines (see Hollingsworth, 1989b, and other related studies of cognitive attention, such as Laberge & Samuels, 1974, or Leinhardt & Greeno, 1983). As a beginning teacher, reducing managerial problems by keeping the class together as a whole gave Leslie the mental space needed to fine-tune her reading program. At the same time, however, the whole class format focused her attention on the larger group where children could give *the impression* of engagement, as Aaron had. Leslie talked and wrote about attention to children and the complexity of learning to teach.

> It could be that the 1st year you worry so much about the material curriculum that you forget to look at the kids. Or it could be that if things are going OK you don't look too deeply. When things aren't going OK, you look into it.
>
> In the beginning years, one does not have a great deal of time to reflect. The teaching days do not provide it. . . . Once you're in the classroom you don't get much of an opportunity to see what else is happening [although] that is probably the time you need it most. And

don't forget that reading isn't the only thing one teaches during the day. . . . [Finally], you can't teach subjects if the children are fighting, if they don't know how to communicate their feelings, if they don't know how to solve problems and work with each other, and/or if they don't believe in themselves and how much they can accomplish.

There is a lot about reality in schools that is not mentioned in teacher education courses, and much of this has to be dealt with and managed somewhat successfully before a teacher can really focus on analysis of reading methods—or on children.

The Importance of Caring for Diverse Children

With Leslie's curricular, managerial, and social routines in place, stories about children and Leslie's passion to teach them began to dominate her attention and our data. She reflected on the fact that children in the school where she taught were unlike those she had worked with during student teaching, and also unlike children she had known in her own suburban Caucasian school experiences. Leslie wondered about the appropriateness of middle-class ideologies and rules with children of diverse experiences. As she described her 2nd year class to Karen, her discussion of children's responses took on a caring and personal, rather than theoretical, tone.

> I think they're the best bunch in the whole school. I'm scared I'll never get such a good group again. They're really enthusiastic about learning. They want to know about everything. . . . They say 'Oh, we get to do our journals today! Oh, it's spelling today! Oh, great!, It's math time!' They just love to discuss. . . . Most of them live in drug-selling neighborhoods where life is chaotic. . . . They're so dear. They really take care of each other. . . . They really need a stable environment at school where the rules are really clear. I have to understand individual cases and make sure my rules, like tardy rules, are benefiting kids, not hurting them. . . . I had one little girl whose mom was always on drugs, and [the child] used to try to wake her mom up in the morning to tell her she needed to go to school—but she couldn't get her mom going, so she did the best she could to get herself to school. The mother ended up in jail. What was the point of discussing tardiness with her? Her effort was heroic, even if it didn't meet the school's policy for proper attendance.

In spite of the complexity and difficulty in learning about her children's lives and how best to teach them, Leslie dedicated herself to the task. "I would much rather work here than [the schools where I student taught] with those [privileged] children. They all knew everything. The teacher was semi-irrelevant."

Aaron did not live with both parents, nor did he have an abundance of economic resources, but he was well cared for. He lived with his mother— who worked evenings so that she could spend time during the day with Aaron and his teenage brother, who helped support the family by working part time, and a teenage sister, who helped him with his schoolwork. Aaron was brought to school by an adult Caucasian baby-sitter, who often compared him to her own children and made negative comments to Leslie about his intelligence.

Leslie did *not* agree. Though her life experiences as a white, college-educated, economically secure woman—and those of her own daughter, Sarah—were far more privileged than those of Aaron and his family, and might have predisposed her to worry about Aaron's potential based on his different socioeconomic status, she did not. She looked beyond the stereo-types and Aaron's often rumpled physical appearance to see him as a member of her caring classroom community. She realized that there were many ways to display intelligence other than through middle-class standards. She found Aaron to be wise, capable, and a good problem-solver: He could comprehend oral information and describe what he knew quite well verbally. He simply had a hard time with printed text:

> He is actually quite bright, very verbal, and has good auditory skills. So bright, in fact, that he compares himself to what other students are doing in the classroom and then he becomes more depressed when he sees other kids around him being able to handle the text fairly easily.

My observations in Leslie's classroom supported her assessment. Aaron *was* bright. He did listen to what was going on and could repeat, paraphrase, analyze, and discuss verbally. He could talk about what he wanted to write. On my third visit to his class, I noticed the differences between his knowledge and his performance, and the resultant effect on his confidence as he worked on his Christmas story. When verbally reporting his plan to me, his small body moved in happy anticipation. Then he changed postures when it was time to begin the work. His eyes dulled, and he became visibly frustrated, shaking his dark curls and looking around the room for cues. Later, provided the words, he had trouble reading back his own cramped written version of the story. I learned that this was not an isolated occasion. Aaron's bright eyes were often sad. Leslie talked to Karen about her concerns:

> Well, . . . he didn't read. . . . I think he had more skills than he thought he had, but because he was so depressed and his esteem was

so low, I think he just didn't try. He didn't make any effort. So I think he pretty much decided that he couldn't read.

Change in Curricular Materials

Leslie found that she could not resolve these concerns by relying on literature alone to teach Aaron to read. A shift in required materials (mentioned earlier in chapter 3) had accentuated this problem.

My 3rd year of teaching began dramatically different than year 1 or 2. The district had adopted a new basal text, had us go to training sessions, and sent out strong memos stating that we were to use the text as the basis for our reading program. Because the text was literature based, there was interest in it on the part of the teachers. At the primary level the stories looked very good. They were the kind we might have picked to read to the children.

While waiting for the textbooks to arrive, I continued to use my own literature-based program. However, I noticed, as did my friends/colleagues/researchers from the university, that a significant number of students were not attending to the text. The wonderful rhyming stories were not engaging them. I continued thinking they needed more time to adjust to school. However, I began to worry.

Leslie in her classroom.

When the new materials arrived, the "grade level" assignments of the literature selections and the outline of skills to be mastered increased her concern. Aaron and his friends clearly were not reading on a second (or even a first) grade level—a fact that had not been obvious with the ungraded literature materials. Leslie needed help. "There was no support from the district with this problem. The other teachers at my school [usually good resources] were also in a quandary and couldn't help. I had reached a point where I had no answers. Even my own philosophy of learning from literature didn't help."

The Support of Collaborative Conversations

Each time Karen and I had gone to Leslie's classroom, we asked her to talk to us about her literacy lessons, the rationale behind their development, and what children were learning from them. Leslie also talked to our conversational group about those issues. We learned that she, like the other beginning teachers in our study, lacked a meaningful way to tell whether students were actually learning to read and write *within* the literacy program. The whole-class format, chanting, and patterned language effectively hid the nonreaders from detection.

> The hardest question I found to answer was "How do you know that the kids learned this?". . . . You don't really know. What do you do? Do you look at their faces? Their eyes? You're so busy thinking about what you're going to say and getting organized that it's really hard to concentrate on how much you're getting through.

Our continued study of her learning to teach, however, encouraged Leslie to reflect on such questions. When Leslie's focus was on curriculum in her 1st year, her responses to our questions about children who were not participating reflected a belief in the popular program: "Right now I think that if we just do a lot of reading, if we keep stressing the reading, and what does it mean and then predict what you think's going to happen and those kinds of things, then they'll get better." Later, her responses reflected a questioning of such beliefs. "There have been times when I've pushed the lesson for the sake of the lesson. It can be a disaster. We talked a lot about that last time. I try not to let that be a focus."

During her 3rd year, when a literature-based basal publisher tried to promote one program for all children, we then noticed a shift from a curricular to child focus.

> [The basal representative] convinced me of that old philosophy—if you hear and read it and spend enough time with it, it will happen. I

think that the other second-grade teacher and I thought that for awhile and thought, "Oh, good, this solves a lot of our problems. And we just have to have faith that this will work." Except that I went back to the classroom and watched, and some kids were engaged and interested, but there were a lot of kids that weren't even on the page that they were supposed to be on and were staring up at the ceiling.

RESISTING CURRICULAR NORMS FOR CULTURALLY DIVERSE CHILDREN: THE ROLE OF TEACHER EDUCATION

"If year 2 was marked by 'If it's fun and interesting they'll learn to read,' then year 3 was marked by 'There is no best way to teach reading.'" Leslie talked to our group about her concerns for nonliterate children.

> Several people have mentioned a fear of having to deal with nonreaders and feeling very unprepared. The [teacher education] program never really mentioned it. We spent our time focusing on kids who could read. So I was really scared, too—in fact, panicked. I felt that I didn't have any skills whatsoever. This is my 3rd year of teaching second grade, and I have a whole-class environment again, but this year I have about 10 kids who just don't seem to be able to read really well, so many that I couldn't ignore it any more. This was exacerbated by the fact that [the new graded] reading books . . . made it more evident that the kids couldn't read.

As the children stood out from the background of the curricular program, so did Leslie's sense of responsibility as a teacher. Instead of attributing students' problems to lack of "ability," or resting her concerns by placing trust in a particular approach to literacy, she saw herself as the mediator of children's learning. "I keep thinking if they can't read when they get out of my classroom they're never going to read. I think they're doomed if we don't get them on the road here in second grade."

Teacher Education for Diversity: A Question of Timing

The teacher education program *did* include information about teaching nonreaders and writers, although Leslie and her peers did not recall it clearly. The information was embedded in critical discussions about diversity and the currently popular approaches to literacy. As a professor who taught Leslie in her credential program, I had supported the motivational and theoretical grounds for using literature and experienced-based writing as a basis for learning to read and write. I also believed in the constructivist stance and the potential for academic freedom that a literature approach provided teachers for creating their own instructional lessons. I cautioned Leslie and the others, however, about adopting this approach as defined and practiced in many local schools.

When visiting their student teaching classrooms, I sometimes noticed children—like Aaron—who were not reading and writing and who were silent during whole-class literature discussions. They were girls and boys of every cultural background—children who demonstrated strong voices and presence in other settings, but who seemed to be almost invisible in this one.[4] The *clearest* contrast between the rich, full voices I heard during recess and the silence during reading lessons occurred with the young African-American males—like Aaron. I learned that cooperating teachers often reconciled the silent voices with the process approach underlying literature-based instruction. It was "O.K."—they told me—that these students weren't reading because they were getting the meaning of the story by listening to the other (primarily Caucasian) students' discussions. Thus all children were achieving the *purpose* of reading: to understand the meaning of the text.

So, theoretically at least, these teachers believed all was well. With enough exposure to "natural" reading and writing activities—even children who were reluctant to do so would eventually become literate. Their cooperating teachers were philosophically opposed to grouping children by ability or giving easier reading materials or alternative approaches to literacy to those who were struggling with print; they were fearful of the stigmatizing effects of diversifying instructional procedures. Therefore, they usually taught the whole class with one text—and one approach.

As we discussed these observations in the university classroom, I asked Leslie and her peers to read articles by Lisa Delpit (1986, 1988) on the potential dangers of failing to provide explicit instruction to children of color. We talked about the differences between middle-class, Caucasian children who came to school with a "language of power," and others who often found classrooms to be socially and linguistically foreign. To redress such inequalities and provide more equal access to literacy, I encouraged the new teachers to try multiple approaches to language instruction—including some mentioned by Delpit that were not politically endorsed by the popular process approach movement.* I wanted teachers to use all available approaches (and invent new methods) to give every child an

---

* Lisa writes to me: "Oh, Sam, I'm such a fool. I must not have done that reading then. I'm reading Delpit now and loving her."

equal opportunity to join in the literacy conversation. My exhortations, however, were overshadowed by contextual factors. A socialized faith in the literature-based approach—as modeled by teachers in the local community—became a primary block for hearing my solitary voice which cautioned against *any* single approach as appropriate for all children. Aaron and others like him were silenced by a general trust in the method.

Leslie talked to Karen about other reasons that she did not employ alternative strategies earlier in her career.

> I'm not sure that you can successfully employ those in the very beginning. You've got too much else that you have to deal with that nobody tells you about. So you just have to hope that you can remember those things when you're ready for them. Or if you're really lucky perhaps somebody will come back when you're really ready for the information. Once you know what you're supposed to do, you can figure out how to do it.

Teacher education became "real" for Leslie and the others in our conversational group as begining teachers.

LESLIE'S RESEARCH INTO OTHER APPROACHES

The shift in Leslie's district to a system that labeled curricular materials with grade-level categorizations which her students could not meet, and her regular conversations with us and other teachers whose students were not learning to read and write, prompted Leslie to ask for and critically evaluate or research other approaches. Though there were differences between Leslie's and Mary's foci and styles of classroom research, there were some similarities between their approaches which Leslie wrote about in response to chapter 5. She began by (1) observing the situation, (2) defining and owning the question, (3) seeking external solutions from those she trusted, (4) conducting her own classroom investigation, (5) coming to conclusions, (6) modifying her methods, and (7) continuing the process again with other problems and issues.

Some of her research supported the normative principles behind a literature-based literacy program, while other findings resisted them. For example, Leslie found it was necessary to have children practice rereading stories a second and third time. She also incorporated a program for systematic, whole-class phonics/spelling instruction she had learned from a colleague in previous years. Other modifications were closer to her holistic philosophy. Leslie insisted that the children take responsibility for their own learning, for sharing their knowledge with others in cooperative tasks, for resolving conflicts, and for organizing and helping her run the classroom.

On a spring visit to Leslie's room, I saw three groups of two children each working on cooperative reports in expository text. The task required that the six children (four African-Americans, one Hispanic, and one Filipino) share the six books. While Aaron and his partner were discussing one book, their second book was "borrowed" by a child from another group who refused to give it back when Aaron's partner requested it. Instead of going to Leslie for help, the other children discussed options for handling the problem themselves. Within minutes, books were traded, and all children went back to the work at hand.

Leslie respected her students, thereby earning their respect in return. Her classroom was a warm and safe environment in which to learn, full of rich language and varied activities, replete with gender and racial equity, and fun! Still Aaron and one third of his classmates were not learning to read and write.

In desperation, Leslie asked me to repeat some suggestions I had made in her credential program. What I recommended was that Leslie try a philosophical and material expansion of her literacy program to include a supplemental approach that worked well for me as a primary grade and Chapter I teacher of migrant children (see Hollingsworth, 1988). It is important to note that I could have suggested many different approaches, many fully compatible with the normative program. My selection was based on giving Leslie a different way of thinking about the problem that would both challenge the normative model and attend to the diverse needs of children, and one that she could manage within the confines of her busy classroom. At this stage of her teaching career, I had good faith that she would not simply endorse the approach I suggested, but modify or reject it to fit both her students and her own beliefs.

The difference between my recommendation and Leslie's approach was the inclusion of systematic instruction in linguistic analyses and phonemic awareness, in flexible groups small enough to allow teacher attention to individual children. The format was based on a program initially developed by Guszak (1985). It supported many of the instructional features Leslie was using with an additional emphasis on inductive and systematic letter-sound practice for children who needed that sort of practice to read independently of the whole class activities and available patterned texts. For children like Aaron, a strong listening comprehension coupled with weak decoding skills identified a perfect opportunity for teaching and learning. The rhyming patterns in the supplemental materials seemed to also serve as a familiar link to "rap" music within the African-American culture.

Providing the scaffolding for Aaron and the others to figure out the processes of reading and writing themselves, and to transfer their new understanding to other materials, was close enough to Leslie's beliefs about developing literacy and her concern about literacy skills for her to give it a try. However, the practice materials and the notion of teacher intervention to assess individual literacy performances in less-than-meaningful text were clearly resistant to the normative curricular approach—and thus challenging to implement.

The continuous support Leslie received from the conversational group while attempting to incorporate this alternative approach into her literature program proved to be important. Unlike most staff development or inservice programs, our collaborative research allowed Leslie to frame her particular problem, ask for help with specific features of the new approach she did not understand, watch me model the approach with her children, get specific feedback about her teaching from Karen and others, and then modify the program so that she felt comfortable with it (see also Teel & Minarik, 1990).

> I think that I've probably had success due in greater part to you [Karen] than I realized or maybe you realized. I saw problems and talked about improvements or modifications, but without you I wouldn't have gotten beyond the talking stage. Knowing that you were coming meant that I tried to do them. I tried harder, and I would reflect on the questions I knew you would ask. Knowing that you were going to be present made me think of what I wanted to do and what I had set as goals.

This nonjudgmental support encouraged Leslie to develop and research her own variations on the new approach that better corresponded to both her teaching philosophy and her children's learning needs. She talked to our group about her revised literacy program.

> The [children] really like [the supplemental approach], and it does help them make progress. Contrary to reports I've read about the negative impact of pull-out groups, these children were visibly delighted at being successful at their reading task and felt comfortable with the small group and increased personal attention. The reality was that they needed a program tailored to their needs to develop the self-esteem and successful strategies needed to become literate.

Leslie's expansion of the normative curriculum now allowed Aaron and the other nonreaders to progress by playing and experimenting with the less literary material. These were experiences Leslie did not feel she could provide when she used the more serious "real" literature. The success she discovered through the alternative approach also served as a stimulus to locate and research additional material suitable for language manipulation and play.

THE NEXT CHAPTER IN LESLIE'S STORY

I went back to visit Aaron again near the end of the school year. His eyes stayed bright the whole morning. His voice was clear and strong as he read a class-composed book, a list of his classmates' names, and a book in his class library written by four classmates, Debra, Jerry, Aaron, and Sam. Entitled *Donatello Fights with Crag*, it contained vivid illustrations of this text:

> Donatello the turtle went for a fight across the slimy, dark, nasty sewer, and around the tin, cold pipes. Over the disgusting pizza crusts [in the] water, past the dead rats, through the gooey dark green slime. Under the hanging black, hairy, wiggly, spiders. And [Donatello] got back for pizza.

Later in the morning, I saw Aaron pouring over three expository trade books about snakes that he and his partner, Debra, were using to write a research paper. His new skills and confidence allowed him to fully cooperate in searching through the texts for "important" information on snakes. He proudly read me something he had contributed to their coauthored paper. "Some snakes have up to 100 babies at a time!" He smiled up at me, and his eyes matched the excitement in his voice: "That's a lot of brothers and sisters!"

Leslie summarized the various changes she had made in her literacy program and reported the results at a monthly group meeting.

> In general I feel very happy about it. I haven't tested them [the non-readers], I've listened. I haven't given them any formal test and I probably won't do that. What I've used for assessment is their changes in attitude. They tend to be children that wouldn't interact with print, were pretty depressed, and exhibited behavior problems.
>
> [Aaron and his friends] engage in print a lot more during silent reading time. They'll go up and try to find books. I've listened to them read and it's a lot better. . . . And they seem really happy. They act now as if they have the confidence to tackle new tasks and materials whereas before they felt defeated before they started.

At the end of the year, Aaron was promoted to third grade. He returns to Leslie's classroom often to visit and read to her. Today Aaron might still not do well on a standardized test of reading, nor would most of the children at the school where Leslie teaches. However, that is not her primary goal. Aaron's improved responses to reading and writing activities, the lifting of his depression, his feeling of accomplishment and pride, his eagerness to tackle new material, his less conflictive interaction with his peers, and his ability to read and write full, large letters and stories on clean sheets of paper and read them back are all part of the process to literacy and the goal itself. Leslie's success with Aaron is also a successful story of learning to teach.

POSTSCRIPT:
WHAT LESLIE (AND THE REST OF US) LEARNED

Because we've "read ahead" in Leslie's story earlier in Part I of this book, we know that a commitment to teaching as continuous inquiry and research was a theme Leslie kept with her during the ensuing years of her teaching. As we met at Karen's cabin, Leslie summarized the inquiry-oriented process of learning to teach literacy.

> It appears that once I finally realized that the class environment was not equitable, i.e., not everyone could read and write or participate (and the district was not going to provide out-of-class support) that I began to look at new ways to make the situation equitable and successful for kids like Aaron. Two things seemed to happen: The first came from a feminist/caring perspective (drawing on myself because there didn't appear to be other viable sources for support). It resulted in (a) group or buddy work for support (sometimes pairing Aaron with a friend who was academically stronger and enjoyed working with him); (b) a noncompetitive environment to prevent lesson failure, and (c) continuation of the patterned, literature-based activities. When the feminist/caring stance didn't fully help Aaron, then I had to move to a new cognitive approach (the linguist readers and small group approach). It seems that, once I began to focus on the children instead of the program, I began truly to understand a lesson I'd heard from my student teaching supervisor about being "in tune with the children." I was with them relationally and rhythmically. I now use this way of knowing to direct the flow of my class and how I approach developing curriculum.

That Leslie was satisfied with a process of determining whether the literacy program worked in her current class did not mean that her learning to teach was complete. In her 5th year of teaching, she still talked about the need for relational and empirical inquiry to establish new literacy programs suitable for the variations in each new class.

Mary and I were laughing as we were driving back from [California Reading Conference in] Sacramento because the whole point of our paper, sort of the conclusion that we had both come to, was that there is no perfect reading curriculum, and that's what we had both discovered. I mean that every year you basically just have to see what class assembles, and then just sort of figure out, then adjust everything, and do whatever the kids need. And yet, you know, you start off each year thinking that you can just do the same thing. "Oh good, this was the same thing I did last year and it will be so easy!" And, then, you try and. . . . I had finally had to admit to myself that no, I couldn't do the same thing I had done last year. I was going to have to come to grips with the fact that this group was not the same as last year's group and I couldn't do the same thing.

As she came to see learning to teach as an ongoing process, the freedom that Leslie gained from this process of inquiring into her own teaching not only contributed to her children's academic success and sense of self-worth, but let her know that she had the knowledge to create and evaluate any reading program she might choose to try. The sense of emancipation that defining success for herself gave her from curricular packages and text was important to her learning to teach. Leslie eventually used that freedom to rally support among her peers to challenge what they perceived to be other inequitable curricular policies. (Leslie's story continues in chapter 9.)

ENDNOTES

[1]This chapter is partially based on an article which was previously published as "Learning to Teach Aaron: Literacy Instruction in an Urban Classroom" in the *Journal of Teacher Education, 43,* (2,) pp.116–127, 1992.

[2] As in Mary's story, the point here is neither to critique a particular philosophical or curricular approach to literacy instruction, nor to call into question Leslie's ability, as a beginning teacher, to interpret the approach "correctly." It is to emphasize the risk that all teachers must take to challenge and critique socialized norms and draw upon their own relational knowing of their pupils.

[3] Leslie's initial decision was based on whether or not journal writing would be "developmentally appropriate" (a major focus of her Piagetian-based teacher education program).

[4] Refer to discussion of multiple literacies in chapters 5 and 8.

7

Reflections on Race, Class, Gender, Self, and Learning to Teach

LISA AND JENNIFER'S RESEARCH ON "CLASSROOM MANAGEMENT"

The narratives across the early years of our conversation told about these teachers' efforts to reconstruct the standard school curriculum for the many-cultured children entrusted to their care. So well-schooled ourselves in the traditional disciplinary structure, academic procedures, and peda-gogical styles of education, many of us in the group (particularly the white, middle-class women) had trouble remembering what we were like before our schooling reshaped us. We had even more difficulty beginning the arduous but necessary task of deconstructing schooling to emancipate and reeducate ourselves. Those of us who had either teaching or life experi-ences of talking without being heard, or sensing that our ways of knowing were less valuable than those in authority "over" us, were particularly eager to pull together the fragmented threads of our diverse selves and stories.

I could recall, for example, thinking that the stories about myself as a child that I shared with my friends were different from those I related to my family or told in school. Though often trying to express my own (and different) sense of personal reality to my teachers and parents, I was most often argued out of that reality. (In school, I was "evaluated" out of that reality.) The "father knows best" message eventually persuaded me that an adult, authoritative interpretation of reality had more value than my own.

In such ways, most of us in the group learned to "behave correctly" in our school settings and adopt both the "managerial styles" and the language of the dominant school culture as our publicly schooled selves, silencing or muting stories that might have reflected competing perceptions or ontologies. Most of us agreed with Anita Plath Helle (1991) that the disciplinary structures of traditional educational courses, academic standards, and authoritarian pedagogical styles silence diverse ways of knowing and being, distort the "educated voice," and even reshape students' sense of self to accommodate an ideological standard.

When—in women's literature, in poetry, in philosophy, and in the feminist press—we read or heard about alternative and even rowdy forms of being, different from the controlled and muted behavior expectations at which we became so facile in school, our fragmented selves found places to rest. Our composure returned with stories of "connected" or relational knowing resulting from the integration of multiple standpoints and multiple interpretations.[1] New theories of the relational self that celebrate the interdependence of body, mind, and spirit, subjectively defined in connection to other (Buber, 1966; Noddings, 1984), have helped us rediscover and articulate our private voices. No longer did we have to submerge ourselves under the hegemonically distancing and self-deprecating rational models, where we, as marginal persons, could never measure up. If anyone could empathize with a need for inclusion and the intimate understanding of other in relation to self, we—as teachers—could. Here's a poem by Linda Hogan that speaks to the importance of the support we gained from each other in risking unknown and undervalued (and thus evaluatively dangerous) ways of learning to teach.

> When we enter the unknown
> of our houses,
> go inside the given up dark
> and sheltering walls alone
> and turn out the lamps
> we fall bone to bone in bed.
>
> Neighbors, the old woman who knows you
> turns over in me
> and I wake up
> another country. There's no more
> north and south.
> Asleep, we pass through one another
> like blowing snow,
> all of us,
> all.
>
> *Linda Hogan*
> *"Our Houses"*

Not all of our understandings were easy to tell or hear, nor did their translations into stories all have happy endings. This chapter contains some of those stories. They reflect on the intersections between race, class, gender, self, and teaching in a complex social setting. They also provide two more examples of teacher research; however, in both cases, Lisa's and Jennifer's research "findings" come more from trust in themselves and their experiences than from objective data. Both are examples of teacher research on what is usually called "classroom management" or social relations, a feature important both in learning to teach and in facilitating the learning of literacy. Both teachers examine that issue, not through generic cognitive or strategic approaches, but through raced, classed, and gendered perspectives. I realize that there may be readers who would suggest that "learning to trust one's observations" is not an example of theoretically sound research: that research procedures have been clearly established, and these approaches clearly fall out of those dimensions. Those of us in our group have struggled with the question of "is what we're doing research?" Though we've often taken different positions on this issue (see chapter 10), I maintain that it is. First, because it makes a valuable contribution to the quest of educational knowledge; and second, because it is information that should be shared with others to assist in the struggle to improve urban education, and not just kept to ourselves as reflection or personal inquiries often are. Further, variations in research practice are not illogical—particularly in feminist practices. Even in feminist work, however, the struggle to maintain variance is difficult. As a society, we are well educated into the need to follow authority, find the best way and use it. It's a difficult trap to get beyond to see the possibility of what might be.

> As feminist theory is presently practiced, we seem to lose sight of the possibility that each of our conceptions of a practice may capture an aspect of a very complex and contradictory set of social relations. Confronted with complex and changing relations, we try to reduce these to simple, unified, and undifferentiated wholes. We search for closure or the right answer or the "motor" of the history of male domination. The complexity of our questions and the variety of the approaches to them are taken as signs of weakness or failure to meet the strictures of preexisting theories rather than as symptoms of the permeability and pervasiveness of gender relations and the need for new sorts of theorizing. (Flax, 1990, p. 179)

I am pleased that we found different ways to interpret and demonstrate the phenomenon of teacher research. It seems not only valuing of our different selves (and as exciting as a new journey!) but educative for our profession. Our differences help prevent premature closure in the struggle for understanding.

JENNIFER DAVIS-SMALLWOOD'S STORIES

In our search for new ways of theorizing, we are fortunate to include Jennifer Davis-Smallwood, an African-American, Native American, and French-American woman and a member of our conversational group. Her stories of multiple yet integrated identities helped to liberate and connect our own. For example, I first learned from Jennifer the method of listening, respect, suspending judgments, and understanding as I came to understand her ways of being through my own cultural lenses.

Although what I'm about to say is clearly *my* language and not hers, Jennifer's stories show how she deconstructs the reality of school and generates meaning internally. She would say that she teaches the way she sees it, not how she's told. I would say that she is not rewarded (as many of us are) by performing according to authoritarian rules or representing someone else's reality of school. I would say she "reads" the "text" of school (how it's *supposed* to be) in a deconstructive manner. Jane Flax would (and did) say:

> Deconstructive readers are disrespectful of authority, attentive to suppressed tensions or conflicts within the text, and suspicious of all "natural" categories, essentialist oppositions, and representational claims. They are willing to play with the text, to disrupt its apparent unity, to rescue its heterogeneous and disorderly aspects and its plurality of meanings and voices. They are not to think of themselves as author(ities) or as un- or dis-coverers of Truth, but rather as potentially interesting members of an ongoing conversation. Their responsibility is to offer listeners a variety of moves from and against which further movement becomes possible. (Flax, 1990, p. 37)

To find out how Jennifer has come to read, deconstruct, interrupt, and challenge the concept of "classroom management" as it's supposed to be in school, we must begin with her biography, which becomes an analytical research tool. That is, Jennifer's understanding of herself as a black feminist led her to structure and analyze the classroom as she did.

Jennifer attended her first four grades in African-American community schools in San Francisco, California. Her mother was the school secretary. Her father owned his own carpentry business in the community. Both Jennifer's family and her community supported standard, middle-class school norms which included "sitting still in class, making good grades, playing ball at recess." Jennifer felt supported and did well. During her fourth grade year, her family moved to San Jose. Jennifer and her sister were the only children of color in the new school. Finding support within that school community was difficult.

> When we went out to play ball, we lined up and the captains chose their team members. No one wanted me . . . I was not only a girl, I was a black girl. After I hit a grand slam homer with the team that "had to take me"— everybody wanted me. I began to see that there were ways of being OK in that group that didn't include all of me. . . . My teachers told me to "stand up straight," ignoring the fact that I couldn't do their version of "straight" because of physical differences in African-Americans' bone structures. . . . The teachers told me I could do better in school if I would just "Try harder." . . . Because I didn't meet their standards for "Trying harder," I was sentenced to the "low groups." What was OK in San Francisco was suddenly not OK in San Jose.

In contrast to the "schooled" evaluation of her, Jennifer's family reinforced her centered belief in herself as an intelligent, worthwhile person. She embraced their support as a means of facing educational rejection and stayed in school. In fact, she stayed through 4 years at one University of California campus where she obtained a bachelor's degree in economics and added a 5th year at another California campus to earn a teaching credential. A personable, humorous, strong, and easy-going young woman who enjoyed the construction trades and soccer during the summer, Jennifer talked with our group for years about her learning to teach. After her 2nd year of teaching, though, she left the classroom. Her story of school in San Jose replayed for her as a beginning teacher.

Jennifer tried to put her own lived theories about cultural difference and self-acceptance to work as she was learning to teach in classrooms with high proportions of children from African-American families. She believed in community and self-regulated group learning to support children of color. Children answered questions simultaneously—often in competing tones. Jennifer encouraged her students to solve their own problems and trust their own intuitions. Noise level problems while working in groups didn't bother Jennifer, nor did children's decisions to switch groups if they changed interests. She was more concerned that the students find ways to do well—to see themselves as successful. Her personal theories and teaching style had been endorsed neither by supervisors in her teacher education program, nor by the individualized and competitive academic policies encouraged by the school where she taught after graduation. In the area of classroom management, for example, Jennifer had been taught to set firm rules for classroom interaction. She was told to "keep control" by discouraging call outs, having students complete their academic work independently and quietly at their seats, keeping the pace of lessons up so the students would stay on task, and punishing any behavior that deviated from those rules.

Jennifer used the same coping strategies her family taught her to value during her elementary school years to research her practices: a belief in her out-of-school ways of being and knowing, and intuitively based confirmation of her observations. Thus, Jennifer continued to feel confident about her own work in the face of disapproval. Her biographical or intuitive research validated her methods. She refused to accommodate to standard "classroom management" rules, and resisted by continuing to do what she felt was appropriate for the children (see Anyon, 1991, for an excellent discussion of accommodation and resistance). Jennifer felt successful in supporting children's personal and academic success. However, after 2 unsuccessful years of trying to convince her school staff that the African-American and Latino children in her classroom were learning what was important to them, and that the style and content of the standard *recommended* pedagogy were not meaningful to these children, Jennifer needed a break. She returned to construction trade work where she felt she had more time and freedom to work on changing the standards of school for such children from the outside. Currently, she is writing proposals to create an environmental education experience for urban children outside of school, where movement and exploration is better tolerated. Meanwhile, she supports herself and her life's project as a substitute teacher and operating engineer.

Jennifer's intuitive research did not change her administrators' minds about the way it's supposed to be in urban classrooms, but listening to her stories, analyses, and insights certainly changed those of us in the conversational group. Her stories helped awaken and validate an appreciation for alternative and culturally appropriate pedagogical styles. For some of us, they led to a clarification of feminist issues and a search for feminist pedagogies committed to include the diverse experiences of women and minority children as part of their self-educations. For others of us, they gave permission to accept what we were already doing in support of our students, even though our instructional styles might not be approved by the majority of our academic colleagues.*

I probably learned more about the importance of taking a nonjudgmental research stance as opportunity for my learning from Jennifer than

---

* Lisa added: "I think Jennifer also helped me see the school system as systematically problematic and to feel comfortable voicing that critique."

from anyone else—because we cared about each other, and because we came to this work together from different places. When I first started observing and listening to Jennifer, the year before this conversational group began, I was still in a research mode in which I was supposed to go into her classroom to see if she was doing it right. Fresh out of my doctoral program, her classroom didn't look like the exemplary models presented in educational research reports. I might have gone away, as others did, shaking my head and wondering why she refused to conform, but something tripped me up. I had a sense she knew something no one else had yet told me. As we worked together over time, I began to sincerely care for Jennifer, and wanted to know why she taught the way she did. I could ask her real questions about her teaching, not just questions intended to trip her up and demonstrate that she apparently hadn't learned what I had taught her (because, obviously, her behavior didn't mirror that learning). Not just to try to have her guess what I wanted her to say and then say it . . . but because I really wanted to know.

Learning from Jennifer wasn't easy. Not only did her teaching not look like anything I'd seen before, she didn't always have the words for telling me why she taught as she did. She hadn't written or published one thing that I could read to understand (my schooled mode of learning). I had to keep going back to her classroom, to watch and listen. Eventually I understood; and the process of understanding Jennifer changed my professional life. I no longer could enter a classroom to research what I thought I already knew and then leave. I no longer wanted to teach by convincing others of what I knew to be true. Jennifer taught me that I didn't know it all. Jennifer taught me to learn.

Later, I realized that Jennifer and I shared a common connection: My own teaching (and my research) often doesn't "look like" the exemplary models. Many of my academic colleagues do not understand my professional approach, and—perhaps because of the competitive and hectic pace of modern life—cannot take the time to learn to care for me. Thus, they sometimes judge my practices negatively. But in an academic community, having a world of colleagues to draw from, I am more privileged than Jennifer was in her small school building. Many of my colleagues *do* try to understand (although they may not always agree), because we share caring relations. They, like Jennifer, have become my teachers.

LISA RAFFEL'S STORIES

Jennifer's stories touched all of us in our conversational group. One fall in her 3rd year of teaching, Lisa heard Jennifer talk about her biographical or intuitive research on "classroom management." That same fall, Lisa was

Jennifer in conversation.

also taking a graduate course from me called "teaching as research." (For more on that course, see chapter 11.) As in Jennifer's case, the class learned that Lisa's life story also helped shape her perceptions as a teacher, and her interest in classroom research. Lisa grew up in Connecticut, living alone with her working mother. As a "latch-key kid," figuring out not just what to do, but why, was important to her survival. She took that sense of herself into school.

> As long as I can remember I've been the kid or adult with her hand up, asking a question. This leads me both to push my students to understand the curriculum and themselves, and myself to understand my students and my teaching. Part of this quest has led me to be extremely reflective. . . . The positive aspect of my reflective process is that once I understand my motives, I can be more clear, more real with my students. As I grow in self-awareness, it pushes my students to become more self-aware. The negative aspect of my reflective process is that I am often too hard on myself. At times I blame myself for all the problems in my classroom, forgetting that the students have partial responsibility for whatever happens in the classroom.

At the beginning of our course on teacher research, Lisa wasn't sure *what* she wanted to use as a research project. She talked of her confusion: "So many things bug me. My low kids . . . management . . . reading. I guess I have about 300." We asked her to describe what stood out as the most serious challenge to her "ideal" classroom. She quickly identified the problem of "management."

I felt the classroom management problems most acutely when trying to get the students to listen and focus. It felt as if I would ask for their attention and then stand there waiting and waiting. As I stood in front of the class asking for focus and not getting it, my feelings were hurt and my ego crushed. My need for approval from my classroom community was not met. I became stuck on their inability to focus the way I wanted them to.

In discussion with the other teachers in the class, Lisa described her ideal classroom image as one with more on-task behavior, where one child speaks at a time and where children pay close attention to direct lessons from the teacher. Lisa's words about her image did not match her personal theories about classroom interaction. Not only had I heard her talk to the conversational group about her experiences in Peace and Conflict Studies at Berkeley, I had observed her teaching in several different culturally diverse settings where she established interactional patterns based on a sense of classroom community and democracy. The teacher–self she exhibited in those settings did not hold the absolute authoritarian role painted by her "ideal" classroom image. They better reflected her life. She wrote about her early life experiences and educational beliefs for a national conference.

I had strong intentions when I went into teaching. I focused on the pedagogy and practice of democratic education and on oppression by race, class, and gender. I felt (and still feel) that our current political, economic, and educational systems were (are) unjust, unfair, and unhealthy. I was critical of society and felt it was everyone's duty to do something about it. I believed I could make my greatest contribution by creating a classroom where students learned both about the troubles of the real world and about their abilities to make changes in that world. Over the years I've learned that this means teaching about controversial issues that they find relevant and teaching critical thinking, self-esteem, communication, and cooperation skills.

One of my personal/political values has been a belief in the importance of community. I think this is important for all people and especially young ones taking risks and trying to learn. So I work to create a sense of community in my classroom. We go on overnight trips together, raise money, resolve conflicts, talk about our feelings, etc.

When Lisa was probed, she admitted that her desire for authoritarian order in the classroom was "what was expected; what she'd been taught." As she tried to conform, the role of the teacher became decontextualized from herself. Regardless of her own experiences or beliefs, then, she felt personally accountable for living up to someone else's picture of a "good, middle-class schoolroom," where children sit and listen quietly to the teacher. Thus, her children's inattention made Lisa feel like a failure at teaching.[2]

Lisa tried many different interventions to solve the problem. She posted "rules for focusing" on the wall. She gave positive rewards for focusing. She took away privileges for not focusing. Some of her interventions helped, but not to her complete satisfaction.

> At the end of many days I was feeling like I had battled the students all day to get them to focus. Driving home I would go over and over in my head what I could do differently, what I had done wrong, and how I really didn't know how to be a teacher. I had tried a few different strategies for improving their focusing. I was rethinking my discipline plan, my reward system, my signal, etc. Some of these interventions helped a little. The real change came when I looked within myself.
>
> I talked to my therapist about my problems. I told her, "My kids won't focus on me and it's my fault." We talked about how it felt when they wouldn't focus and why it was so important to me. She asked me to remember what happened last year when I asked my students to focus. I remembered, "They focused."
>
> "So," she said, "could it be this group of kids?"
>
> We went on to discuss how I actually was getting the students to focus this year, it was just different from last year. They were louder, slower to focus, and had a shorter attention span. By releasing my feelings and acknowledging my fears, I was able to see my classroom with some perspective. Letting go of the huge emotional hook of being a total "failure" or "success" as a teacher freed me to analyze my classroom situation and learn some important lessons. . . . Most importantly I realized that whether the students focused or not was a function of not only my abilities, but theirs as well. This realization helped me to feel better about myself. As my feelings of self-worth increased I would be easier on myself with the knowledge that this particular group of students had difficulty focusing the way I expected.

In our teacher research course, we began to untangle Lisa's "ideal" classroom expectation through a close examination of the "real." I videotaped her classroom and brought it back to our graduate class for group analysis. Together we watched footage of Lisa's students at break time, then observed her calling them to order, then saw them take a moment or two to settle down. It was clear to our class that the "focus" problem, though not perfect, was minimal. Some teachers suggested that the students' behavior was quite appropriate given the mix of ages, cultures, classes, interactional patterns, and Lisa's democratic expectations for them. Given our feedback and that of her therapist, Lisa began to revise her image to look at herself and her own expectations. She began to realize that what she perceived as lack of focus was not such a problem when she broadened her image to include not only a focus on the students "as they're supposed to be" but herself and her beliefs about teaching, learning, and life in relationship to the students. Reexamining the class with her revised image, she saw the children's behavior simply as a reflection of the individual differences she valued. She became more relaxed in her instructional approach with the children. They responded in kind. She resolved the "focus" problem by teaching with a new image as a result of the research—an image more consistent with her beliefs on difference and community. Lisa was ready then to work on some of the other problems that were out of focus in her new image. She had begun to adopt a perspective of teaching as research, using a feminist rather than a traditional approach to classroom inquiry (see Table 7.1).

So much of how I learn to teach comes from the experience of being in the classroom with students. I learn from watching myself and my students and thinking about what I've observed and felt. I try something in the classroom and then evaluate the results. In a way the students teach me everything. All the goals, objectives, and lessons only have meaning in relationship to the students. At times I'm rushing around so much that I forget that. I have a hard time stepping back and watching the students to learn from them.

I watch them doing academic tasks and interacting during their free time. I ask them as a class if they understand and to explain their understanding. Sometimes I question individuals so I can grasp the students' perspective. I evaluate their written work, their drawings, and their answers in class. I've learned invaluable lessons in this process, too many to list all of them. But some of the important ones: students often need background knowledge development before delving into a new topic, students use each other as editors naturally but need some guidance, students need time to clean up and transition to new activities, and students crave opportunities to be successful at school.

Lisa's natural propensity to reflect and her developing skills as observer of children, however, was largely unsupported in her school as a means to develop other than "standard" expectations for classroom management. In her 4th year, she left the classroom and returned to graduate work. She talked about her decision at a national conference (Raffel, 1990).

TABLE 7.1

Teacher Research

Traditional Approach	Obstacle	Feminist Approach
In isolation	Single Perspective Lack of support	In conversation
Begin with questions from others' theories	Projects are too large Lack of ownership	Begin with observation of own experience Discover own voice/theory
Reproduce others' methods to collect data	Inflexible methods Inappropriate analyses	Notice where personal theory and standard classroom image clash Clarify differences by gathering information
Use others' analysis schemes to reduce data	Data are molded to fit scheme Fear of failure Ignores broader context and external constraints	Create tentative new classroom image to incorporate focused data Suspend image; allow it to shift dialectically Listen to alternative theories, images, examples Data are coded by incorporating personal and alternative theories Data are interpreted within school, social, and political settings
Summarize at end	Overlooks influence of research interactions	Continuous re-imaging or summarizing
Results take standard written format	Often inaccessible to other teachers	Results are tentative and nonprescriptive
Only significant results are reported	May be significant, but meaningless	Results help clarify personal voice and others in multiple form
Change in researcher is not reported	Ignores both richness and reality of research	Personal transformation is an important result

I decided to change jobs for a number of reasons. First I am simply ready for a change and a new challenge. I've always wanted to work with college-age students and I look forward to working in the area of peace and justice again. But the primary reason I'm changing jobs is because I'm exhausted and burned out.

I believe any kind of teaching is hard, and teaching the kinds of kids I work with is especially hard. It's not the kids themselves that are difficult; they are wonderful. For me it's the glaring realization that the current system is not working. I have all these questions and not enough support to handle them. All the support of the collaborative group helped me through 3 years, helped me be reflective, productive, and to grow. But it wasn't enough, especially at my school site, to bury my deep disillusionment with public schooling. I felt myself a cog in the grinding reproduction of inequality. Maybe by working in a different educational context I'll come to understand some of the reasons for those dilemmas.

Lisa's currently back at Berkeley in a doctoral program and working with California Tomorrow, a small, nonprofit organization that conducts research, formulates policy, and serves as advocates for the multicultural student population in California. Lisa's role within the organization is to help teachers understand how to manage, support, and teach the culturally diverse children within their classrooms.

CONCLUDING STORIES

Lisa and Jennifer's stories have given us diverse and compelling examples of teacher research that underscores the importance of reconciling "situational" and "substantial" selves (Nias, 1989) through raced, classed, and gendered perspectives as we are learning to teach throughout our careers. That is, though our current biographical or intuitive senses of self can easily become lost in various evaluative or judgmental settings, they are important to try to reclaim, for teaching and—perhaps—for other practice situations as well. The stories in this chapter, like those before and after, have not given us solutions, but ideas to "push against" as the conversation continues. Our collective narratives are, of course, the beginning. In freeing ourselves to celebrate and include our own diverse selves, we have uncovered another way to tell our own stories, and to hopefully make spaces for others to tell theirs. The following chapter contains other examples of teacher research in middle-school settings that employ still different approaches to inquiry and are intended for different purposes. It is important to remember, as you read through the stories in Part II, that our pedagogical changes began as we learned to listen to the stories that were and are becoming us.

ENDNOTES

[1] While not intending to promote connection and relations as stereotypes of gendered experience (i.e., women's), we want to make clear the importance of those concepts—and the educational settings in which they can be developed—for learning to teach. We hope that their importance will lead to valuing and promoting connection and relations for both women and men in teacher education programs.

[2] Both Jennifer and Lisa, reviewing this chapter, expressed amazement at how little they had articulated that their perceptions as teachers had to do with race and class. Lisa told me, "I can't believe that we didn't say more about those issues. Obviously there was much to say about Jennifer being black with a bunch of black kids, and me being a white woman with black kids. It's just not coincidental that our problems were based on being 'approved' by what white teachers might do. I didn't talk about it because I was scared. There was no support in my teacher education program or my school for raising such issues. Maybe we should have been braver. Maybe Jennifer's perspective on what black kids need should be taken seriously. It's about differing opinions and different kinds of knowledge. Now I can talk about it because, at California Tomorrow, it's part of my job. I get supported for thinking in those ways. But it's still amazing that we didn't say more about the role of race in teaching while it was happening."

8

What Happens to Literacy After the Elementary Grades?

THOUGHTS AND RESEARCH ON URBAN EXPERIENCES

As school curriculum has traditionally been organized, the responsibility for literacy instruction rests with elementary-grade teachers. By the time students reach middle school, they are "supposed" to be competent readers and writers and ready to move into subject studies in depth. Moreover, according to developmental theory (Piaget, 1961), which was heavily promoted by the conversational group members' credential programs, by seventh and eighth grades, students are ready for formal operational or abstract thinking about knowledge. As any teacher of the middle and higher grades knows, however, that goal is far from being realized, particularly in urban school districts. Many students reach middle school without the knowledge of how to read and comprehend difficult content area texts. As a result, the drop out rate increases dramatically. A series of recent studies on urban education which I've cited earlier in the book clearly supports that. For example, Jonathan Kozol contrasts the differences in urban and suburban schooling across the United States. In one chapter, after reviewing the drastic difference in basic skill competencies between urban and suburban districts in New Jersey, he describes the statistics on secondary dropouts. "The high school dropout rate of Jersey City [is] 52 percent, [translating] to some 2,500 children every four years. The corresponding rate in Princeton, less than 6 percent, translates to only 40 children" (Kozol, 1991, p. 158).

Though society as a whole has been slow to react, there have been excellent attempts within teacher preparation programs to deal with this phenomenon. Almost every state requires a course in literacy instruction for credential candidates who will teach secondary subjects. Yet, because of the demands of the 50-minute class structure, the pressure of testing standards to get content material covered, and the lingering belief that literacy really IS NOT the responsibility of secondary teachers, the problem continues (see Hollingsworth & Teel, 1991). After extended conversation about these dilemmas in our conversational group, the middle school teachers—Anthony, Karen, and I—decided to conduct some research on our own teaching to see what was possible.

Anthony Cody, you will remember, joined our conversational group as an eighth grade life science teacher in an urban middle school. He was interested in remaining with the group of (primarily) elementary school teachers for reasons that he explicates in this chapter. In the 3rd year of our work together, Karen Teel also returned to the classroom as a part-time teacher of seventh grade world history. In our 5th year, I also decided to return to the classroom as a collaborating teacher in eighth grade world history. This chapter, then, explores our collaborative and individual investigations into ways we could teach literacy as we taught social studies and science. Like the elementary teachers in our group, we chose to deal with these questions in different ways, although we were informed by our conversations with each other. Each of us will tell our stories about how we chose to incorporate literacy instruction into our disciplinary areas, then we will try to summarize what we've learned about literacy, disciplinary subjects, our students, and ourselves at the end of the chapter. The stories will demonstrate the importance of teacher research as a means for reversing the "literacy" problem in urban middle schools. We'll begin with Karen Teel's story, who came into our conversational group with 10 years of experience in middle school. The description of her research begins with a discussion of how she became aware of and interested in content-area, literacy instruction. Karen, speaking in the first person, tells the story herself:

KAREN'S STORY: TEACHING HISTORY THROUGH LITERATURE

My (Karen's) initial role in the collaborative conversation group was that of a doctoral student and researcher—not a teacher. At the meetings I listened for changes in the beliefs expressed by Anthony, Mary, Leslie, Lisa, and Jennifer in their teaching practices. One of the most interesting aspects of the experience for me was the process of discussing, analyzing, and trying to make sense of the issues we raised as a team. The group problem-solving process was new to me, and it raised old and new questions for me about my own teaching.

When reading became the focus of our conversations during the 2nd year, I learned a great deal about the benefits of attention to reading problems through reading practice. I'd always known that students needed to be good readers to succeed, but I'd never really thought much about how to promote reading in my own social studies classroom. These conversations provided information and an impetus for self-reflection. I became more and more curious about how to address all of these critical issues— particularly with African-American students who populate many of our secondary schools in the Bay Area.

Following the 2nd year of our collaborative group, I decided to return to my tenured position as a classroom teacher in the Richmond Unified School District, California, and to become a teacher–researcher. I wanted to work with African-American students from inner-city Richmond. I arranged to teach one class of seventh grade world history at a middle school.

Naturally, my interest and role in the collaborative group shifted when I became a practicing teacher as well as a researcher. The other teachers in our group were as interested in my experiences as I was in theirs, and the issues discussed took on a different meaning for me. I found striking similarities across teaching assignments and age groups between my classroom struggles and successes and those of the other teachers. Our relationship became a more reciprocal one in that we shared stories and could better support one another. It thrilled me to have genuinely interested colleagues listen to my stories, give me feedback, and above all, support my philosophy and efforts. That validation built up my confidence and resolve, and helped me to believe in my ability to find better ways to work with my students.

After years of listening to the collaborative group's conversations about reading issues and proposed programs to address reading problems, I was determined to promote reading in my seventh grade world history class. The students resisted reading the text. Many of them couldn't read, and the rest didn't seem to find details of the Roman Empire interesting at all. I thought, to get them interested, I needed to find a way to validate my students' own present cultures. I wasn't sure exactly how . . . so, like Mary and Leslie, I systematically observed students' responses to my teaching. At first, I took some time out of each 50-minute class to read what I considered to be high interest literature to the students. Though the students appeared to enjoy the stories, some of them asked to read their own choice of books. When I took them to the library, I discovered that most of the African-American students selected biographies and historical fiction about their own culture. I then encouraged *all* of the students to pick out books that pertained to their cultural heritage as a way of acknowledging cultural diversity.

At this point, however, I wondered whether my students understood the concept of cultural diversity. I wondered if they really knew about their cultures, how culture influenced their lives, and how their cultures were different. A fellow graduate student suggested that the students write about their ancestors who first came to America. So, the students researched this topic with their families and then wrote about where their ancestors originally came from, who they were, and how they happened to arrive here in the Bay Area. The students' stories, along with illustrations, were printed and bound in a book that we called *Coming to America*. Each student received a copy of the book to share with their families.

Based on what I learned about my students' interests in books, from talking with reading specialists like Sam, and from reading about Marva Collins (a very successful African-American teacher of inner-city children in Chicago; see Collins & Tamarkin, 1982), I created a reading program for social studies. We continued to study world history from the school text, but I now required and provided time for additional reading outside of the text. I hoped that it would give them another way to learn history

Karen and class.

and also improve their reading, writing, and speaking abilities. I announced to the students that they would be required to read a book about history each month, to fill out a book report form, and to represent what they learned from the book in some creative way such as in a drawing, skit, or model. I was going to give them 2 days of the week to read their book for about 15 minutes. Over the course of the year, I changed that schedule so that the students had 10 minutes, at the beginning of the period, 4 days of the week to read their books. During that 10 minute period, I read along with the students. The rationale for both the more frequent reading practice and for my reading with them, which Sam suggested to me, was that learning to read requires regular and frequent practice, and that role modeling by the teacher is very effective in influencing student attitude and behavior.

I gathered together approximately 150 books that made up a classroom library. The books came from book stores, from the Salvation Army, from my own children, and from other teachers at my school. I selected books that represented the racial and ethnic diversity in my classroom and represented a variety of topics. Our classroom library consisted of books written by and/or about African-Americans, Asian-Americans, Hispanic-Americans, Native-Americans, and European-Americans. With regard to the reading levels of the books, some of the books I purchased were either simplified versions of the originals (such as the classics) or were written with readers in mind who have weak reading skills and little motivation to read. The books ranged from second grade to adult reading levels.

When the reading session was about to start, I took out a timer and set it for 10 minutes. Then, I told the students to begin, and I started reading my book. The students were expected to do nothing other than read during this time. I walked around the room reading and checking on the students' progress. Sometimes, I stopped and quietly asked individual students how they liked their book so far. Other times, I asked a student to quietly read a sentence out of the book. I tried to use the time not only to read my own book but to monitor the students' reading as well. When the timer went off, I encouraged the students to mark the place where they stopped reading. Often, it was hard to get some students to close their books.

During the 2nd year, the students kept track of their reading progress on 5 x 8 cards. Each day they read, they listed the date, the name of their book, and how many pages they read in the 10 minutes. I introduced the cards because I decided that the 2nd year's group of students needed more accountability built into their reading. I got the idea for the cards from my son's ninth grade English teacher. The students received credit for their reading efforts through the 5 x 8 cards and for telling about their books in what I called, "book talks." During the "book talks," which most students gave at least once each quarter, the students appeared to be very proud to describe the stories in their books about young people and adults from a variety of cultural backgrounds.

The results of my program were promising. Since the African-, Asian-, and Latino-American literature they read and presented was just as respected as stories of Greek, Roman, and European history authorized by our text, the students in my class experienced some validation of their cultural heritage. They also learned about world history. And they improved their attitudes about reading.

How did I know? By their choices, reactions and conversations. The books were all around them every day, and even my poorest readers were looking at them and making an effort to read them. The African-American students, in particular, almost invariably chose biographies or historical fiction about African-Americans—such as Harriet Tubman, George Washington Carver, Jackie Robinson, Bo Jackson, Dr. Martin Luther King, Jr., and *Sounder* and *Escape to Freedom*. Periodically, I heard them talking to each other in class about Harriet Tubman or Martin Luther King, Jr. It appeared to me that they enjoyed learning about the black slaves' struggle for freedom and about the Civil Rights movement. Some of them seemed more intrigued with the classics. One black student said he liked learning about the myths represented in the book, *Dracula*. Some students read "choose your own adventure" stories about ancient Egypt or Rome while others read about Asterix, the cartoon character who lived in Gaul under Roman rule. Many students were also able to recognize similarities between events within their own cultures and those we discussed from our history text. Thus, another benefit of the reading program was the students' growing familiarity with the classics and with important topics in world and United States history which they could now better connect with their own cultural heritages.

I asked the students during class and during lunch time how they liked the reading practice they were getting. Some of them really liked it. When I asked them why they liked it, some responses were: "I think I'm reading faster." "I didn't like reading but now I do." "It helps me to read more." "I'm reading better, I understand more, and I'm learning more about history." "I like it because I don't really have time to read the books at home." "I learned that history is exciting." "I like the wars and how you have to protect yourself." One student said that reading historical fiction and biographies at the beginning of social studies class was a good way to get her mind in gear. Another said it was a good way to "rev up his brain." Some students even suggested that more time be provided for reading in class. Only a few of them said it was just so-so.

My research didn't end with a conviction that I ought to make time for self-selection of culturally relevant literature in world history. I had many more questions to research about the content of the course and the best ways of teaching that content. I found the help I needed to pursue those questions. In our ongoing, collaborative conversational group, we continue to talk about ways to promote literacy across grade levels and disciplines. We have also addressed the issues of racism and classism, both institutional as well as personal. I perceive our reflection and teacher research as processes that move in and out of the classroom. Our collaborative meetings provide a forum for reflection on our classroom experiences and encourage us to continue on with our classroom research. So much happens in classrooms, and teacher research can be a lonely process. Our collaborative meetings give all of us a place to share our growing insights and revitalize ourselves as teachers.

SAM'S STORY: MULTIPLE LITERACIES, SOCIAL STUDIES, AND COMMUNITY

The next story told in this chapter is about my own (Sam's) teacher research in an eighth grade world history class in an urban community in Michigan. In the 4th year of our collaborative group, I moved to a midwestern university, but I still traveled back to California for monthly group meetings. I had become excited about Karen's experiences as a part-time, world history teacher, and decided to try some similar ideas in the Midwest. I hadn't taught secondary history in 12 years, so I had to catch up on the literature and rely on teachers with current experience for guidance. In Michigan, as a member of a professional development school, I worked with 12 teachers in an urban junior high, and most closely with one teacher, Paul Abram.[1] Following lessons based on our collaborative planning, I taught the 1st hour of his 8th grade, world history class, and he taught the rest of the day. Susie Standerford and David Kubel, graduate students at Michigan State University, also served as facilitators and researchers in that class. Margie Gallego, a professor at Michigan State, also participated in this project, as did several teachers from Paul's school community.

THE CONCEPT OF MULTIPLE LITERACIES

Paul's world history classroom was situated in a large brick and oak building of a 1940's vintage in a working class area. The tall brick smokestacks of its physical plant flagged its geographic location. Though students represented primarily African-American, Caucasian, and Latino backgrounds, the school also had many Asian- and Native-American students. Paul's classes were filled with diverse, bright, and interesting students with something in common: Most had poor standard literacy skills. Students with better skills, primarily Caucasians, were scheduled into a section of "creative" world history. I soon learned that Paul's students were quite capable of communicating to function successfully in their own communities outside school, but were somehow less able to replicate literacy behaviors required for school success.[2] Therefore, many of them made poor grades in other classes, were segregated from higher achieving students, appeared to be disinterested in most school subjects, and were at high risk of dropping out.

As our team discussed Paul's students and my teaching with our colleagues in Michigan and with my colleagues in the California conversational group, we found a focus for this work. We decided to look at the "reality" of the situation differently in order to make a difference. Although it is the diversity in *students'* communication and comprehension styles within urban schools that has often been seen as the "problem" contributing to school failure, we thought about it differently. We chose to define the students' failure in school as "problematic" (and not simply attributed to student deficiencies), and to redefine the problem as one of the content of social studies instruction being too separate from school and community-based literacy processes. We hoped that recognizing and integrating students' own personal and community literacies might both increase their understanding of "school literacy," and increase their success in disciplinary studies.

Similar to Mary's story (chapter 5), we learned how to recognize the need for and accomplish the broadening of "standard" or "school literacy" by looking at the students. Although Lucinda stated adamantly that she didn't like to read and, in fact, WOULDN'T read the world history text, I noticed that she carried a paperback romance novel with her school notebook. Danny was almost always out of his seat and inattentive, but when I sat and talked with him one on one, I found out he knew an incredible amount about sports. Though Tyrone was often absent because he was suspended for fighting, when he was in class he asked provocative questions—showing a sensitivity to issues not only in his local community, but in our vastly changing world. Yet Tyrone couldn't read the eighth grade text well enough to comprehend it. The text didn't interest Danny long enough to sit still to read it. Lucinda wouldn't even try. She told me that she always got bad grades in school and she always would, so she wasn't wasting her time and energy.

What's interesting about these stories is not that they're new or unusual, but when I shared them with the research team and the conversational group, not one member blamed the students for their behaviors. Some of us thought they acted that way in eighth grade because of their repeated failures in school. Others pointed to the irrelevance of history of "dead, white, European males" to their lives and worlds. Others talked about their need to be validated for what they did know. Some of us wondered if they knew that their failures were not their own faults, but were part of a larger societal problem involving power and poverty and care. And we all agreed that they needed to be taught standard literacy before they could be expected to perform well in eighth grade social studies. That was *our* responsibility as teachers. Therefore, our goals were to teach them by (1) increasing their various literacy levels, (2) connecting school and community life, (3) enhancing their feelings of self-worth in school environments, and (4) raising their levels of academic achievement in social studies. A diagram of the activities and attitudes we used to accomplish those goals through developing multiple literacies in the world history class is found in Figure 8.1.

The following is a narrative account of how our goals were achieved, documented, and celebrated through attending to activities that drew out students' multiple literacies.

COMMUNITIES OF POWER: A SIMULATED GAME

To learn more about the students' understandings of community and societal issues, and to prepare them to learn about historical communities, we asked the class to play a simulated society game, *Starpower,* twice during the first semester.[3] The first episode was used as a *pretest* to uncover the students' ideas about how one gains power in society and the ethics of those in power. We assigned students to social classes (Triangles, Circles, and Squares) on the basis of their ability to gain colored chips of higher values. Students could "move up the social ladder" with economic ability and luck. The students who moved up into the ruling class, the Squares, replicated external society by making rules that would be to their benefit. When mobilized into the "squares" group, Danny, who had asked for justice for all classes as a member of the "triangle" class, now made a new rule for his triangle peers: "No sleeping on the park benches!"

As the Circles and Triangles lost power and hope for improving their lot in life, they quit the game. The class had an interesting discussion about the power of the underclass, since the ruling class has no power when the lower groups resist. They also wrote about their experiences.

Today was real boring because I didn't get no gold and I'm . . . I went down for trading chips .

The game rules really sucks everybody poor should go on protester so they don't have nobody to take the money from the circles and triangles (the lower classes).

I wish we can be in they group so they no how it fells to be poor.

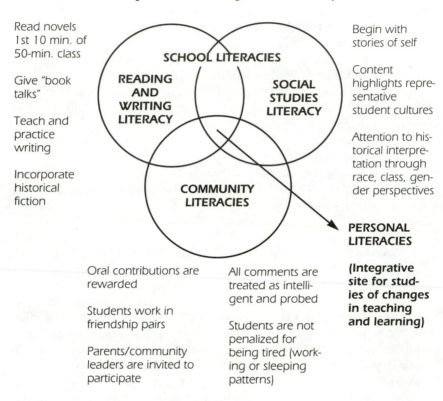

FIGURE 8.1
Multiple literacies in 8th grade world history.

Read novels
1st 10 min. of
50-min. class

Give "book
talks"

Teach and
practice
writing

Incorporate
historical
fiction

Begin with
stories of self

Content
highlights repre-
sentative
student cultures

Attention to his-
torical interpre-
tation through
race, class, gen-
der perspectives

PERSONAL
LITERACIES

**(Integrative
site for stud-
ies of changes
in teaching
and learning)**

Oral contributions are
rewarded

Students work in
friendship pairs

Parents/community
leaders are invited to
participate

All comments are
treated as intelli-
gent and probed

Students are not
penalized for
being tired (work-
ing or sleeping
patterns)

Class goes out into the community

Community Literacies: the appreciation, understanding and/or
use of interpretive and communicative traditions of community and
culture.

School Literacies: the interpretive and communicative processes
needed to adapt socially to school settings, maintain a good sense
of self, and gain a conceptual understanding of school subjects.

Personal Literacies: ways of knowing and beliefs about self and
personal communication norms arising from historical or experimental and gender-specific backgrounds.

The students had few ideas about how they might help create more egalitarian societies, but they had little trouble connecting the game to their lives.[4] We decided to focus on the idea of learning to create an egalitarian society as an end-of-semester goal for social studies, while we worked toward standard literacy. In the meantime, we accepted their dialectical differences (an example of community literacies) and their preferences to communicate and study in separate gender groups (an example of personal literacies).

MAKING LITERACY AN INTEGRAL PART OF CLASS

We began doing something similar to what Karen was doing in California, using the first 10 minutes of every class for reading of self-selected books, followed by 5 minutes for students to give book talks. Second, we explicitly taught literacy strategies that would connect the subject matter with students' life experiences to increase their participation in their own learning. Third, we encouraged students' natural tendency for social participation allowing them to work in social groups. Further, we gave them extended writing practice, beginning with personal, community-based experiences. Other teachers in Paul's building also helped him plan the writing activities.

Providing Time for Reading and Book Talks

The first instructional change we made was the setting aside of the first 10 minutes of each day for students to read self-selected novels. Paul's school librarian and Ann Tracy, a librarian at my Midwest university, provided a wide variety of high interest books for the class. Everyone in the room (i.e., students, teachers, university folk, visitors) spent this time reading to model the importance attached to reading by the adults. In the beginning, there was resistance—to put it mildly—to the quiet reading time. Students were not accustomed to entering a classroom and immediately focusing on independent assignments; most were not in the habit of reading for pleasure.

To wear away the resistance, the team members circulated each day before the class bell to remind students that they could earn credit if they were reading before class started. Gradually, the students began to pick up their books as they entered the room, and all but a few began to read immediately. By November the room was usually quiet and all students were reading before the first period bell rang.

At the end of each reading period, we asked students to give voluntary "book talks" as Karen had done in her class. This activity provided students conversational practice in locating important details and events, in summarizing information, in speaking before the group, and in fielding questions about their talks. The book talks also generated interest in books and helped develop a climate for respect; students listened attentively to each other and asked questions about each other's books.[5]

Paul summarized his feelings about the benefits of adding reading activities to social studies class.

> It does calm them down, and for some strange reason, they like reading. We have used other things like point systems—but with this you don't have to tell them. They just come in, get a library book, and sit down and read it. The students really like talking about their books, and they like hearing other people talk and hearing themselves talk. It kind of brings the class together in a community type way because they all like hearing each other and talking. Some may feel it's not school, and they get enjoyment out of reading, but I think it's really helpful to encourage people to read because we all read. Teachers read, everybody in here reads, all adults read, so they can see the importance of it. It sets the tone for the class.

By the end of the first semester, many students told us that history was their favorite class! When asked about the unfamiliar practice of reading novels in a history class, the response was also positive.

> RITA: The advantage is that if you read more when you get older you can read better.
> SAM: Is that what you really think or what you think I want to hear?
> RITA: Sort of . . . so we can read good books.
> LUCINDA: Before, I didn't like to read, but I'm starting to read more now. I don't understand because when we read these it's not like reading history books. With these, we get a choice and with the history books the teacher tells us.
> JAN: If you read everyday, it gets easier.
> SELINA: I like it cause it is better than reading a textbook.
> DANNY: I don't know if I like it. . . . I like to read, but them books. . . .
> SAM: You want more exciting literature?
> DANNY: Yes.
> SELINA: Every Friday should be a reading period for the whole period.
> LUCINDA: I think the librarian should let us choose our own books.[6]
> BUD: I like it.
> ATKIN: Why?
> BUD: 'Cause it's better than doing work.
> ATKIN: Now we're getting into a new concept, 'cause that's not what we are doing it for.

SAM: What are we doing it for?

ATKIN: To help us learn. I like it 'cause it helps us learn to read.

SAM: Has reading gotten easier?

ATKIN: Yes.

SAM: How many of you think reading has gotten easier? (Seventeen boys and four girls raised their hands, twenty-one of the twenty-nine students.)

With a strategy to improve their reading in place, we began to look at ways to increase their comprehension of social studies.

RESEARCHING AND WRITING PERSONAL CULTURES

In an effort to have students identify culturally with the study of history, they were asked to investigate their own cultural backgrounds through an "archaeological dig." I disguised myself as a famous archaeologist, "Dr. Snoop," and brought in artifacts from my home. Students had to tell me as much about my culture as they could from the artifacts. The students then used information gained from these archaeological digs of their own homes, along with anthropological family interviews to write about their own cultures. Applying Mary's research, I allowed them to work together in friendship groups. Gladine wrote an especially insightful and poignant essay, explicating some topics that displayed part of her community literacy.

> My mom culture is Africa American. I want to know why Racism still exist in 1991. My mom said that racism was worse than it is today. And today people still hate one another. What do society want from people of color. My family believe in honesty, and spending time with relatives and going to church every Sunday morning.

Gladine's African-American partner, Selina, wrote similar comments about her family's concerns and traditions. These cultural essays were combined into a class book, which the university published and bound, and distributed to all class members. Other writing practice occurred in the form of a class newsletter on the Renaissance, and annotated illustrations of historical events.

Valuing Oral Contributions

In addition to introducing writing practices reflecting their lives, we also worked hard at validating and building upon the students' oral strengths.

It was clear that these students knew much more than they could write about (an example of "community" as opposed to "school" literacy). Therefore, during class discussions, we would have one student come to the overhead projector to write down all comments made by class members. That seemed to help students attend to and build upon their peer's comments as serious, and to take themselves seriously (as attested by the increasing complexity and thoughtfulness of the comments). The preserved overhead transparencies also gave us a record so that we could reward (give credit to) their oral contributions.

Of course, we also had to work hard at not allowing the boys in the class to dominate the conversations (and the African-American boys to dominate the Asian boys). In one class, I reported the research to the students that boys usually speak 80% of the time in class, and girls only 20% (Sadker & Sadker, 1985). I asked them if they thought that was something we might want to experiment and learn to do differently in our democratic classroom. "No!!!" yelled the boys. "Yes," the girls countered, somewhat more softly. I gave the girls' weaker response an 80% handicap rating on their responses and went ahead with my experiment. For the first 80% of the class, I explained to them, only the girls could speak. We would save the last 20% of the class for the boys. After I settled the boys' protest, I began the discussion of the day's topic and waited for the girls to respond. I ignored any boys who tried to jump in. I waited for 15 minutes. When the girls did (tentatively) begin to speak, the boys were silent, but many were visibly agitated. After about 5 minutes, Atkin, our class mayor, yelled out, "OK, you've had your 20%—now it's our turn!" We spent the rest of the class period discussing this phenomenon and why it exists in school classrooms. Although that exercise could not reverse that strong socialized pattern for girls to listen and boys to speak, it brought the issue to our awareness for continued work.

Raising Academic Achievement Through Critical Thinking

We wanted to give all students an opportunity to speak because we wanted to monitor how well they were learning to think critically about various interpretations of historical events—as they related to their own lives. We asked students to investigate particular events, prepare arguments for and against the issues raised, and debate with classmates about contrastive interpretations. Sometimes the content was selected for study because it reflected the students' cultures in our class. When we studied cultures not represented, we tried to choose issues of focus within the content that were also current for the students. One example was the issue of women's rights in ancient Greece. We asked students to take a position on the practice of denying Greek women full rights of citizenship, to prepare arguments for a Greek Assembly meeting, and to debate the issues in a simulated assembly meeting. They spent time working in small gender-specific groups to investigate the pros and the cons, and to prepare their debates. Then, as students delivered their arguments, the audience members were asked to critique the issues, the thoroughness of the arguments, the persuasiveness of the teams, and finally, to vote for the resolution of granting women full rights or denying it. Here's an example:

AGNES: We want equal rights because women are just as good as men.

KAWANDA: We believe that fact is true, but also the role women should play in society is that they should stay home and nurture the young.

GLADINE: Housework and raising children do not fill up the entire day. That means women have too much time, too much idle time. They would rather be in the assembly making working decisions that they are capable of doing.

LUCINDA: Women should not be watching soap operas all day long. They should be cleaning the house and doing laundry.

RITA: Women can and want to achieve if given citizenship. Some women have left their dull lifeless existence to become liberated Greek women. Clearly, women are as capable as men in intelligence. To think otherwise is to be blindly unreal.

The debate format allowed students to hear, examine, and appreciate different personal literacies—or the way personal attributes such as gender affect their opportunities to communicate and participate in society. Doing written critiques after the debates forced them to identify and record opposing views. We held similar debates on issues relating to Greek colonization and slavery in ancient Greece. Because of the diversity of the group and the relevance they saw to their own lives, interesting and opposing viewpoints surfaced on all issues.

AT THE END OF THE SEMESTER

To see how the reading practice and changed attitudes affected their reading levels, eight students with varying reading abilities were pre- and posttested using the *Ekwall Reading Inventory* (1979) in September and in January. The students all showed gains of at least 1 year in their school literacy levels in both word recognition and in comprehension. However, we realized that neither informal nor standard reading instruments (designed to measure "school" literacies) could hope to validate the fuller ranges of literacies present in students' school lives, so we also looked elsewhere for evidence of their progress. For example, we recorded the development of their writing skills and the conceptual knowledge of history through portfolio analyses. We noted their oral contributions as well as their written. We understood that some students did not have the same opportunities for participation because they were often tired in class (had working or sleeping patterns that were part of their lives but over which, as teenagers, they had no control). Finally, we asked the students to repeat the *Starpower* simulation in December as an end-of-term posttest to see if students' ideas about their own roles as powerful transformers of history had been critically challenged throughout the semester. We hoped that their experiences had not only taught them some facts about world history, but also helped them value diversity of opinion, read history critically, resist current and historical norms, and imagine the possible. Our hopes were realized. This time the students decided not only to use game chips to represent economic values, but education, leadership qualities, personality, and family connections as well. Students had learned that people could achieve power and wealth through a variety of means and that power should not belong to only the wealthy. The students in the poorer groups offered ideas for rules, rather than giving that right up to the rich. By the end of the game, the class as a whole agreed to give each person in our classroom "society" the same number of chips. Atkin, our elected class mayor, announced that the class had achieved an egalitarian state!

The instructional changes we made not only increased students' standard or school literacy levels, and their understandings of the connection between school and community, but their feelings of self-worth, and their academic achievement in social studies. While not avoiding controversial or difficult concepts that were central to both the students' lives and their study of world history, we offered students an opportunity to take part in democratic procedures within the classroom, to experience and analyze inequities in society, and to investigate their own cultures as well as the cultures of ancient civilizations. This calls strongly into question the heavy dependence on developmental pedagogy based on fixed age levels. For the students in Paul's classroom, connecting and concretizing abstract historical knowledge was critical to their learning it. By implementing a variety of evaluation means to determine the *quality* of their *ideas* as multiple literacies, and not just their standard *writing and reading* abilities, we found that they became engaged with the subject matter, willing to offer their own ideas, proud of their own backgrounds, and aware of broad themes throughout history such as power, conflict, and equality.

I was happy to return to a conversation meeting in California at the end of the term and report Lucinda's response to the interview question: "Who is really smart in class?" She replied, "We are all smart in our own ways."

REFLECTIONS ON OUR COLLABORATIVE CONVERSATIONS: ANTHONY'S STORY

Every time I (Anthony) leave our collaborative group, I feel buoyed by the reassurance that there are people really working to find solutions to the problems we face as teachers every day.

In my classroom, I try to look at how I am relating to students, and I work to overcome my various biases. My background is one of social activism; fighting the Bakke decision against affirmative action in the seventies, against militarism in the eighties. When I first became active, and was challenged over sexist or racist attitudes, my first response would usually be defensive. After many long discussions, however, I began to step back and disown some of the attitudes I had accumulated. I realized I would only be able to change what was going on in society if I was willing to make some changes in myself.

After working part time as a park naturalist, I decided teaching science was the best career for me. It brings together several of my passions: a love for learning about the natural world, a joy in working with young people, and a desire to serve and educate the disenfranchised. My credential program offered a mixed preparation. The small cohort of secondary science teachers that met weekly was a source of support, and I found common ground with several participants. However, many of the issues we faced while student-teaching in urban, largely minority, low-income schools, were not addressed. I felt many of my fellow student teachers were not equipped to deal with the educational environments we were moving into, and worse, some held truly racist ideas, which were not being challenged.

I raised this issue in several teacher education classes, with little result. One class, supposedly about social issues, focused almost exclusively on the governmental and political processes affecting education. In the discussion section for this class, week after week, one other teacher and I would refocus the discussion on issues of educational equity and the need to deepen our understanding of the cultures and experiences of the communities in which we worked. The discussion at times became quite heated. One person responded to a suggestion that we really needed to get more exposure to what was going on in the African-American community by saying, "What do you mean? Should we go spend time in the bar on San Pablo Avenue?" In the same discussion he asserted that Felix Mitchell (a slain drug kingpin who had recently had an elaborate funeral) was a more important cultural figure to his African-American students than was Martin Luther King, Jr. Many of these teachers knew very little that was positive about African-American or other minority cultures, and actually thought they were doing their students a service by imposing their white, middle-class values.

When Sam first invited me to join the conversational group, my first fear was that the participants would be similarly closed-minded. What I found instead was a group struggling with the very issues I had raised. The group has kept me experimenting and thinking of ways I could do things better. It has also caused me to reflect on how I project myself in the classroom. As a male teacher, more than six feet tall, I have often heard the comment, "You shouldn't have any trouble at all with discipline!" as though one accomplishes class control through physical intimidation. My size does come in handy occasionally, in breaking up a fight, for example, but 99% of the time, I discipline through other means.

My 1st year teaching gave me a taste of the folly of trying to rule by intimidation. My last class of the day included about six of the most troublesome students of the school. They were often disruptive, and I responded with frequent detentions and strong words of disapproval. I spent a great deal of class time attempting to control their behavior, and the remainder of the class became turned off and bored. The content of the class ceased being science, and instead became the contest of wills between these students and me. I tried changing tactics towards the end of the semester, but it was too late. Since then, I have tried to be more sensitive to the dynamics in a class. The following semester, I got a similar class, again, late in the day. Rather than focus on conflict, I praised the class at every opportunity, and tried to isolate and downplay the disruptions. I

Anthony and class.

provided fun activities, and linked them to cooperation. A few students continued to cause problems, but they did not set the tone, and the remainder of the class was not alienated.

Some students, particularly at junior high school age, bring a lot of anger to school with them. Sometimes it surfaces with any authority figure, but often it is strongest with men. The students' fathers may have left home, or they may have abused their children. This anger comes out in the form of defiance, rudeness, or profanity. Sometimes the goal is to anger and infuriate me; to provoke a confrontation. Sometimes the challenge is too strong to overlook, and I must write referrals and send the students from the room. More often than not, however, I respond by trying to defuse their anger, bringing the focus back to our task in the class. Last year I had one student, Felicia, who was often moody. She would refuse to work, and become very hostile when I asked her to get her materials and work. I called her mother, who told me that, earlier in the year, a group of boys had sexually assaulted Felicia on the way to school.

In these circumstances, attempts at physical and verbal intimidation are worse than useless, and would link me with all the oppressive males in these students' pasts. Instead of intimidation, I have tried to work towards student ownership of the class. Karen and I have experimented with a variety of approaches. Each month we select officers at random from each class. These officers carry out tasks in the class, and help establish a team spirit for the class as a whole. Choice is introduced as much as possible; in reading material, project topics, and group partners. Student contributions are valued and leadership is developed.

The traditional approach to teaching at a secondary level is to place course content in the forefront. As a teacher of science, I spend much of my time researching new techniques in science education. Little attention is given to broader issues, highlighted by our group, such as how students really learn, what role literacy plays in subject matter learning, and how they relate to school and to us as teachers. Our group has helped me to learn how to open up to exploring these issues in an ongoing way.

At Karen's urging, for example, I got serious about increasing reading levels for my students. I had taken a course on reading in the content area in the teacher education program and done well, but my focus on science in middle school had been so consuming that I didn't really know how to work it in.[7]

I started my classroom reading about 100 science books, most featuring color photographs and vivid graphics. Students chose these books from our classroom library with high interest, but I was troubled by a tendency of many of them to merely flip through the books looking at pictures, often not even reading the captions. I then assigned projects based on the reading, with limited success.

Anthony and his family.

Photo © 1993 Francisco Garcia

I had also picked up about 40 or 50 paperback novels, mostly science fiction or animal stories. These were popular, but there were management problems involved in having only one or two copies of each title, and students from 5 different classes reading the same book.

My latest scheme is to choose about 5 titles from a range of reading levels, and get 15 copies of each. Students will choose from those 5 and be responsible for reading the book in class and doing some sort of project based on their reading. This should increase accountability and solve some of the management problems. I feel positive enough about this approach that I'm starting a project in my school to share it with my colleagues (see Figure 8.2). If this plan doesn't increase the literacy levels of my science students, the collaborative group will help me revise it. Our discussions help us reevaluate our experiences and learn from each other.

Is this a feminist approach? I think it is. The teachers in the conversational group and I are speaking up and taking control of our classrooms and course work. We're breaking traditional "glass ceilings" to minority student success. In our schools, we are often treated as passive implementers of curriculum funneled from above.[8] From the state level down to our school sites, teachers are rarely really involved in decisions that they are expected to implement. This powerlessness mirrors society's lack of respect for the teaching profession. The history of teaching in the United

FIGURE 8.2
Bret Harte Reading Rhythm

Overview

Reading, similar to writing, is a core skill students need to succeed in almost every subject. Students who are poor readers often avoid reading, and fail to improve their skills in spite of years of school. Reading Rhythm places books of high interest, at appropriate reading levels, in students' hands, and asks them to read. Through practice, with high interest materials, student abilities, confidence and interest in reading should grow.

Starting with teachers in Social Studies and Science, classes are provided with funds to purchase roughly 50 books, to create a classroom collection. Books will be read at least twice a week, for from 15 to 20 minutes at a time. Students who have both science and social studies will thus get almost daily reading practice, in addition to the reading they do in English class.

Program Goals

1. Increase student reading abilities, particularly targeting those of low ability.
2. Engage and excite students about reading.
3. Reinforce disciplinary content in Social Studies and Science.

Strategies

Participating teachers in Social Studies and Science will receive a budget of $200 with which to purchase books. The criteria for book selection are as follows:

- Books of a wide range of reading levels should be chosen, so all children can read materials at an appropriate level (4th to 12th grade levels).
- Books should be high-interest.
- Books should relate to the content of the class in which they are read.

Teachers in each department should compare lists before ordering to avoid duplication in the lists from one grade level to the next (duplication at the same grade level, from class to class, is fine.)

Recommendations

- It is recommended that at least five copies of each title be ordered, so that students can read their first choice book.
- Students should keep a daily reading log to help the teacher keep track of their reading. Teachers may wish to give credit as students read as well, to reinforce participation.
- Social Studies may wish to pick two days on which to do reading, and Science could pick two other days, so that students are reading almost every day.

Implementation

Participating teachers should turn their lists in to Anthony Cody. We can get the books at a 20% discount from Cody's Books. Please include on your order: *title, author, price,* and the quantity you wish to order. Sample reading logs will be made available.

States as a predominately female profession is key to understanding this. Similar to nurses, teachers are regarded as natural nurturers, mother surrogates. As nurses' and mothers' work is undervalued, so is the work of the teacher.

Our group has embraced some aspects of this identity and rejected others. I, for example, value children and our roles as nurturers. Teaching is not a technical delivery of curriculum appropriate to a child's developmental level. A great deal of attention must be paid to understanding the needs and life circumstances of each child. In particular, I am aware of the factors of race, gender, and economic status that we and our students bring into the classroom. But I challenge the idea that teachers are passive implementers. Those in our group, including me, do not accept being told to use materials inappropriate to our students' reading levels. We work to democratize our classrooms, to empower our students and ourselves.

ENDNOTES

[1] This is not "Paul's" real name.

[2] Others have noted similar patterns. See also Bernstein, 1977, and Delpit, 1988.

[3] Karen Teel had previously used *Starpower* in her classroom with much success.

[4] We also had hoped to take the class on a field trip to visit governmental agencies, but could not arrange it because of limited school funds.

[5] This was one of the most important ideas I learned from Karen, Anthony, and other members of our California group. Treat every student's comments with respect, even silly comments. Eventually, the students begin to take themselves and their knowledge and their voices seriously.

[6] Students in the "regular" (as opposed to "enriched") classes were not allowed to check out books from the school library because they had often failed to return them.

[7] For more on the topic of reading in the content areas, see Hollingsworth and Teel, 1991.

[8] Since this was written, Anthony has led a group of teachers in his school to bring literacy into their own classrooms, has collaborated with a university researcher on a project to teach his methods to the entire 200+ member faculty, and was invited to speak at a regional conference for California administrators. His topic will be a critique of expensive (and ineffective) staff development workshops done by "experts," and the encouragement of more conversation among teachers about their own classroom research.

9

Taking Social Action

One afternoon on a monthly visit to California, I was driving away from Leslie's school, when the words of this not-yet-popular song came out of the radio in my sports car and flew up into the clear, deep blue of a West Coast sky:

> From a distance
> We all have enough
> And no one is in need
> *Julie Gold*
> *"From a Distance"*

The song reminded me of the television special that had aired the night before about the new educational plan in Leslie's district, known as a "system of choice." From the distant stance of public television, smiling supporters told us that the newly reorganized school district brought the promise of better education for everyone. The TV cameras did not close in on Leslie's school—situated in a crime-plagued urban area where few would choose to raise their children if they had a better economic choice. Only that morning, Leslie had watched one of her second graders become the victim of a gang fight on the playground. Leslie called for administrative help five times without anyone coming. She jumped in to help the child, pulling off the older third and fourth graders, but they turned their fists on her and she had to stop. I arrived soon after the event. It was understandably difficult for her to bring her mind back to teaching literacy or math, so she reconvened her class with a discussion of caring and conflict resolution.

That evening our conversational group met at Leslie's home to talk about the incident, the new system of "school choice" and the relationship between the two. Leslie began the conversation with a reference to the television program that had aired the previous night.

LESLIE: The people speaking for choice haven't been to my school. They don't know the lack of choice that the kids there have. They don't know the lack of choice that teachers have in choosing schools, classes and programs.

ANTHONY: It really sounds like another program where white, middle-class parents can choose to keep their children out of schools like ours.

MARY: I agree.

SAM: So where do our choices come in? We don't really have a choice to ignore the problem. It's too late because we've already become aware of it—and we're concerned about it. Is our choice to keep working at the problems of equity, safety and educational opportunity until there is real choice for all kids? Where will we get the energy? Who will support us?

LESLIE: Well, we can't always count on administrators, that's for sure. As soon as we get someone who seems to understand the problem and can vocalize it for us at the district and state level, he's pulled away to another school.[1] It's as if someone, I don't know who, wants to keep our kids down and out. Even when we protested what such an action would cause, we were told, "teachers do not run schools."

JENNIFER: How can we get people to see that it's the system of education, and not the kids, and not the teachers who are at fault? How can we get the wealthier people in this country to care enough for all kids to give up some of their own privileges so that we all. . . .

ANTHONY [SARCASTICALLY]: But this country was founded on "rugged individualism"!!

JENNIFER: How did "we" get to think otherwise? What influenced us? Why don't we figure that out and educate everyone that way?

MARY: Teachers have to educate themselves. I wish more of them had groups like this.

Our conversational group, as usual, had raised a number of issues without immediate solutions. Yet Leslie still had to go back to work the next day and the day after and keep on facing whatever came up at her school. Jennifer felt compelled to keep on writing grants for out-of-school experiences (without success), trying to get "the system" to let her try another way to educate urban kids. Mary, as a teachers' union representative, kept on trying to sort out and articulate the major issues in her district's teachers' strike to administrative boards. Anthony kept on trying to explain to his urban colleagues that his middle school kids might be having problems because of difficulties with school literacy, not because of their race or class. I kept trying to find new insights "from the world outside of our group" that would give us direction and hope. That night, like many other nights, we didn't come up with any brilliant ideas that would solve the problem on Leslie's school playground, yet we kept coming back to these conversations month after month and year after year. At this particular time in our country's history, with urban areas growing more and more violent (*America the Violent,* 1993), these are issues to which we just could not close our eyes.

Why did we keep on? How did we learn to cope with such challenges? Where have we found the energy together to keep asking questions, risking solutions? Those issues are too complex, too compelling to let go. Therefore, in this chapter, I've chosen to have us focus on our collective research into those questions, drawing from conversational data across our years of work together and trying to articulate what it was about this group that opened our eyes to the inequities in urban schooling and encouraged us to keep working toward equity.[2] It is one thing to know and value equity in urban education, and quite another to enact that knowledge within the existing power structures of schooling. How did these teachers resolve such tensions? Clearly, such issues are important for educating other teachers to understand and act upon the societal, structural, and political issues of schooling, should they happen to find themselves at graduation, as these teachers did, working in urban settings. This chapter is organized around five story sets from our conversations and writings that speak to these teachers' experiences with (1) a foundation in the ethic of care, (2) the politics of voicing school problems, (3) the tensions between knowledge and knowing, (4) the validation of collaborative teacher research, and (5) locating cultures of support. It is around those themes that these teachers gained the courage, the knowledge, and the support to change their practices in support of urban students.

A FOUNDATION IN THE ETHIC OF CARE

If we've made one point clear across this text, I hope it's that these teachers found the passion and courage to do what they do because they deeply cared for urban children. Nel Noddings also speaks to us about the challenge to care in schools.

Classrooms should be places in which students can legitimately act on a rich variety of purposes, in which wonder and curiosity are alive, in which students and teachers live together and grow. I, too, believe that a dedication to full human growth . . . will not stunt or impede intellectual achievement, but even if it might, I would take the risk if I could produce people who would live nonviolently with each other, sensitively and in harmony with the natural environment, reflectively and serenely with themselves.

A child's place in our hearts and lives should not depend on his or her academic prowess. Lots of young people see through today's educational slogans. We preach constantly that "all children can learn"; we even suggest strongly that they all can learn anything the school has to offer if they are taught well and try. If they don't try, they are made to feel like traitors, even though they might work very hard at tasks over which they have little control and choice. Thus, despite our determined optimism and insistent everyone-can-do-it, students complain, "They don't care!" They suspect that we want their success for our own purposes, to advance our own records, and too often they are right. (1992, p. 13)

Throughout all the stress and complexity of learning to teach, across changes in administration and curriculum, across changes in her own knowledge, Leslie cared. She concluded that "The children are wonderful. That is the only unchanging truth." Leslie's words came on a spring night, sitting alone at her computer at home, as she reflected on her day. They clearly demonstrated an ethic of care as the foundation of her teaching.

I'm tired. I wasn't so tired earlier. It is not a physical weariness. It is a case of wanting to forget—an emotional weariness.

I came home with my bag, full as usual. Tonight I planned to review the rest of the year and get an idea in my head of what the children should work on before we leave for summer vacation. I want to make sure we don't miss anything. I want the end of the year to be important for them. They deserve a good send-off to third grade. I'll miss them. All of this goes through my mind. Instead of my work I'll probably read my mystery book—which I keep on my nightstand just for these occasions—when I need to forget for a while what is happening in the "environment" I spend my days in. If the environment were just my room and the children I wouldn't feel this way. The reality is that the "educational environment" is my room and the children AND the administration AND the community. How many people who write about education include these other areas? And I keep hearing the words of a gentleman at last year's [professional conference] in

Boston who spoke of the need to teach teachers to teach better and to teach them to learn faster. . . .*

I can't help thinking of a particular student. He has been on my mind. He was so special. He transferred into my room late in the year. He was so depressed and out of touch with school. He got into trouble, and yet he had turned around. Someone very special from our collaborative group came to work with him each Friday. His reading was so much better. He smiled. He came to school each day. Now he is gone. Last week I ran into him in the hall during my prep-time. He had lost the smile on his face. His mother brought him to school to say she was pulling him out. He wanted to tell me. The reasons behind his mother's action are private. We talk about them at school. We don't print them. Maybe we can't. I heard he is in a foster home now. I—we—can't help him. I feel he is lost, and except for the tears I'm shedding now, I try to forget all about this because if I hurt too much for him I can't do a good job. I have to stay to teach the others.

The children are wonderful. That is the only unchanging truth. That is why I do what I do. And I keep hearing the voice of the nice gentleman who wanted us to learn to be better teachers. Does anyone from the "outside" ever spend any time in a classroom? Maybe they all want to forget more than we do.

I feel better now. I don't know why.

Leslie began her teaching career not only with a deep sense of the ethics of caring for children—not just as she generically defined care, but in specific relation to these children in ways that they responded to as caring. Sometimes teachers' care for children fits their definition of "care"— such as having all of them read books that match their grade level, but if the student rejects that care (e.g., the student cannot read the text and feels frustrated and humiliated), then, in Noddings terms, a caring relation does not exist. Leslie also wanted to be involved in caring relations with her school leaders. Having come through the school system herself pretty well intact, she initially placed her faith in school, curricular, and researched guidelines—trusting that those guidelines would be safe for her students. When she observed that wasn't the case, she asked the school leaders to allow her to modify the "rules," trusting that they, too, would care for the individual children assigned to Leslie's room, more than they

---

* Rereading this chapter, Leslie noted: "Years later this statement still angers me!"

cared for district curriculum policy. That's when Leslie's transformation as a teacher really began . . . as she describes it herself.

Perhaps it started when our district adopted a new literature-based reading series. Previously, I had been doing a "whole-language" program as the district was in transition and wasn't very definitive about what we were to use. However, when the new series came out the other second grade teacher and I decided to give it a try. It turned out to be mandated by the district in several memos we later received. We immediately sensed a problem. We knew our students enough to know that many would not be able to achieve any degree of success with the grade level book, so we called downtown and asked if we could have classroom sets of the third and final first grade books. The response was a loud "No! Your students should be reading on grade level." Both of us thought this was rather amusing since the district frequently let us know how our test scores were in reading on the achievement tests. The amusement faded and we felt abandoned. The message was that they didn't really care about the kids.

A second example that caused Leslie to lose faith in what those in authority thought was best for her children happened in a similar way, and it involved not just curriculum but the school structure. To show fidelity to the district "rule" of student choice of schools and curriculum, she would have to be uncaring to her students. She spoke about the tension between her experiences, those of her students, and the new district policy. Because the classroom reality did not reflect the principled and theoretical mandate for structural changes, the policy felt "uncaring."

In theory, the district's new "system of choice" would give every student access to all sorts of electives and would give them a balanced program. In reality, what about the student who took P.E. classes twice a day and never signed up for a science class? What about the students whose parents could not read or understand the program and let their 8-year-old fill out the program. Some teachers wondered if there was value in having a student repeat their cooking class or lego class each trimester, because they liked you and felt secure in the "known" as opposed to the unknown of other classes, even though the curriculum was the same each time. As a parent, I know from experience that it took some time and quite a bit of negotiating before my husband, our daughter, and I came up with a schedule. My daughter thought tap, jazzercize, art, and drama were great. We checked to make sure there was a reading, math, writing, science, or some other academic subject to balance her program.

Leslie's sense of fidelity remained with her children. Her care for them led her to question authority and find other ways of teaching them. Jennifer's ethic of care for urban kids took a different and even stronger form of resistance: it led her to leave her full-time teaching position—and to leave us with some provocative questions about urban education.

> I believe that there is a great advantage in not buying into the system. But I have my degree. So I'm going to teach these kids that they don't have to? It's kind of like, well, is it fair to them? But . . . when I buy into the system, what am I buying into? What am I teaching these kids by teaching them to read about dead white men? What am I teaching them about the value of their life in war-ravaged American cities? You know? What are they really learning?

Karen's sense of care took still another direction. In acknowledging the emotion running through their communities at the time of the Los Angeles riots following the court decision regarding the police beating of Rodney King, she raised some questions about a time and place for voices of rage in schools.

> On Friday after the Rodney King decision, my kids came in and they were just off the walls. I mean, you know, in a positive way as far as I was concerned. Yet most of them had settled down and were sitting down when the bell rang. The principal, vice principal, two security guards, and a counselor came into my room with panic on their faces. I just looked at them. They said, "What's going on?" And I said, "We're talking about Rodney King." And the principal said, "You're not talking, you're screaming!" And I asked, "Isn't this happening in every classroom? I mean—this is very serious, important, meaningful stuff? Isn't this . . . ha . . . no. . . ." And I said, "Oh." And then they left.

THE POLITICS OF VOICING THE PROBLEM

Karen's experience was not unlike others of us who chose to teach in relation to the urban students. The response of others who expect teachers to comply to a set of school norms often in contract to their relational teaching is often negative—and sometimes frightening. Without the "sphere of freedom" (Arendt, 1974, p. 30) we were constructing for ourselves in our conversational group to speak in our own voices, it would have been easy for us to feel powerless, victimized, and overwhelmed in the face of such persistent norms.

Maxine Greene (1988) helped me to give words to the spaces for freedom of knowing we were creating for ourselves. In quoting Jean-Paul Sartre, she spoke of the praxis we were learning to devise: "the project of acting on our freedom [which] involves a rejection of the insufficient or the unendurable, a clarification and an imagining of better things" (p. 5). Greene tells us that to take action toward our freedom as educators we must first "name the obstacles" that stand in our way. We should make public the blocks to freedom and point out that they are simply artifacts or human creations. School norms for discourse that prevent either teachers or students from creating spaces in their schools where they can "take initiatives and uncover humanizing possibilities" (p. 13) is an example of such an obstacle. "When oppression or exploitation or segregation or neglect is perceived of as 'natural' or a 'given'; there is little stirring in the name of freedom" (p. 9).

Leslie and the others found that trying to identify obstacles on the paths they had to travel to teach their students to be a daunting, but important activity. It was certainly too simplistic and ineffective to simply "blame the administrators" or the school district, who were probably acting under the authority of those even higher up. In one conversation, we took this to the length and suggested blaming the President! Even had we done so, it would not have made school better for children in Leslie's classroom. What we had to learn to do, though, was recognize and vocalize the issues and visualize solutions.

None of those three tasks was familiar or common ones for school teachers. Recognizing the problem was Leslie's first problem, as it was for all of us. Once the problem was identified, acknowledging it and speaking to it (instead of hoping it would go away, or feel helpless to face it) was another difficult matter. Both required great courage. Obviously, not all teachers choose that path. Many teachers spend their careers in teaching, and either work in school sites where equity is not a problem, or perhaps do not feel they have the power to do anything about the inequities that exist. Those teachers remain in schools for many reasons, and often show a strong sense of fidelity to the job and to children. Yet others make different choices.

Similar to Hirschman in his classic 1970 volume on "exit, voice, and loyalty" in the business world, I've found a feminist correlate to the dilemmas of schooling. Though teachers sometimes have significant critiques of school structures and curricula, they often go publicly unvoiced. Remaining in the classroom out of loyalty to an employer is a choice made by many female and male teachers. When the difficulties become unbearable (or unheard if voiced), a second choice for teachers is to abandon the loyal position and leave the school. That ending became a chapter in both Lisa's and Jennifer's stories.*

The middle ground—where teachers choose to stay—is noisy and messy. It's the place where private truths become public; where the inequities of "choice" become clear and where loyalty, recast as fidelity, becomes a relational way of being (Noddings, 1986). It's the place where real and intimate relationships are formed, public policies and statements are challenged, and shifts take place so that teachers can not only stay, but also potentially contribute to social change. It's in that middle ground, where the theory meets the road, that Leslie and other beginning teachers who have remained in the classroom are located. It's there, where risks occur, that the story of these teachers takes place.

The Feminization of Teaching

The risk involved in naming the obstacles to teaching urban students was often a topic of conversation for us. The risk involved making vulnerable not only our jobs, but the quality of our professional lives—if we were to threaten those with more power than we. And those power differences often looked unbreachable. Leslie speculated with us on why teachers are afraid to speak out.

> It shocks me, having come from a number of years in the business world, that teachers aren't more vocal. Perhaps it is historically the role the United States gave teachers who were female mostly, certainly perpetrated by districts who don't ask teachers their opinions and who cringe at the thought of "site-based decision making." As a matter of fact, at a recent meeting between the teachers of an elementary school and the superintendent over a change in personnel which the teachers thought was not in the best interest of the school the teachers were told that "teachers do not run the schools." And further, from my observation, the lack of teacher voice comes from university researchers who are involved in education, who write research papers that influence district policies, yet who don't ask teachers their opin-

---

* Lisa added: "I left that school to go to another (the university) to keep on working on the same issues, but from another perspective."

ions, who do not work in the reality of classrooms daily. Teachers are silent because no one wants to hear.

Further, I believe there is some guilt. Teachers often see the failure of students as a mother sees the failure of her child. It must be our fault. We should have done more. This is often reinforced by parents (parents of my daughter's friends for example who sometimes forget I'm a teacher) who complain about teachers for not giving their child the very best education without consideration at all for the makeup of the class or the policies of the administration. Does anyone ever complain that a teacher has to teach a combination class? I was naively shocked when my 1st year they gave me a second and third grade combination. Heavens, throw me in a classroom without any support and then give me two jobs to do simultaneously. Get real! Yet I am supposed to meet each child's needs. And then maybe put several children in who have learning disabilities or who belong in special day classes, but who are not placed there by the administration—who would prefer you just do your job and be quiet. After a while you begin to believe you should be able to do it all or you're a "bad teacher."

Sometimes when a teacher at my school is particularly depressed, most often about kids who need special help and who are not receiving anything, another teacher will whisper, "You know you can't do it all," but we wouldn't announce that out loud to anyone outside our group of trusted insiders. Teachers are supposed to do the best for each "of our children" regardless of the lack of support or actual hindrances placed before us.

Leslie's message speaks clearly to the burden of female and male teachers' challenge to "do it all" in silence. In our group, we learned that we could claim the right to know and to speak, as Leslie's words clearly demonstrate. On many occasions we talked about the challenges we had to overcome to speak about our work with some integrity. Our discussions take off from Leslie's analysis about the gendered nature of teaching to look at the power of school boards, parents, local administrators, and even our peers and students that tends to socialize us into silence. It begins with a school norm not to admit that any school problems exist: not even our own.

The Discourse of Having No Problems

ANTHONY: I think at the school site you try to project a certain image both to the students and to the other staff, you know, that you've got things under control. Because that, if you, if you project an image that you're having problems, then that generates problems, you know, and so. . . .

MARY: Gee, I just learned that this year.

ANTHONY: I learned that from reading my evaluations. My evaluations I think were a reflection of my reputation among the staff and among the students. Cause they weren't based on observations really. They were based on those things. You know, so I got positive evaluations because I had pretty good interaction with the other staff. And in general I was, I didn't have anybody complaining about me or anything and so I think if, you know, if you really had a lot of concerns that you were, you know, complaining about, then I think you would be, if you were up front about all the problems that you had, then that might be reflected [in the evaluation]. You know, that so and so has a problem with classroom management. You know?

KAREN: Right.

ANTHONY: You may have a problem with classroom management but if you don't go around telling people that then they may not perceive it because they think you're classroom management is no. . . .

KAREN: That's right.

MARY: It's like trying to talk to people at our schools about what's happening in our classrooms like we talk here. Instead of just listening to someone who's saying "This is what I'm seeing in my classroom," and "I'm wondering about this," all of a sudden they're trying to give you a solution. You know how that bugs me? I don't find that to be collaborative at all. I find it to be real hierarchical. I mean it's like "Oh, oh, if your students are doing that—well then, this is what you should do"—and it's like bullshit! That's not what you should do. You know, the person should be listening to you. And it wasn't until this year that I finally sorted out what you were just talking about because I was having just a hideous time with classroom management. I had a child . . . that child I told you about who was berserk in my classroom.

ANTHONY: So what would you say that you'd figured out?

MARY: Well, what I figured out was the more I presented these problems the more they became *me* rather than something that the school should take on. I mean the retort would be, you know, like, "Ha ha, what are you doing in your classroom to cause all these problems?" It wasn't all ribbing. There was some seriousness behind it.

Perhaps Mary and the other teachers (or I for that matter) would not have noticed that there were institutional rules for presenting an unblemished image of ourselves without our conversational group, where it was safe to do so. Yet banding together with other like-minded teachers to talk about problems within school was not always safe either. The competitive nature of the school, and the rule of discourse for fidelity to the institution were powerful incentives to silence.

Silencing Critical Discourse

From a distance
You look like my friend, even though we are at war
From a distance
I can't comprehend what all this war is for
> *Julie Gold*
> *"From a Distance"*

MARY: I'm working in a teacher research group at my school, but I don't feel comfortable talking about the same things we discuss here.

KAREN: But the interesting part is that, I mean, I would never feel that way, and that's because I'm tenured, and there's nothing that anybody could—

ANTHONY: Even tenured teachers, you know, there's lots of things you, you know, that's what we were talking about. You still get evaluated, your schedule is a reflection of how much political power you have to some extent and—

KAREN: So you have to be careful about complaining, especially.

ANTHONY: Right. And, I think for the most part my administration I wouldn't feel uncomfortable admitting certain things were wrong, but—

KAREN: Well, it's interesting because . . . it's like a double-edged sword. On the one hand there can be a lot of benefit, a lot of growth involved, a lot of helping you to clarify your views and help you to shift in how . . . your practices and all that sort of thing from talking to people. Hearing what other people are doing and having people react to what you're doing and just that whole thinking process. But on the other hand, there can be some real risks involved. People can perceive risk and decide that they're not, they're not really comfortable being honest or being really frank about how they feel, or what they're really concerned about. They may just be bringing up some superficial things. But, so, . . . you know, how can one advocate collaboration?

Anthony's suggestion to this dilemma is that teachers join cross-site collaborative teams, as our conversational group had. The rest of us agreed on the importance of that, particularly for having a safe space to acknowledge and voice the problems of practice—and for finding out that our voices were valid and strong. But finding places to speak critically was only the beginning of the work of praxis. Conversation alone would not improve students' lives in urban schools.

KNOWLEDGE AND KNOWING

Across this text I have emphasized the importance of feminist epistemologies with respect to teaching urban children. The importance of not only employing someone else's knowledge (even after "owning" it) but constructing one's own tentative "knowings" in relation to others was important to these teachers' learnings. Leslie's story of learning to teach was an example of such an epistemology. Her success in her second grade classroom required that she partially challenge her own personal beliefs about literacy instruction, what she was taught in her teacher education program, the district's mandated literacy curriculum, the literacy program publisher's recommendations, her peers' convictions about the best way to teach reading and writing, professional development plans that discouraged her from interacting in professional conferences, the community realities of the district's new choice structure, and her feelings about the personal cost of her efforts to her own family life.

But Leslie began with a different attitude that caused her to close her classroom door to conversations about things other than the knowledge of curriculum. Because she thought her new career depended upon such a narrow focus, she closed herself off for awhile, from knowing about and transforming her practice—limiting the opportunities she had to learn to teach. She told Karen:

> Given the focus of student teaching and now teacher evaluation, it seems there's only one shot at getting it right. It's very different from a career phase—as in an apprenticeship in the business world.

Permission to Learn

When Leslie eventually returned to our group, she appreciated the space to be a learner instead of an expert. In fact, all of us thought that feature of our group particularly important. Anthony and Mary talked about the importance of a space where our knowing voices could be tentatively heard and validated in our group. They hypothesized that we could speak without absolute certainty because most of us were beginning teachers. However, they also noted that such a space for articulating *tentative knowings* was not the norm for us in other educational settings. Most of those spaces were for learning and/or articulating *certainties of knowledge*.

> ANTHONY: But the bottom line is . . . everybody started out as fairly new teachers and didn't have very much confidence and it was able . . . part of it is you're able to be more up front about your incompetence because you're not necessarily expected to be, you know, fully competent as a relatively new teacher.
>
> MARY: Yeah, and I think built into that is the fact that we all know that there is always a level of incompetence that we will have. You know, as competent as we were gonna be, that there's always something that, I meant that's the sense that I have, that we're always trying to fine-tune our classrooms or work on the curriculum or . . . I can't get at this, so that there's always some level that we're maneuvering to do a better job, which implies that you know, we're not completely perfect.

Having certified or authorized "knowledge" about the issues was not a prerequisite for speaking in our group.

Classroom Stability

One interesting feature that we noted about our group was that, after some initial shuffling from one class to another, the teachers basically stayed at the same grade level for a few years. Mary and Leslie, for economic reasons—such as combining classes or teaching on a year round calendar—sometimes even had the same group of students more than 1 year in a row. Both situations seemed to contribute to their abilities to develop relational ways of knowing their disciplinary curricula and students.

Respect for Relevant and Different Knowledges Within the Conversational Community

A final point that we should make about our learning in our collaborative conversational group was that, while we felt safe to construct and create our own knowledges of urban literacy, we did not feel compelled to adopt anyone else's knowledge; nor did we need to "intervene" so that our discovered knowledges were accepted by others; nor feel rejected if our knowings were not adopted by others. Leslie explained this important aspect of their perceived freedom to take social action in their own ways to a representative of the British Columbia College of Teachers, where she was invited to speak as an expert on collaboration.

> It is my opinion that our group has stayed a working community because we are committed to a common belief: that we must discover how to be better teachers for the sake of children we were all deeply committed to. . . . In the beginning, I thought of leaving several times because it was hard to find the extra time and because it was often emotionally unsettling and wrenching to deal with the issues we talked about and to have to face what I was doing. It was hard some-times to make a leap of faith and trust that the time spent would be worthwhile because it did not look like a traditional place where we could find answers to our classroom problems. But I learned to trust. And I always felt that something important was happening—an opportunity that I could not in good conscience pass up. In addition, the group gave us an opportunity to throw out unformulated yet frus-trating questions or thoughts without judging us as "ineffective" for not knowing. Without having to take anyone else's solutions. New ideas shared by one of us led to a discussion by all and in that way in some aspect touched something in us that we could eventually use to understand similar dilemmas in our own classrooms. Our group sup-ported our roles as intelligent identifiers of problems and of knowl-edgeable professionals able to find solutions. . . . It gave me the confidence to say I have the power to shape the learning that goes on each year in my classroom and that I have the tools to do it. It is a very powerful notion. It is exciting. It led me to see that there are some very strong connections between environments that bring out the best in students and those that bring out the best in teachers.
>
> I wondered the other evening why I haven't adopted more of Mary's reading program. I have listened to her as she has created and recreated it over the years. I admire her tremendously and respect the research she has done in this area. Then I ask myself if the goal of a collaborative group is to improve teaching and/or the educational environment for students, then why had I not replicated a working program, researched by a respected and committed teacher who had made no effort to foist her knowledge on me? It was clearly because our collaboration, while encouraging and supporting improvements and social change, also respected the knowledge we all had as partici-pants to judge what we needed, and supported our freedom and respected our wisdom of choice to modify and make our own which we knew to be personally relevant to our best interests and those of our students.

Summary

All of these issues were those that the teachers had come to know in our group and were worth speaking about. Though they continued to draw upon and critically evaluate others' knowledges, they increasingly valued their own ways and instances of knowing. Once Leslie "found her voice" and felt free to talk about a wide range of issues, she couldn't be stopped! The topics of her learning ranged from literacy programs to school systems. Her continued critique of the "system of choice" is but one example. She prepared these remarks as part of a talk for an international conference.

> In the "choice" program, many elementary schools now have periods, much like junior high schools. Students choose a number of elective classes. In brief the new program was to increase students' enthusiasm for school and thereby increase their test scores.
>
> Teachers were not consulted about whether we thought the program would work for our students. "Open forums" which we were asked to attend to discuss the new program, tended to discourage teachers from asking questions, making suggestions or presenting modifications. Teachers had a number of concerns, but I believe the two most serious from their perspective were (1) that moving around between four to five different teachers and student groups 4 days a week would be very difficult for many of our students who come from unstable family situations and who need bonding and consistency; and that (2) less time with their primary teachers who know them well could result in a less solid educational foundation.

Leslie was not only naming the obstacles to her freedom to teach and her students' freedom to learn, but also, in Hirschman's (1970) terms, she was breaking traditional loyalty with the institution. Following Noddings (1986), she had recast loyalty as fidelity to herself and her school, not in the way it *is,* but in the way it *could be.* In Weiler's terms, Leslie was developing consciousness.

> Women's consciousness includes both hegemonic ideas from the male tradition and the possibilities of critical consciousness of what Gramsci (1971) called "good sense." . . . We must interrogate our own consciousness, language, and ways of knowing in order to come to see the realities of our own relationships. In this way, feminism asks for a radical reappraisal not only of our practices, but of consciousness itself. (Weiler, 1988)

Leslie had learned what she needed to transform her own knowledge of what it takes to teach urban children. That is, she changed her beliefs about her rights to search out tentative knowings, to transform and own authorized knowledge, to reconstruct the boundaries of knowledge—the "truths" of knowledge, and to claim the power of such ways of knowing to teach for social change. The "proof" of her transformation, as with the other teachers, was in her work to effect such changes in her students. Here's an example of Leslie discussing her teaching about gendered rights.

> LESLIE: Every year I've heard it. "Well, the girls can't have the ball. They're girls."
>
> SAM: Oh, dear. This is only second grade.
>
> LESLIE: And the girls—
>
> MARY: The girls don't want it either.
>
> LESLIE: Yes. But there are always some girls, if they could have the ball, who want it. So I bring it up and we'd spend some time talking about it . . . then they play with it.
>
> SAM: Under protest from the boys! I remember an example like that one day this year when I was visiting.
>
> LESLIE: Yes. That day the boys really didn't want the ball, but they wouldn't give it up. The boys would say, "They're girls . . . they can't —
>
> KAREN: There's only one ball?
>
> LESLIE: Yeah.
>
> SAM: The boys play with the ball and the girls jump the rope.
>
> MARY: And if you give the ball to the girls, they usually give it to the boys.
>
> LESLIE: So I keep bringing it to their attention. I put it into stories. Girls and boys can both play with balls and jump ropes. . . . If I wanted to spend time and energy on a study of ball socializing, I'd have plenty of data!

THE VALIDATION OF COLLABORATIVE TEACHER RESEARCH

As our stories across Part II have made clear, the teachers' sense of competency was supported not only by their becoming aware of their knowledge and ways of learning, but by their confirming their instructional actions through classroom research. Knowing without action seemed of little use in transforming urban schools. Many examples of their praxis have been presented and will not be repeated in this chapter. However, it is important to note that their ongoing experimentation and evaluation of instructional strategies by systematically attending to students' responses were part of the reason that they could not only value different ways of urban education, but take action to change their practices.

It is also important to remember that even though the teachers were conducting classroom research projects on their own and presenting them at conferences by the end of this book, (although they still had the regular support of the conversational group), that they had begun the work of teacher research in collaboration with our research team. At a national conference in Boston, Leslie spoke to the support that Karen had given her to help research new methods which led to alternative solutions (see Teel & Minarik, 1990).

> The voice that I have found, has in part resulted from my participation with the collaborative group. While we started off rather traditionally, the fact that Sam listened to the "stuff," and talked it over with us gave it validity. In addition, Karen, who spent much time with me in the classroom, also felt a need to change our teacher–researcher relationship so that we ended by tackling issues that I, as a classroom teacher, really needed to deal with to be a good teacher and they weren't always "curriculum" issues.
>
> I really thought material curriculum was key in my student teaching, and I think that's not a real priority, not to say that a teacher shouldn't know her curriculum well and study curriculum, and be well-versed in a variety of curriculum. But when you actually teach, that's of secondary importance. It's the students and what's happening and how they're getting excited, and what their problems are and where they are. That's the number one priority. And then the curriculum interfaces with [the students]. That would probably be the most significant change, I think I've made, in the way I see things.

As valuable as both Leslie and Mary found relational inquiry for establishing their programs and assessing student progress, however, self-initiated inquiry of any type was devalued by Leslie's school district.

> No one gives us credit for the research we do. I conducted systematic research all last year, wrote papers, presented at conferences. I applied for professional development credit [for that work] and I was turned down. They will give me credit for mentoring another teacher, or for attending a workshop, but not for critically examining my own teaching.

Mary found more support from her district for her inquiry-based innovations. Her administrators have even checked with her frequently

Group at conference.
Left to right: Susie Standerford, Margie Gallego (and Esmé Allison), Karen,
Jennifer, Deborah Dillon (discussant), Sam, Mary, Anthony, and Leslie.

about the progress of her work in our collaborative group. Others at Mary's school were also cognizant of the larger importance of their research efforts and have recently secured state funding to assist Mary and other teachers at their school with part-time aides. They are further supported in a teacher research project through their professional development center. The same support was available for Anthony, whose school supported him in many different types of research ventures.

LOCATING COMMUNITIES OF SUPPORT

> From a distance
> There is harmony and it echoes through the land
> > *Julie Gold*
> > *"From a Distance"*

Though our conversational group was the longest-running source of professional support these teachers had while learning to teach, their transformative work might have been short lived had they not begun to develop like-minded communities within schools to sustain their efforts and broaden their base of support across schools (see Liebermann & Miller, in press). Although, as we have seen, there was more than a degree of risk in doing so, they were committed to that risk. The commitment seemed to come both from the care they had for their students, the developing senses of their own knowledge, their classroom research, and the support of our group. Locating communities of support in their daily professional lives was not an easy task in school settings noted for isolation (Little, 1990).

Teacher Support Groups

In spite of their acknowledged danger of joining others at their schools to improve the lives of their students, the teachers talked at length about what those groups would and did look like. The conversation began with Anthony suggesting teacher groups use a "grass roots" strategy for change, which he had learned in his preteaching life.

> ANTHONY: One of the concepts I learned about organizing is that you start by organizing yourselves. And then you start by organizing people you have a common interest with. And we're teachers, so it makes sense to organize ourselves as teachers.
> LESLIE: Well, I honestly believe this. It sounds depressing, but I think that it's really true. If you can't get, at least a majority of your staff to be thinking in terms of change—
> MARY: All you need is 12%.
> LESLIE: Then you've—
> ANTHONY [TO MARY]: Is that from—
> MARY: I think Ho Chi Minh said that.
> LESLIE: Once you form a group, you've got a collective vision.

Leslie talked to us about a group of teachers at her school she had joined. The group had one thing in common: a criticism of the "system of choice" for urban students. Leslie's critique incorporated not only the other teachers voices, but her students' voices as well.

> Teachers at my school grew increasingly uncomfortable knowing that the ideological appeal behind the plan was one thing (who could be against free choice?), but the reality was another. In actuality, there was discrimination against many children. They were not all getting the best education. So the primary teachers quietly met, on their own time, to devise a system that would insure that each child got science, computer classes, etc. We also were uncomfortable with the fact that there were no reading and writing classes offered and less core time to

help students who needed extra work. . . . After many hours, the teachers devised a program. Volunteers were to teach classes that we agreed were best for the students. Several teachers even put together programs in basic math and phonics because many of their children "needed" such instruction. There was a great feeling that we would really be able to help the children. It was done quietly and discreetly, with the approval of an administrator who was willing to look the other way sometimes. Unfortunately, a number of circumstances changed at the district level (including having to relocate to another earthquake-safe school site) and the program was never realized, but we haven't given up. We are trying again, working with and around the district, if necessary, to do the best for the children.

One evening Leslie talked about the strength of a culture of support for visualizing school changes—and for the emotional support needed to take action toward social change.

> LESLIE: You know, I came home and I was just so angry I could have stuck my fist through a wall tonight, but after this conversation, there are so many things that we can do. . . . To believe that we can change things only takes a faculty that says, "Yeah, this is a good idea." You know, agreeing that you'll try different things in your classroom, that you'll spell each other when things get bad . . . it just takes people to really believe that it can be done and just, you know, just do it. . . . It can be so easy.
> ANTHONY: Yeah.
> KAREN: Yeah. When it doesn't happen, you have to wonder . . . are we in the minority?
> LESLIE: Well, we believe—
> ANTHONY: We can fly! We can fly!
> KAREN: Do most teachers not believe?
> ANTHONY: Well you just need 12 percent according to—
> LESLIE: Ho Chi Minh?
> ANTHONY: Mary and Ho Chi Minh.

The importance of humor in our group's serious work should not be underestimated.

Administrative and Parental Support

As the years we were together increased, so did Mary's involvement as a political activist as a union representative in her school district. The stories about her work were solidified by her belief in teachers and her trust in her own abilities, as they were tempered by the care she felt for urban children.

> It's interesting, you know the big budget crisis in the state? Well, we had a union rally. Jennifer was there. It was really serious. Our jobs were being cut, our benefits were going. Teachers were more or less "blamed" for the problems of school, and therefore we should make the sacrifices. A couple of nights later we had our union meeting, and the action committee got together afterwards and said, "Okay, so what are we going to do?" And the teachers said, "Involve the parents. Everybody's going to say, 'Oh, it's a bunch of teachers trying to save their jobs.' We can't be the only voice." So then we had a discussion about how to approach parents. "We can't come on too strong. There's this fine dance between how we're going to show them that we care about education . . . about their kids, and still stand up for ourselves."

As I listened to these teachers talk about their work and their caring for their students, it seemed increasingly important that they should be in the same sort of caring relations with those whose children they teach and those in authority over them. That perhaps, to be heard and acknowledged as one human being to another was at the base of their political need for voice and action, and for both the male and female teachers to be valued for their good ideas, their careful reflections on their practices, and their caring relations with their students. When such occasions happened in the teacher's schools, they were celebrated in our group.

> LESLIE: I want to relate an experience I've been involved in at school. Some of the teachers wanted to create a group to talk about a vision for our school—where we could talk and think about a program where all our ideas would be valued. Mary called such conversations "over the fence," to illustrate how teachers, mostly female, undervalue their conversations because they are not presented in the dominant form of "traditional, serious" discussions following a predetermined agenda. The group turned out to be just all women, basically, except for one fellow who comes from a feminist perspective. He doesn't even know it, I don't think . . . but he has it. And, anyway, we all came together because we needed to talk about this stuff. We didn't really have words or definitions, but we intuitively understood that there needed to be a lot of this—talking over the fence for awhile.
> And then this principal, who is really a wonderful person,

came in, and said, "Well, this is really nice." He found out what we were doing and started to lead the group. He approached it from the way that he always knew how to do these things: he pulled out graph paper and started to write down this stuff. He tried to organize us. He said, "OK, so what are we going to be in January and February?" And the teachers didn't want to do that, and he didn't understand why. Now I understand. It's because people hadn't talked enough to come to consensus. . . . So they said, "We don't want to talk about January" and he said, "Well, what about March, then?" He was trying the best that he could from the way he knew best and we were all trying our best and. . . .

Well, anyway, it broke down; someone politely excused the inability to communicate "because we were tired." The meeting adjourned, and everybody disbanded, and that was the end of it.

SAM: What we have here is an imbalance in power. He wasn't willing to communicate.

LESLIE: I think he was willing to share power. He just didn't understand this feminist process.

JENNIFER: I wish he hadn't walked into the room because you guys had a plan. If you guys would have just sat there and jawed . . . and—

LESLIE: Well, we didn't quit. We talked about what had happened, and then we realized what the problem was and then we went back and explained better to him what we wanted to do, and he listened. And we told him that there was no point in just giving up and walking away because it was worth caring about and putting energy there. So we went back and helped him understand how we needed to process stuff. And I honestly think it's going to work.

ANTHONY: Well it's good that he learned that—

LESLIE: But, you see, it would have been real easy to walk away and say, "drop it." This is another classic example of somebody in power. But that wasn't the case.

Leslie's story demonstrates not only her conviction of the importance of teacher groups to create school change, but to involve administrators in caring relations. Her sensitive response in listening to the administrator's confusion instead of his words perhaps gained the response to care back from him in return. Leslie's story teaches the rest of us another way to look at the problem of power.

The Gift of Family Support

Leslie was fortunate—as were the rest of us—to find the support she needed at home to work in urban settings. Actually, it was more than support. The narratives of our lives outside our schools, and the support and challenges we found there cannot be underestimated in our learning to teach. Leslie's daughter, Sarah, and her husband, George, were continuous sources of joy and strength which lightened her work. Occasionally, though, Leslie's new ways of viewing the world also created transformational waves in her family. She talked with our group about her husband's coming to understand feminist perspectives.

> George and I are talking about this with each other right now. It's been a tough conversation. To George, the idea of a feminist epistemology was a foreign concept. It was hard for me to communicate, and harder for him to understand. . . . Then George had a personal experience in his work where he had to attend a seminar on management styles. Everyone had to write down their ideas about solving [the same problem] and the solutions varied widely. Perhaps because it came in the middle of our own conversations, he suddenly could grasp the notion of a totally different way of looking at life.

The fact that George was willing to struggle with such a foreign concept and not simply dismiss it had a great deal to do with the care Leslie and George had for each other and their desire to understand one another. The support of such family interaction patterns might have been a precipitating factor in Leslie's sensitivity to her school administrator's confusion.

CONCLUSION: THE VALUE OF TEACHERS' VOICES IN EDUCATIONAL DISCOURSE

> It's the hope of hopes
> It's the love of loves
> It's the song of everyone.
> *Julie Gold*
> *"From a Distance"*

As a former classroom teacher myself, and being in long association with these teachers, it has always surprised me that teachers' voices are not considered as educative for setting school policy. It seems that the idea that teachers should remain publicly silent is based on an epistemological position that

Students are the passive recipients of knowledge. The role of teachers then becomes that of the dispenser of knowledge. . . . [T]he vision of . . . feminist teachers and administrators is deeply opposed to this view of learning and teaching. Instead, they emphasize that students are knowers and creators of knowledge. (Weiler, 1988, p. 122)

Kathleen Weiler's critique suggests that not only students but administrators and teachers are creators of knowledge. Leslie not only changed her beliefs about what curriculum to teach her children, she changed her understanding of what it meant to be knowledgeable. Tracing Leslie's transformation of voice through a perspective of feminist epistemology (Belenky et al., 1986), we see that she has changed the way she perceives herself as a learner. From believing that she can trust her knowledge and critique advice from all-knowing authorities, she now believes and acts as if she is herself the creator of knowledge. As this chapter has described, Leslie acquired her constructive and political voice through a perspective of care for herself and her children.

Recent research (as translated to us by district official and textbook publishers) suggests that reading groups by ability are bad and should be abolished. Heterogeneous grouping is the new program. . . . A salesperson for the new literature based reading series told us that if a nonreader just sat in a heterogeneous group long enough the student would learn to read. "Trust me," she said. "Even the ESL children will learn to read!" An observant teacher knows that this is not always the case. I have finally gotten the courage to stand up to inappropriate university research recommendations. I use flexible groups to teach children who need particular forms of instruction. And I have documented success for these urban and culturally diverse children.

The rule for me now is watch the children, trust them and other teachers, take papers with a grain of salt and don't trust anybody who hasn't spent a long time in a classroom and don't assume that your children will get any outside help.

I love teaching. I have loved every one of the years I have been teaching. I have never worked with a group of people whom I admire as much, who are as dedicated to their jobs. No matter what is done to frustrate them, ignore them, or put roadblocks in their way, teachers do their job to the best of their abilities because the children deserve it.

The issue of improving teaching is more than finding out how to teach teachers to teach better and more quickly, and teachers know this. If we are to truly make the improvements in education that are desperately needed we all need to take a more holistic view of the problems including the teacher, the classroom, the curriculum, the structure and habits of school districts and administrators and the parents and community who send their children to us. One small way to begin is for teachers and researchers to join together in collaboration and respect. It can not be well accomplished separately. We need a unified "voice" to make the changes our children deserve. We need to meet each other in a new role.

Leslie's and the others' stories show that teachers' capacities to create knowledge do NOT have to be limited by the socialized traditions of their roles.* Learning to teach can reach beyond the boundaries of the curriculum into the political mind and voice of schooling. It can name the obstacles to new visions of equity in schooling. It can ask questions about the theories, truths and knowledges of school, politics and available choices, and whether they are equitable for all children. And, although, like Leslie's challenge with boys and girls and the ball, it may be hard to challenge the politics of education with regard to the socialized rules of *who* gets to keep the ball most often, Leslie's story reminds us that learning to work in communities for change may be a matter of knowing how, and having a commitment to that work that, with persistence and support, leads to action.

ENDNOTES

1 Leslie is referring to an administrator who appears in her story later in this chapter.
2 I deeply appreciate the encouragement our editor, Brian Ellerbeck, gave me to refocus this chapter. My first version was written primarily in my political voice rather than in Leslie's and the other teachers'. With Brian's help, I think there is now a better balance.

---

*Leslie tagged a clarifying phrase onto this sentence: "or by an administrative structure that often sabotages their power and ability to create, reflect on, and implement knowledge."

10

A Conversation on Teacher Research

REFLECTIONS ON OUR WORK IN PART II

MARY: I was thinking about this teacher/research idea, and what it means for a practitioner, and what its future was going to be. Like is this going to be mandated?

This culminating chapter in Part II illustrates one of the times (increasing more often across our 6th year together) that I am not present at a collaborative meeting. This one is in Leslie's home. The conversation is taped, as usual, and transcribed. The topic of this evening is "teacher research." The conversation seems to speak to many considerations for advocating teacher research for learning to teach literacy in urban classrooms. Therefore, I will draw upon these teachers' words as they speak to these issues and questions: (1) the promise of teacher research, (2) is it real?, (3) a feminist rationale, (4) a close up on children, and (5) the possibility of revolution.

THE PROMISE OF TEACHER RESEARCH

In the segment below, Mary begins the evening's conversation by talking about a teacher research conference sponsored by her district.

MARY: What was wonderful about our teacher-research conference was the audience: They were colleagues—other teachers from our schools.

183

KAREN: In the district? Other schools in the district?

MARY: Yes. And some principals. But, what was really nice was the feedback that we got. It was not just—you know, "Oh, I liked your paper," but the fact that they came. And were really support- ive. I got a positive feeling . . . wow! Maybe, there's something to this movement which will help us learn to appreciate each other!

KAREN: Do you think they were sincere?

MARY: Absolutely. Absolutely.

JENNIFER: What was [your colleague] Nate's research study?

MARY: Reluctant readers and writers. He looked at five kids.

KAREN: Oh, I'd love to see his report.

MARY: He chose kids who had problems with reading and writing.

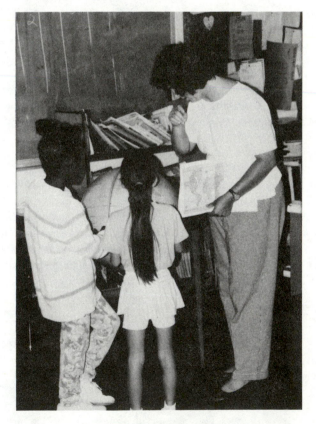

Mary in her classroom.

JENNIFER: So it was kind of like mini case studies.

KAREN: Did he come to some kind of conclusions about how they were different?

MARY: Well, you know, I think everybody came to some sort of conclusion. Mostly they were personal conclusions, not something you could disseminate and say, "Well, try *this* in your classroom," but the kinds of things that worked for them.

One clear benefit of teacher research is that it gives teachers an action-oriented process for working through instructional dilemmas particular to their students and their classrooms. Another promise which might not be as clearly evident comes through in Mary's words. Teacher research supported by her district created conversational spaces for teachers to come together to see the possibilities of their creating changes in urban classrooms. It also helped develop a conversational community across schools for teachers and administrators. Such spaces challenge traditional knowledge domains, roles, and responsibilities for establishing curricular and instructional policies for classrooms.

In spite of such promises, the question of the validity of this work came up in our conversation, as it does in almost every discussion of teacher research.

BUT IS IT RESEARCH?

LESLIE: But, we can't really talk about our research, because it's personal. If it's not universal, then you can't share it with anybody, and so it's of no value. And yet, teaching is such an enormously personal sort of thing.

ANTHONY: But could it be done so it was less personal?

LESLIE: You know you get into kind of a problem area there. If you encourage teachers to be reflective researchers and improve situations in their own rooms—

KAREN: Then we don't worry about whether it's transferable—

LESLIE: Exactly.

MARY: Right.

LESLIE: Who cares if everybody in the whole world can't replicate your experience? I think that's a major problem with a lot of university research. That everybody comes up with something that works, that's universal, but you know—as a teacher—that it really isn't.

ANTHONY: Well, we've talked about that, but then there's another problem.

LESLIE: But, if it's from university research, then everybody's got to do it, whether it really works or not.

ANTHONY: Which is you can't just say, "Do research because it's therapeutic, or it's useful." I mean it's useful for you as a teacher. But the whole point of research is to gain insight into some general principles that could be applied by other people.

LESLIE: No, it's not.

MARY: Not necessarily. I mean that's *one* definition of research.

KAREN: No, there's a lot of different thoughts . . . opinions about that. . . .

(laughter)

ANTHONY: No, I mean I agree. You could redefine research, and I think that's perfectly valid.

KAREN: Oh, but you mean—

ANTHONY: To redefine the purpose of research. And, you know personal understanding is my approach to this group frankly. But the ostensible purpose anyone else would be interested in reading what you say is, presumably to apply it to themselves.

JENNIFER: I think this discussion is really good.

MARY: Some of the things I got from other teachers [at the district teacher research conference] were more astonishing to me than, than the information I got out of my own research.

LESLIE: You know, I have even gone to presentations on math where the ideas didn't actually apply to me at all in my grade level or anything, but I do sit there and think about math . . . about how I could maybe adjust my math program, or what I needed to do.

Anthony: Sure. Well but that's, I mean that's, that's the value of any decent presentation.

LESLIE: But it only worked for me because the person who gave it was a teacher, you know? I was willing to go because it was a teacher. So, if it were anybody else, I wouldn't have gone, I wouldn't have believed it could work for me. But if one teacher had decided to go off and try something different, and he had success with it, and he was feeling better about his whole math program, and it was sort of like there was hope for my math program.

ANTHONY: Yeah, well, that's what's frustrating though. I think that it is a schism between what is research and, this concept of teacher as researcher. And I'm not, I still feel unresolved about the, the gap between the two. Because I think, what is research? I think what research is defined as . . . and, you know, I found myself thinking this when I was reading your papers, you know, where are the numbers? What validity does this have. What . . . .

KAREN: Oh, good. I want to talk to you about that.

ANTHONY: You know, is this just anecdotal. Is this just your tale of teaching in an inner city? I mean, you know what I'm saying?

JENNIFER: Yeah, but what's wrong with that?

LESLIE: Yeah, but. . . . I just get livid about that attitude!

KAREN: So what does teacher research mean?

JENNIFER: It's a kind of research.

MARY: It's action research.

ANTHONY: I think, you need to develop a rationale that distinguishes it from, or somehow defends it from comparison to the other form of research.

LESLIE: Well, it's certainly meaningful for me.

ANTHONY: So if you could prove it statistically then.

KAREN: No. . . .

LESLIE: No, longitudinally.

MARY: A longitudinal intuitive study.

KAREN: Yes.

LESLIE: I would do histories. I would do . . . I would do sacred stories[1] of people over time to find this out.

ANTHONY: They're going to say that's not research.

KAREN: Right. And I agree. That is not "that kind" of research. It's totally, totally different.

ANTHONY: It may be that we want to embrace the term research, and we want to try to redefine research. . . . I think that's what Sam's saying. And I think if we're going to the conferences, where we're presenting to those people . . . right? I mean we're not just sitting here at Leslie's eating dinner, you know?

KAREN: It's true. We're not just presenting to the teacher–researchers.

Anthony has raised an important question which many people outside of our group have considered. Marilyn Cochran-Smith and Susan Lytle's work on this topic is somewhat helpful. Their formulation of teacher research as another genre of educational research sets it apart from traditional considerations of experimental research, yet speaks to its validity.

Comparison of teacher research with university-based research involves a complicated set of assumptions and relationships that act as barriers to enhancing our knowledge base about teaching. Researchers in the academy equate "knowledge about teaching" with the high-status information attained through traditional modes of inquiry. They fault teachers for not reading or not implementing the findings of such research, even though teachers often find it irrelevant and counterintuitive. Yet teacher research, which by definition has special potential to address issues that teachers themselves identify as significant, does not have a legitimate place. . . . Regarding teacher research as a mere imitation of university research is not useful and ultimately condescending. It is more useful to consider teacher research as its own genre, not entirely different from other types of systematic inquiry into teaching, yet with some quite distinctive features. But it is also important to recognize the value of teacher research for both the school-based teaching community and the university-based research community. (1990, p. 4)

There is yet another way of thinking about teacher research as a means of self-validation of knowledge from a feminist perspective that is less often found in the professional literature. Our group spoke to my preference for the feminist argument behind teacher research. It was brought up as a rationale for the teachers' impressions of the value of this approach to knowledge.

A FEMINIST RATIONALE

JENNIFER: It makes you think about what it is you're doing and makes you discover how it is you learn what you learn.

LESLIE: I have a real personal feeling for this because for years and years I had to live by a sort of code which required . . . a certain perception of life and reality and academics. I had to quote other people, not myself. And for years I accepted that as the standard. And so for a long time I felt as if I had no intelligence, my point of view was invalid, and it got to the point where I was reduced for awhile to not saying anything. I felt a lot and I thought a lot, but it was all sort of anecdotal, and it was intuitive. And so, this group, who happened, by the way, to be men—

ANTHONY: You couldn't justify according to them.

LESLIE: Well, yeah. My ideas were completely shot down and I felt really bad. It took me a decade before I got to the point that I understood that an intuitive, anecdotal way of understanding human beings is very, very valid. And that in fact, you know, I began to feel very proud of myself. My way of doing things and dealing with people actually produced better relationships, produced greater understanding of people, gave me more sympathy for people. Led me to be able to change myself and make conditions better for myself and for other people. Because of those wasted years being silenced, I have a lot of anger now. In my own experience, it happened to always be men who decided that there had to be this code and there had to be this rationale, and there had to be numbers.

KAREN: In my life it was the women.

LESLIE: And I understand now that, my, my way of doing it was very valid too. It doesn't mean that we can't arrive at valid conclusions from this different perspective. It is annoying and frustrating to me to have someone say, "No, this is the way and because, yours doesn't meet our standards, that you don't have numbers and you don't have graphs and you don't have charts . . ." I would almost venture, just for the sake of argument, to say that perhaps anecdotal intuitive kinds of analysis of human beings might prove to lead us to a better world.

ANTHONY: And I think it's kind of, we need to gather our defenses somewhat, and develop a theoretical rationale for what we're doing. I think Sam has an argument, an intellectual rationale. That's what I wanted to discuss more. And I think you have from your own experience, an argument which you could carry into a meeting.

KAREN: Well, we did. Sam talked about it. At Stanford.[2]

LESLIE: Sam takes that argument into the meeting every time.

KAREN: Every time.

JENNIFER: Every time she practices

LESLIE: Anything she does.

ANTHONY: Well. . . .

LESLIE: A feminist epistemology. Yeah.

KAREN: Do you know what it means? I'm still not sure.

ANTHONY: Alternative ideas on how we know what we know, based on research on women.

MARY: Yeah. It's a way of knowing, and I think a way of knowing . . . you know, that's not valid in our culture, in our dominant culture.

ANTHONY: In the dominant paradigm.

MARY: The kind of things that we have been talking about . . . just different ways of—

ANTHONY: Well, see, my problem is, the cross that I bear, so to speak, is not only that—

MARY: You were born a male!

ANTHONY: No, not only my pesky Y chromosome, but, but also, my training as a scientist . . . a science teacher. I tend to take that approach, which, which really, looks at the validity of everything, and tries to compare it not only through my experience, but also, to what objective measuring sticks are being to explain it, other than the person's personal experience.

Anthony didn't convince them. Conversely, the women teachers didn't convince Anthony to abandon his preference for the scientific objectivity—nor could they convince others with similar backgrounds. The point that Leslie and the others made very well, however, was that "objective measuring sticks" don't always validate everyone's points of view. For many women, male and female teachers without education in the scientific form of objectivity, and people of color, other measuring sticks are called for. The case in point: the failure of urban students in schools run on principles of "objective" measures. One major promise of this work is how teacher research brings forward the lives of the children out of scientific objectivity to be seen close up and personal. The conversation continues.

A Close-up on Children

MARY: Teacher research is so personal.

JENNIFER: It makes you think about . . . how kids learn what they learn. That's what it, to me that's what's interesting about it. And that's what's interesting is that it *doesn't* say, " I studied 100 people and 50 of them said this and 50 of them said that." Well, to me that's, you know, you can always find fault with numbers.

LESLIE: Take Jarvin, who I was studying last year. And take a university-based project studying the norm. Jarvin is not the norm, so he's not mentioned in the study. I can't learn how to help him from the study. An anecdotal story might be more helpful and encourages me to try . . . a pattern of observation that will help me understand him.

I have done several questionnaires in the last few weeks for a program that is supposed to help children with possible emotional problems. The questions are lousy. I filled out 30 of them. But, they do not give a profile of the child. The woman in charge insists that these profiles will help me understand who needs help—will tell me who my children are. I know who my children are. I watch and listen to them. I don't need these idiotic questionnaires. Shame on her for not knowing this.

JENNIFER: But the thing is, we are making an improvement with teacher research . . . I mean how many people have been touched . . . how many kids have we talked about . . . really talked about.

KAREN: It may seem much too small.

JENNIFER: It may seem like you're not doing anything, but any time anybody comes in your classroom or talks to you, or interacts with you, or any one of us, and if they are doing the same kind of work and hear your stories, something has changed. I mean, the fact that we're all sitting here—

KAREN: I agree.

As I read these words, it reminded me again of Noddings' sense of an ethic of care that these teachers displayed in their intellectual deliberations and their optimism.

> To care and be cared for are fundamental human needs. We all need to be cared for by other human beings. In infancy, illness, or old age, the need is urgent and pervasive; we need caregiving, and we need the special attitude of caring that accompanies the best caregiving if we are to survive and be whole. But at every stage we need to be cared for in the sense that we need to be understood, received, respected, recognized.
> We also need, but not all of us learn to care for other human beings. Some people genuinely care for ideas, great causes, objects or instrument, man, animals, or plants. . . . Caring cannot be achieved by formula. It requires address and response; it requires different behaviors from situation to situation and person to person. (1992, p. xi)

JENNIFER: Just the idea that we've discovered in our research is going to be on a tape and Patty . . . the transcriber's going to hear it. Maybe she'll talk to somebody, and maybe, you know, it's like, just, as soon as you open your mouth you've affected 10 other people at least. Maybe people will start thinking about the possibilities for these kids instead of looking at them as hopeless statistics.

THE POSSIBILITY OF REVOLUTION

The evening's conversation closed with the potential of teacher research as a revolution for transforming education. Now, it's important to note that the critiques of teacher research as a "glorification of teachers' knowledge" (Zeichner, in press) are well founded. Not all teacher research leads to social transformation—much of it, in fact, leads to replication of the inequities of schooling.

> Teacher research is not fulfilling its potential to play a part in the building of a more just world. When I go to a meeting of action researchers, I always expect to feel a certain sense of solidarity and a shared sense of outrage at the condition under which many of our fellow human

beings are forced to live, and the growing gap between the rich and the poor, at the erosion of democratic processes. And I expect to experience a shared contempt for that most painful of all situations that allows an enormous number of children to live in conditions of poverty. . . . There is little apparent concern over these matters of educational equity and social justice in the teacher research community. Sometimes it seems as though teacher research and the empowerment of teachers are pursued in ways that are totally oblivious to the current situation for the people who, by anyone's definition, do not share equally in the rewards of our society. Sometimes teacher research seems too self-serving. (p. 35)

The teachers in this book would agree. They would also add that university research on teacher research is also self-serving if it doesn't include, and use the language of, teachers in classrooms who are in the center of the struggle. If it doesn't value and validate research as these teachers are doing toward equity in urban education. It calls for, in Leslie's words, "a revolution" in power, in voice, in research, and in collaborative action. The last part of the evening's conversation shows how the revolutionary impact of these teachers leaving their classrooms to attend an international conference on teacher research.

> LESLIE: You know, I am so discouraged. I think that there's got to be some like, revolution.
>
> JENNIFER: Sure there's got to be a revolution.
>
> LESLIE: I'm talking real revolution. I'm not talking about dinner parties anymore. I'm talking about—
>
> ANTHONY: Revolution and not a tea party.
>
> LESLIE: And maybe a revolution is happening . . . in the last couple of years of our giving papers at research conferences, there's been more impact because of the teacher research movement. More people actually listen to me and you and you, because you're a teacher.
>
> ANTHONY: Who are these people?
>
> LESLIE: People in universities doing research at university level talk to teachers now.
>
> MARY: "You're the expert, I'll listen to you."
>
> JENNIFER: Right.
>
> LESLIE: And we're being heard at these conferences. I remember Jennifer standing up at Stanford and talking back to that man [3] . . . Telling him that his "researcher's language" describing teacher research was totally incomprehensible to teachers. That he wasn't telling her story, nor the children's stories.

MARY: Jennifer had the whole room in an uproar.

ANTHONY: Yeah, but come on, I mean, in 5 years, in 5 years, those people won't remember. They're tenured professors. They're going to be writing the same, you know—

LESLIE: You should have been there though. I mean, no seriously, you should have been there because, because . . . it was like seeing that the revolution has begun.

MARY: I think Jennifer made them totally uncomfortable.

LESLIE: I thought about that small group of teachers there (us) with all those people. When Jennifer spoke, I looked around, saw hundreds of university people sitting up in those seats, I thought the impact was incredible. I thought it was, the strongest voice I had heard in any kind of conference setting. It wasn't the kind of atmosphere I've gone to before where people talk and everybody agrees. I thought there was tension and there was disagreement, and . . . movement.

Jennifer at conference.

MARY: And Leslie spoke up there too. She said to them, "I haven't heard you talk about the children once." I mean . . . that was—

MARY: Jennifer said, "If this was my classroom, I'd be walking around wondering why people weren't more engaged." I loved that, I just thought you presented it so well. You said, "There's nothing happening here. It's boring." It's, it's like, it was great. "If, if I were the teacher in charge of this classroom, I would be really worried about my effectiveness."

LESLIE: But all of a sudden they listened and then they all applauded. And then they asked questions that nobody could understand but they really tried to interact. It was like we used two different languages.

JENNIFER: Oh, it was incredible. That guy said more words . . . I wish I'd made a list or something. I've never heard anybody talk like that in my life.

LESLIE: But if you listened to the less public talk afterwards amongst themselves, they started asking, "Are we doing anything valid? Is the format that we've set, the way we've arranged this conference, acceptable anymore? Should we rethink these conferences, and the topics of these conferences. Should we rethink who comes to these conferences? Should teachers actually be invited to these conferences?"

JENNIFER: Especially when you call it a teacher–researcher conference?

ANTHONY: Perhaps not. After this experience maybe that's what they'll decide. But what will be the university's motivation to change, other than their conscience? Is that going to be sufficient to shift them?

JENNIFER: There was a big discussion about that too. Sam said to those guys [Sam's colleagues], "Lets' face it. One of the reasons we're interested in teacher research is that we, at the university have to—

MARY: . . . publish or something—

KAREN: Right. Let's admit it. We're all here using the language we do to speak to each other, not to speak to teachers.

JENNIFER: People took her to task for that. They said, "Oh, no, we're here for teachers," and Sam responded: "Where are they? There are few teachers here." (Only those who came with her.) It's like, "The teachers do the teacher research, but we're the ones who take credit for the research, we talk about it, publish it and get our names on it and get tenure and stuff and those teachers are still down at the school.

KAREN: She was being ironic. Of course she's doing this work for the

teachers—for the kids. She was trying to make a point. To insti-
gate some change.

JENNIFER: I think we saw a little bit of the revolution at that conference. I think the system will change when the people who are
most affected by it are changed. And I think that our way of
teaching does that. And our research does that. But we can't do it
alone. We have to educate teachers differently. And teacher–educators differently.[4]

ENDNOTES

[1] Leslie had just heard Jean Clandinin talk about "sacred stories" at a conference at Stanford (see Clandinin & Connelly, in press).

[2] This is the same conference as referenced above, the 1st Annual International Conference on Teacher Research held at Stanford University in April,
1992. Our group presented in an alternative setting: recreating our conversational meetings around a "dinner table." Anthony was not present.

[3] The "man" was John Elliot, sometimes known as the "father" of action
research. John not only heard Jennifer, he and his colleagues later invited her
to speak at an international conference on classroom research.

[4] After reading this chapter, Lisa wrote: "This conversation is extraordi-
nary. It is beautiful, moving, honest—full of people trying to understand each
other, education on all its levels, and how to make change. I respect these folks
so much!"

III

Lessons on Pedagogical Re-Vision

11

Redesigning Literacy Course Work for Teachers

IN SEARCH OF TRANSFORMATIONAL LEARNING

Part III of this book tries to take seriously Jennifer's comments as she closed Part II: "We have to educate teachers differently. And teacher–educators differently." After participating in transformational learning with regard to our thinking about literacy, schooling, teaching, and research in our conversational group and in the teachers' classrooms, I became interested in what I could do in my classroom to transform literacy education course work—for myself and others. I knew that the task was not an easy one: traditions and habits within an institution (and within ourselves) are hard to change.

> It should come as no surprise that many [educational] reforms seldom go beyond getting adopted as a policy. Most get implemented in word rather than deed, especially in classrooms. . . . Seldom are the deepest structures of schooling that are embedded in the school's use of time and space, teaching practices and teaching routines fundamentally altered even at those historical moments when reforms seek those alterations as the goal. (Cuban, 1990, p. 9)

Cuban's historical review describes a formidable challenge to my quest. Except for my experience watching these dedicated urban teachers change their practices, I might have given up. Yet they had taught me to consider the problem of learning to teach differently—by imagining a different epistemology of practice, a different theory of coming to know about teaching. Instead of educating other teachers only about the current knowledge in literacy education, I wanted to create a climate for learning that would help them develop the self-confidence and the courage to face the social and political challenges of teaching urban children. Jennifer and her peers taught me to begin to look at the transformation of teachers' classroom practices in conjunction with an examination of my own classroom practices. Others agree with Jennifer.

> In the education of teachers probably no one factor is more important than the social attitude of the faculty of the professional institution. . . . Each staff member should be encouraged to know at first hand how the less-favored among us live and feel. . . . In every possible way, we must work for the more intelligently social outlook within our staff of our teacher-preparing institutions. Without this, we can hardly hope for socially prepared teachers. (Kilpatrick, 1933/ 1991, p. 29, cited in Liston & Zeichner, 1991)

Kilpatrick suggests that teacher–educators' social attitudes heavily influence how we structure our classroom practices for teachers' learning. I would add that such attitudes also influence the epistemological philosophies that we adapt to frame our teaching. For example, if I believe that public institutions of education, in their current forms, prepare all children to live democratic, healthy, and pleasurable lives—I would find out what the best teachers do to achieve those goals within the institutions, and ask teachers-in-training to model after them. My social attitude would be to approve of and replicate the current society through education. Changes in my practices would be those of improvement within the same epistemic framework. If, however, my social attitude were more critical of the results of public education, I would have to deviate from that framework (even if it had "successfully" prepared *me* for life) and imagine another way to educate socially critical teachers. My life experiences—my son's school traumas in particular—led me to adopt the latter attitude.[1] I had to reject the way I was being prepared to teach, as I was only provided with epistemic experiences that led to social reproduction. For years I wasn't quite sure what to do to construct other ways of teaching.

So, as you'll see at the beginning of this chapter, changes in my classroom practices before the experience of our conversational group, took the form of tinkering within an epistemology of practice that ignored my own social attitude. The rhetorical question I asked myself to guide instructional changes was, "How can I get these teachers to know everything about literacy education that I do?" By the end of this chapter I am reflexively asking, "What is the impact of my teaching on their perceived freedom to learn? And their learning on my perceived freedom to teach? Am I preparing myself and the teachers entrusted to my care to be knowledgeable about existing social realities *and* brave enough to trust in their own ways of imagining those realities differently? Are we coconstructing an epistemology of teaching practice that might reverse the inequities in urban literacy education?"

Those questions are organized through a chronological review of the various changes in the way I understood my role and responsibility as a teacher–educator. The beginning of the story describes a sense of instructional responsibility to develop subject or content expertise in teachers, and what influenced me to modify that perception and see myself responsible for educating teachers to become expert "children-watchers." The conclusion of this narrative describes my current sense of responsibility for developing a sense of collective social responsibility and, as a result, effecting epistemological changes in myself and in the teachers I teach.

Jennifer, her peers in our conversational group, and other voices in the educational literature challenged (and supported) me to write this story. They encouraged me to look critically at the process and the outcomes of my learning to teach across my career—as I have asked them to do. I offer this chapter in the spirit of that challenge, joining many of my colleagues who have also faced themselves critically.

PART I: RESPONSIBILITY AS THE DEVELOPMENT OF EXPERTISE

In the initial days of my teacher education career—as a doctoral candidate instructor in reading at the University of Texas, Austin—my sense of responsibility was closely bounded by university classroom walls. Following timeless examples from my own educational experiences and new examples from research experiences required by my graduate program, I felt it was my duty to *cover the content* of reading theory and instruction, then measure how well my teacher–students had mastered that content. I was influenced by the information-processing models and schema-theoretic accounts of scholars such as R. C. Anderson and David Pearson (1984) and John Bransford (1979). My sense of appropriate pedagogy was influenced by the teaching effectiveness literature as reported by Jere Brophy and Thomas Good (1986). My graduate education occurred just before the time that research on reading and writing would merge into literacy, and qualitative studies of bicultural students' literacy acquisition would seriously question the psychologically based reading models (see Bloome's review, 1989). Even so, from a yet-unarticulated and less well-read (but highly experienced) place in me as a woman–teacher, I sensed that something was missing—I just didn't know what.

So, for the most part, I employed a traditional lecture, discussion, text-based teaching style to help students learn all the content I knew to be valuable. For example, I presented a theoretical umbrella of varying perspectives on reading and writing, then described the instructional strategies that grew out of the varying approaches. I recommended that students consider those appropriate for teaching their future pupils. I then used objective measures to define how well they'd learned what I'd taught. Though no one really told me to, I also felt an intuitive sense of responsibility to engage the young teachers-to-be, who were not always interested in attending class, but I didn't quite know how. I assessed subjectively whether I had fulfilled my duties in that area by noting increased interest and attention in our work together. I did not worry much whether teachers-to-be would apply what they had learned in classrooms. My job ended when they graduated. Satisfactory pre-/post-measures of course content learned by more than 85% of my students let me put to rest my question of responsibility.

In the next part of my story, the requirements of my job as a teacher–educator changed. I was now asked to supervise student teachers as well as teach them. Thus, I began to explore notions of actually increasing content knowledge by taking advantage of the field experience. The boundaries of my sense of responsibility expanded to include both my new instructional assignment and a growing understanding of the social nature of learning; that is, I was now reading authors such as Lev Vygotsky (1978) and Walter Doyle (1983) to make sense of my teaching in this new context. I saw the power of using teachers' practice settings as a place to learn about literacy instruction through its enactment with children.

I was fortunate enough to collaborate with Jim Guszak and John Shefelbine, professors at University of Texas, Austin, during these experiences. Both men were committed to using the practicum to develop appropriate pedagogical approaches to literacy that would lead to social equity in schooling for all children—but particularly ethnic minorities. An additional influence on my teaching was the research culture in my own institution and the literacy faculty's focus on phonemic awareness as a central feature of reading acquisition (see Bryant & Bradley, 1981; Gough & Hillinger, 1980). As a result of my own social and educative context, I now evaluated the success of my eclectic pedagogical approach by collecting data through course-based measures *and* through observations of student teachers' classroom practica/performances. I watched and recorded the student teachers' instructional interactions with children and analyzed their understanding-in-use of the concept of phonemic awareness. I also asked the student teachers to keep systematic records and prepare reports of children's progress. These data helped me evaluate the effectiveness of my approach. Here's an excerpt from Brenda Beams' (1986) report about her work with Gracie, an 8-year-old first-grade student from a Mexican-American migrant family:

> [Gracie joined my literacy group] with two years of kindergarten behind her and still no letter–name or sight word knowledge. . . . All three children in Gracie's group (and their teacher!) read independent texts continuously for 20 minutes a day. . . . [Gracie] read and reread her stories, self-correcting her own mistakes. Through the successful repetition, she not only built-up a strong sight word knowledge, but was able to abstract phonetic cues (such as letter-sounds at the beginning of words) which she applied to other unknown words. In the remaining 25 minutes of our daily work together, she participated in choral rhyming activities to further develop her phonemic awareness, became an eager writer of her own text, listened to stories read to her, and slowly began to join our small group discussions about our reading.
>
> Her success began to spread into other aspects of her life. At the end of our daily 45 minute session together, Gracie rejoined others in a "readiness" group established by her classroom teacher. Near the middle of the semester she became—for the first time in her school career—a star. She was reading fluently as the rest of her group struggled. She was able to help her peers. Her status in the classroom changed. Gracie became a leader. . . . Her classroom teacher noticed that her new confidence also transferred to her efforts in mathematics work. (Gracie's teacher later asked Brenda to teach her about our approach. For more information, see Hollingsworth, 1988.)

Brenda's success with Gracie was much more meaningful to me as a teacher–educator than were her perfect responses on a final examination over the literacy content. Similar findings from over 90% of the other preservice teachers in my class suggested to me that I had met my responsibility—as I then defined it—to have an impact on classroom practice. Ultimate transfer of this eclectic literacy approach to teachers' own classrooms *after graduation,* however, seemed beyond my absolute responsibility, given both my job description and my then current research focus. Besides, I *assumed* that these well-informed teachers would transfer what they'd learned to their own classrooms.

PART II: RESPONSIBILITY AS TRANSFER TO
CLASSROOM PRACTICE

The next chapter of my story as a teacher–educator began as I graduated from University of Texas, Austin, and took a job as assistant professor at the University of California at Berkeley. My sense of responsibility again shifted to match the new environment. The graduate-level elementary teachers-to-be practiced in classrooms as they studied with me over the course of a full year. To satisfy my interest in their learning to teach and to meet the requirements of a new professor to engage in a program of research, I collaborated with research assistants to study my teaching systematically, as an influence on 28 new teachers' learning in two literacy courses. Most members of our conversational group were part of those cohorts. We tape-recorded class sessions, conducted interviews, and collected written responses to simulations as evidence of the class members' evolving beliefs and understandings about literacy. The research assistants gave me formative reports of private interviews, which revealed general patterns of teachers' learning (to preserve their confidentiality), and then a summative report after the course ended. These collaborators and I also followed approximately one third of the new teachers into their practicum classrooms and wrote running narrative observations of their teaching. We did not supervise, coach, or evaluate, but simply recorded what we noticed. We then analyzed those triangulated data across the course and classroom sites using Glaser's and Strauss' (1967) constant comparison approach.

Like any teacher who has difficulty attending both to the flow of the lesson and the sense students make of it, I found this sort of pulling back to be very useful. Systematically analyzing these longitudinal data allowed me to become more precise in my understanding of preservice teachers' content learning. I began to see where the new teachers' attention rested and what seemed to be blocking their learning and transfer of literacy to classroom settings. Results of these analyses told me that they paid much more attention to the *activities* of reading instruction than to their purpose. They didn't know to question *what sense children made of the activities,* a questioning that seemed important to flexible and responsive classroom practices. They assumed that interesting and well-executed activities would motivate children to become literate.* The results of this study influenced the next.

I revised subsequent courses to have new teachers "pay attention to

---

* Lisa asked: "Do you think this was partly because of the overall focus of our program (and maybe not you)?" I responded, "Probably both and more."

student learning." I reduced both the content density and the assignment loads to encourage the teachers to know and teach something well, then to look in classrooms and see if children learned from their teaching. An example of my attempts to achieve that goal and still provide a scaffolded but flexible activity structure was to introduce a framework for direct or explicit explanation based on children's metacognitive understanding of text (Duffy & Roehler, 1989). I hoped teachers would use that activity to determine the sense children made of their reading, incorporate varying reading strategies to meet particular children's needs, then guide the children to use the routine and clarify their own thinking. After modeling the approach with class members, I asked teachers to videotape themselves using a routine *modified to suit their particular children,* then to analyze the results and discuss them in class. My initial impression from those public displays led me to believe that students were moving in the direction I had hoped. However, Marcia Cantrell, a research assistant and member of our conversation group whom we met in chapter 1 of this book, also attended these public discussions, privately interviewed the teachers, triangulated their responses with their videotaped performances and audiotaped transcripts of the actual course content, and later wrote a report of their learning:

> One preservice teacher reported to me that many, including herself, "just did it, even though we didn't know WHAT we were doing.". . . [T]he sample of preservice teachers with whom I spoke all reported that they *thought* they would use the framework in their teaching, but found the steps Dr. Hollingsworth required too cumbersome. The few that could articulate their modified plans left out guided practice and analysis. . . . Ironically, it is perhaps because Dr. Hollingsworth did not spend class time [guiding the teachers' practice] that the teachers did not see the usefulness and importance of this step. (Cantrell, 1988, pp. 11–12)

At the end of the course, I compared the *public* statements in the multiple data sources with the *private* data the research assistants collected, then combined course-specific findings with reports from practicum observations and follow-up surveys after graduation. Using a constant comparative analysis, I found little consistent evidence of either shifts of attention away from existing classroom activities or a broadening of theoretical perspectives that would allow them to notice children who were not doing well.

Some of the preservice teachers, including members of our conversational group, did go further. As I described it then, those preservice teachers moved beyond a focus on classroom management and teaching subject-related activities in student teaching to be able to understand what their pupils were actually learning from classroom tasks, modify instructional situations to foster that learning, and become what I called "task aware." I based this description on Doyle's construct of an academic task—a situational structure that organizes and directs both thought and action in the classroom by defining the goals of the task, as well as the cognitive operations, and available resources needed to accomplish the goals (Doyle, 1983; Doyle & Carter, 1984). The preservice teachers who became "task aware" learned to integrate managerial and subject knowledge and establish teaching routines (Rosenshine, 1983) to give them the attentional capacity necessary to focus on what students were actually learning (Doyle & Carter, 1987). Finally, those preservice teachers tested their newly acquired knowledge by working with cooperating teachers whose ideas were somewhat incompatible with their own, but who would also allow them to try out their own ideas in different contexts (i.e., with groups of students differing in backgrounds and abilities) while giving supporting and content-specific feedback.

Leslie's story contains an example of task awareness. In an earlier study of these teachers' cognitive change (reported in the *American Educational Research Journal:* Hollingsworth, 1989b)—written before we realized the importance of using our real names in this work, and before we became comfortable with the risk that encompassed—Leslie was known as "Lynda." In any case, it was *Leslie* who moved full cycle (as I then defined it) through the complex learning to teach process to (1) clarify, then modify her beliefs about learning, managing, and teaching, (2) establish a balanced managerial system to accomplish specific content instruction, and (3) become "task aware" or understand what pupils were learning from text—and what she needed to learn to teach them. For example, Leslie realized early into her second semester of student teaching that the higher level sixth grade students in her classroom were simply "going through the motions" of completing worksheets and getting grades without really learning anything.

> Those [workbook] activities were not challenging enough for [the advanced] group. I had them talk about what they were reading, what they interpreted the author's message to be, then to challenge each other on their interpretations. They really began to learn about what they were reading instead of filling in the blanks to guess what the workbook author thought they should learn!
>
> With the low group, though, I'm at a loss. They can't read the words well enough to do what the high group's doing, and I don't know how to help them. I need to learn more about working with slower readers before I can do a good job with them.

Leslie's task analysis not only showed sensitivity to children's learning, but showed her the direction her own learning needed to take.

To learn whether Leslie and the other "task aware" teachers took that awareness into their classrooms, I continued to follow, observe, and interview them, as described in earlier chapters of this text, into their 2nd, 3rd, 4th, 5th, and 6th years of teaching. The follow-up studies were part of my own task analyses. I learned that I had omitted attention to information in my course, which they saw as necessary for understanding and changing classroom practice especially in the urban environments, or hard-to-handle classrooms, to which beginning teachers were assigned, as well as understanding socialized or normative beliefs about teaching and learning that countered my suggestions, and the means of seeking continued education and support in those difficult beginning years.

I also found that I had taught them much more about research-based literacy content than they were able to process or remember. For example, about half of the teachers could not remember particular strategies I'd covered in class, even when provided with evidence from course transcripts and their own interviews that they had "learned" those particular strategies earlier. I also found, as Part I of this book made clear, that until the new teachers had an opportunity to talk about their basic concerns with social interaction and relationship issues, most of them (those employed in urban classrooms) were not able to attend well to the content of literacy, much less attend to what students were learning from that content.

PART III: RESPONSIBILITY AS FEMINIST EPISTEMOLOGY

The result of such analyses in relationship to these teachers led me to a new chapter in my career as a teacher–educator. It appeared that to enable teachers to overcome both the limitations of university course structures and the uncertainties they would face in their classrooms, and given the tremendous contextual influences to stabilize practice in schools, I would have to radically change my conceptual approach to their learning and my own practice. My new sense of responsibility as a teacher–educator moved into the philosophical and moral realms. I no longer saw value in encouraging teachers to make cognitive changes by learning what has worked for others. It was also clear that the teacher–students had questions and misperceptions that I could not coach or guide because of the institutional structure of separating course work from fieldwork. I wanted them to construct their own learning in action. Like Lisa's story in chapter 7 and Leslie's story in chapter 9, I hoped other teachers could also expand their ways of knowing about literacy instruction by first identifying the *learned and lived* paradigms for teaching and learning, then critiquing their own and others' ways of knowing.

To work toward those goals, I encouraged teachers in my classes to own and articulate their practical experience as valid knowledge. I started the process by giving examples of my own personal and experiential knowledge—although it was somewhat frightening and challenged my learned sense of what a teacher–educator "ought" to do. As I've tried to illustrate throughout this book, having experiential knowledge validated by external authority sources is not a common experience for many adult women—nor for elementary school teachers, male or female. It is less stressful to defer to established knowledge and practice. To comfort myself in the risk of self-authored knowledge as part of *my* teaching, I read scholarly works on women's epistemological and moral development (e.g., Belenky, Clinchy, Goldberger, & Tarule, 1986), feminist theory (e.g., Donovan, 1988; Flax, 1990), feminist methodology (e.g., Harding, 1987), and feminist pedagogy (e.g., Weiler, 1988)—works where other women academics risked new ways of knowing as well.

Of course, simply claiming our experiences as knowledge was not sufficient for learning to teach literacy to urban children. It required an understanding of the politics of knowledge—and the power of praxis or research in action to achieve social change. Thus, I invited teachers' practice-based experiences into our course, asked them to identify research questions within their practices, then had us collectively work on methods for analyzing and solving those questions. I encouraged teachers to develop a critical perspective of *teaching as research* described earlier through which they could *contain, evaluate, and create responsive literacy knowledge for particular schools and children from a perspective of social justice*. Given the politics of that perspective, I could not attach their praxis to alternative (and less political) concepts such as "reflection-in-action," "inquiry," or "practical argument," because of their relation to some higher-ranked and externally authored notion of "research."*

To learn to conduct classroom research, we suspended attention to established research programs and methodological procedures until we were clear about our own projects and questions, how those questions came from our own personal or lived theories of teaching and learning, how they varied from public or external theories, and how teaching could

---

*After reading this chapter, Mary wrote: "Ranking and teacher research is also a potential problem in my district. Some see teacher research as a way to 'move up' instead of a way to grow personally/professionally. I'd like to blame it on 'the university-sponsored' influence, but it's not. It's the need for hierarchy."

be viewed as research. In other words, I asked the teachers to make a commitment to stay "in the question(s)" that arose from their current life experiences (Van Maanen, 1990), rather than finding principled answers to generic questions from other experts' investigations. Because this approach was so different from their usual experience of school, I asked them to deconstruct, readjust and clarify their senses of education, teaching, research, and self in writing and conversation (Greene, 1988; Jagger, 1989; Lather, 1991).

This new understanding of instructional responsibility as a political as well as cognitive epistemology of practice, predictably caused me to change *my* teaching practices. I drew from what I'd learned in our conversational group to effect those changes. For example, I began to use aspects of the feminist pedagogy we had constructed—such as connected conversation, self-evaluation, continuous critique, shared agendas, and a valuing of specialized knowledge each of us brought to our relationships. I tried to recreate the commitment we had to the safety, challenge, and intimacy of conversation as a pedagogical tool to develop our autobiographies, our personal theories and interests in teaching and learning, and the course curriculum.

I've come to articulate those pedagogical processes through my own experiences as they are reflected in other feminist pedagogies in the literature. For example, like Liz Ellsworth (1989), I know firsthand about the difficulties of putting together an emancipatory curriculum. Like Sue Middleton (1993), I know the importance of writing my own life into my teaching. Therefore, I begin each class with discussions and assignments to tell each other who we are and why we think about school and teaching as we do. Because sharing ourselves with strangers is a tough business, I try to reduce the risk by allowing the shape of the autobiographical exploration and the portion made public to rest entirely with each teacher. I try to reconstruct "written assignments" prepared for an instructors' judgment to become a means for nonjudgmental reflection, sharing, and responding (see Natalie Goldberg's suggestions for writing as meditative practice, 1990). I want our writings to reflect our discoveries, changes, and rearrangements of power through reconstructed narratives (see Clandinin et al., 1993).

To address the issue of power pedagogically, I moved externally authored text to a secondary position in favor of actual projects in progress and set up a loose framework for topical discussions about teaching as research. I strongly encourage ownership of knowledge and theory or voice by minimizing the risk of failure. I also try to remove myself from the position of ultimate authority by inviting the class to help establish the agenda, to decide the mode of evaluation we will use, and to make myself and my ideas open to challenge. In Kathleen Weiler's (1988) words, I try to reconstruct "course instructor" as participatory and self-critical. In an effort to further remove attention to what research questions or procedures I might favorably evaluate, and thus achieve the desired outcome of epistemological ownership and change, I encourage teachers to self-evaluate their learning.

Finally, I do not distance myself from their learning. By talking with the classes about my life experiences and the changes I've been through, I attempt to model both the exhilaration and the pain and discomfort that come with changes in our perceptions and our actions (Jersild, 1955). I also want to share with them what I had learned and was learning. In other words, *I* still had expert knowledge about literacy that I wanted them to "know"—or at least consider—as I did when I thought of my responsibility as content coverage. The difference now is that I could see that each of my students had valuable forms of knowledge that I had shut out when I considered my university colleagues and myself the only experts (see Table 11.1 for an overview of this feminist pedagogical approach).

Analyses of this process using a constant comparative approach showed that most of the teachers enrolled learned to identify specific problems in changing classroom practice that came from previously unvoiced ways-of-knowing, developed methods to collect information leading to a resolution, experimented with their findings, and reported the outcomes to the class. An example of this process inside course work was presented earlier in chapter 7, with Lisa's research on classroom management. The problems and questions did not always directly involve the *content* of literacy instruction, as we have seen in this book. Sometimes there were more pressing problems requiring attention before teachers could then focus attention on literacy instruction and learning. Reflecting real practice dilemmas, teachers' studies most often involved looking closely at relationships with children (which is what I had wanted of previous classes) but also involved identifying, analyzing, and developing responses to other school-based obstacles that caused them to uncritically adopt established classroom practices (matching the public or dominant paradigm in vogue), regardless of the needs of children.

WHAT I LEARNED AS A TEACHER–EDUCATOR: SOME SUMMARIZING THOUGHTS

At this point, I'd like to step out of the narrative and attempt to summarize what I've learned. The themes noted here refer to cross-case and

TABLE 11.1

An Overview of Feminist Pedagogies

Feminist pedagogies involve both political and epistemological
critiques of knowledge. They:

- Challenge academically dualistic divisions of knowers and who/what is known, subjectivity and objectivity, expert/novice, science and nature. (Harding, 1990; Reinharz, 1992)
- Assume that knowledge is born in the relation of praxis. (Stanley, 1990)
- Are standpoints (lived), not perspectives (learned). (Hartsock, 1987; Smith, 1990)

  Such views of facilitating research designs for courses in research for
  teachers are "feminist" because they:

- Ask questions which lead to social changes in women's (and, in relative definition, men's) lived experiences and political struggles which had been previously considered unproblematic. (Nielson, 1990)
- Acknowledge that teaching is a "woman's profession" in the broad sense—both male and female teachers in the U. S. are socially situated in workplaces where relations between teachers and students are underpowered when compared to the power of others who distance themselves from students and stand in authority over teachers. (Apple, 1985)
- Develop through dialectical tension (Westkott, 1979) between women's concrete experiences in patriarchal values.

- Validate and include both cognition and rationality as epistemological frames, and also value emotion, intuitive leaps, and other less verbal feelings are traditionally and problematically associated with (and devalued as) "women's" learning. (Gilligan, 1982; Noddings, 1984)

  The features of feminist pedagogy I came to develop in my courses:

- A place for literacy as nonjudgmental reflection, sharing, and responding, where we can celebrate our discoveries, changes, and rearrangements of power through reconstructed narratives. (Clandinin et al., 1993; Goldberg, 1990; Middleton, 1993)
- A commitment to the safety, challenge and intimacy of conversation as a pedagogical tool to develop our autobiographies, our personal theories, and interests in teaching and learning, and the course curriculum. (Hollingsworth, 1992)
- A view of curriculum defined "within students' and teachers' biographical, historical, and social situations that they bring to the classroom, as well as within the relational classroom experiences that they share with texts, with education structures, and with one another." (Miller, 1990)
- Working to reconstruct "course instructor" as participatory and self-critical. (Weiler, 1988)
- A deconstruction, readjustment, and clarification of new (and temporary) knowledge standpoints based upon both personal and external information. (Greene, 1988; Jaggar, 1989; Lather, 1990)
- A commitment to staying "in the question" rather than finding principled answers. (Van Maanen, 1991)
- An acknowledgment of the pain and discomfort that come with changes in our perceptions and our actions. (Jersild, 1955)

cross-class analyses completed across the years of my research on my classroom practices.

Classroom Boundaries as Influences on Pedagogy

My initial sense of responsibility involved passing along what I knew from the experts to novices. The perspective was one of a professional duty or obligation—backed by positivistic arguments for information processing and the culture of my graduate education in educational psychology. The goals for my instruction, bounded by the classroom walls, were straightforward and easily met: "Learn what I know." As long as I was sure of what I knew, that pedagogical stance was sufficient.

When the boundaries of my literacy course broadened to include children, and I could "see" that some of my theoretical assertions weren't holding in urban schools, I became less certain about my knowledge. My standpoint changed, I could no longer meaningfully employ a single paradigm as the basis for my teaching, nor for evaluating other teachers' learning. Using the best expert knowledge of literacy theory and instruction was also insufficient to counteract my own pedagogical limitations and the full range of constraints against changing instructional norms that teachers found on the job.

Self-Knowledge

Continuing to research and change my teaching created conflict about the appropriate role for myself as teacher. The changes I made were more than intellectual exercises. Both shifts in instructional study designs and interpretations came about because of a quest for meaning in my own life. For example, only when I realized my own need for connections and responsiveness in my personal life as a feminist scholar and the institutional constraints on my own teaching practices, was I able to see the appropriateness of that role in my teaching and make a paradigm shift.

Teachers, too, needed to give voice to the role conflicts between internalized goals for care, connection, and inclusion and externalized expectations to be subject matter experts, rational disciplinarians, and dispassionate evaluators. With such self-knowledge as instructional content, these beginning teachers were able to tap deeply submerged beliefs about their roles, then naturally (but not easily) modify established classroom practices. The result was not only an ability to challenge standardized expectations that did not seem appropriate for particular children or teachers, but a better balance of internal and external expectations as well.

Beyond a Disciplinary Focus

As I examined the transfer of knowledge from the literacy course to the classroom, I learned that the preservice teachers couldn't assimilate and really didn't use all the disciplinary knowledge I tried to teach them early in my story as a teacher–educator. Systematic analyses of the data showed that they required more guided practice than I provided to learn new literacy content and strategies. Evidence from postcourse stories showed that new teachers also required more opportunities to discuss and critique the existing literacy strategies and activities they were seeing as standard classroom practice. As this book has made clear, it wasn't enough to present research-based alternatives for fixed groups and prepackaged commercial instruction, for example. To critique and change existing practice, it was necessary to talk about standard practices with reference to personal experiences.

These new teachers came to understand values, caring, and relational interactions as content. Although I failed to address those issues in course work, they consistently came up as important topics of concern after teachers were on the job. Though not the only essential feature of learning to teach, coming to terms with relational issues was critical if teachers were to remain in the classroom, let alone change existing practices.

The Need for Alternative Evaluation Methods

To gain the depth of understanding necessary to acquire self-knowledge and effectively teach children, these teachers seemed to profit from the freedom from evaluation of what *I* knew as content knowledge. To obtain a good grade, preservice teachers in my early course designs often gave *my* knowledge back to me but failed to struggle with their own. I had to collect both privately held or lived evaluative knowledge as well as that more publicly displayed to evaluate their learning accurately. Again, modeling from the process developed within the collaborative group which DID change classroom practices (and where I had no evaluative power), I gave students in my classes opportunities to articulate and compare their own grounded beliefs as inservice teachers, to create their own knowledges, critique that of others, and to evaluate their own growth.

The Reality of Resistance as Perspectives Change

Asking new teachers to look inward to understand and critique external data caused much discomfort and confusion. In the preservice classes of which the teachers in this book were a part, resistance to critical thought was often heavy. Many student-teachers wanted to focus on rehearsing and learning reading strategies. Their requests were not unreasonable given that they *did* need activities to teach.

As the research assistants helped me to see, I actually set up a climate for resistance which I established in my single-minded and oppositional attempts. I wanted them to attend to students and remained fixed on that goal. I'd forgotten my earlier study findings that new teachers seem to first attend to issues of management and subject (because of the immediacy of their job requirements), and only when those domains were integrated and became routine did they shift attention to children. Later, as I began to understand the conflict between my "expected" instructional role and my unvoiced values of caring and connection, I came to see that I needed to take their concerns into account. I began to both understand and model how to make authentic connections in the evolving relationships with my students. Then I was able to lead them into the world of discovery and research in a less forceful way.

However, because of the authenticity of our relationships, resistance and discomfort is still often present in my classrooms, as it is in our out-of-classroom contexts. We are different people with differing values, backgrounds, and practical settings. But our teaching–research conversations—based on principles of care and response that shape my interpretation of feminist pedagogy for educators and incorporate critical consideration of expert knowledge from differing epistemological perspectives—eventually provided most of us with both the safety and the challenges needed to interrupt less socially aware classroom practices.* With these teachers, I'm becoming less resistant to seeing how we might significantly impact the history of classroom practice.

ENDNOTES

[1] My son, Jon Christopher Hollingsworth, a loving, energetic, and gifted child before entering school (he transformed his simple record player into a stereo, for example), was diagnosed "learning disabled," placed in special education, and struggled with literacy instruction. He was so badly judged and mistreated educationally that he left school by 10th grade. Today, he's happily integrating literacy, math, and science in a passion for piloting aircrafts.

---

*Lisa: "What a wonderful paradox—I agree!"

12

Educating Teacher–Educators

THE NEXT STORY TO BE TOLD

This culminating chapter of this book demonstrates both the promises and difficulties of trying to incorporate the ideas of sustained conversation, relational knowing, and ongoing research or critique as a feminist pedagogy into course work for teacher–educators. The chapter describes my attempts to construct a course called "Research in Teacher Education" in collaboration with teachers and teacher–educators who were graduate students at the University of California at Berkeley. I predicated the course on the theoretical elements of a feminist pedagogy that developed, for me, from teacher research—my own and that of the teachers in our conversational group.

As I hope examples across this text have made clear, my study of learning to teach taught me that teachers need personal and political knowledge as well as disciplinary knowledge to teach literacy in urban classrooms. Yet, it seems they are denied access to that knowledge in many programs of teacher education. It occurred to me that perhaps that phenomena had to do with the preparation (or lack thereof) of teacher–educators. Perhaps teacher–educators, like many teachers themselves, didn't know that teachers, as a class, work under less-than-professional conditions with increasingly complex demands for academic, social, and psychological expertise in demographically diverse settings. Yet teachers are often asked to conform to a narrow set of ideological standards that denies this diversity and shapes their reflections. These standards—stated as credentialing requirements, teacher and student evaluation measurements, curricular mandates, and even appropriate research paradigms for advanced degree work—have been historically established by people outside the classroom in positions of power (mainly men) without benefit of teachers' voices and opinions (mainly women) (see Apple, 1985). Let me say more about my reading of "the way it is" for teachers in the United States, and "the way it was for me" as a teacher and teacher–educator, before moving into experiments of "rewriting reality" and "the ways it could become" for future teacher–educators.

A BRIEF HISTORY OF THE "REALITY" OF AMERICAN EDUCATION

American education, developed as an industrial model dividing management and labor, places both male and female teachers (as a class) in the position of "other" where "one's existence is necessarily outside of and apart from the public flow of discourse and meaning" (de Beauvoir, 1952, p. xvi–xxix). In other words, the majority of teachers and administrators who support the management/labor distinction becomes the "us," the "normal," the "neutral," the "good guys." Those holding minority views (e.g., teachers and administrators favoring equalized power) are categorized as "the other." Of course teachers can and do accept their places as labor under managerial authority, and "strike" to get their voices heard.

But the problem begins much earlier than the entrance into the job "market." Teachers are currently educated in institutions of higher education where ways of knowing, valuing, and being that are traditionally and problematically associated with masculinization (the powered majority) are often devalued (Martin, 1981). "The 'male epistemological stance' becomes everybody's stance" (Brittan and Maynard, 1984, p. 204). The gendered positioning of teachers as "other" becomes an issue for feminist critique. Glorianne Leck tells us:

> Of central importance in the feminist critique is the examination of the primary assumption of patriarchy—that activities of male persons are of a higher value than activities of female persons. This precept is woven into the entire intellectual paradigm that is foundational to current schooling practice. For this reason the feminist critique orders a challenge to the epistemological roots of educational theory as we know it. (Leck, 1987, p. 343)

The narrowly cast paradigm to which teachers must conform is not new. Jurgen Herbst tells us that, since the beginning of the early nineteenth century, Prussian-inspired movement to educate teachers in the United States, school reform standards have moved in the direction of a "science of education" in order to create a respectable, permanent, career profession for "white men" (Herbst, 1989, p.183), and away from the temporary, female workforce, where "teaching children . . . was a female occupation par excellence" (Herbst, 1989, p. 27).

The amazing feature of this situation is that, having existed in the fabric of this "norm" for so long, many teachers—even at the elementary school level—do not realize the political and epistemological implications of their own social position. As we have seen in this book, teachers are placed in positions of compliance with a narrow set of decontextualized and polarized educational standards that, taken without challenge, devalue many of their own standards and limit their opportunities to know and critique the institution of education in which they work. This position of *compliant reflection* can lead to accepting such notions as: (1) logic-based analyses have more validity than intuition-based analyses, (2) math and science, as subjects of study, have more value than rhetoric and art, (3) teachers who raise test scores are "effective," while those who do not are "ineffective," (4) students who score higher on standardized tests are "smarter" than those who score lower, (5) pedagogically, content coverage is better (for meeting standardized test goals) than content depth, and (6) affective learning is less valuable than cognitive learning.* Compliant reflection with such simplistically banded and polarized ways of teaching leads to analyzing and answering questions in fairly predictable ways, not posing new questions and developing new solutions. That might be a reason that new approaches to teaching urban children are so difficult to imagine and sustain.

Teachers who sense that broad and encompassing ways of knowing and acting are valid and necessary for reflecting on their work with these children—those, like me, who take issue with more narrowly cast public or professional standards—might sometimes engage in *dissonant reflection*. Remember how Mary reexamined the issue of student evaluation when a student's grandmother came to protest the standard system? Reflection on the distance between public expectations and private understandings causes a clash of frames—and, creating discomfort and even social rejection, is often avoided. Yet acknowledging the tension also creates the potential for change.

It occurred to Jennifer and the others in our conversational group that if teacher–educators were prepared to engage in dissonant reflection (NOT Jennifer's words) about their practices, then teachers with whom they work might also. In the last chapter, I talked about changes in my course work

---

* This passage received many enthusiastic endorsements from our group: Mary: "I like it." Leslie: "Wonderful! Yeah! The Truth!" Jennifer: "Did you make this up your own self?"

for teachers to notice and reconstruct compliant frameworks for reflection, based on my coming to understand that teaching school was a feminist issue. This chapter describes how I am attempting to translate that perspective into a course for teacher–educators. My pedagogical perspective is grounded here, as it was in my work with young adults in chapter 8 and with teachers in chapter 11, both in my own autobiographical experiences and in participatory study as a learner with those I teach. My experiences led me to view the process of teacher education course work as epistemic *re-search*—a process of formulating new theoretical frameworks for reflecting and knowing from an interaction of socially and politically authored norms and the personal experiences and values that underscore teaching practices. I'll talk briefly through two instances of transformation in this work: through a reflective autobiography of my own evolution as a teacher and with a critical look at variations in reflective stances and the process of change within and beyond a course for teacher–educators.

A Brief History of My Own Reflective Frameworks

I was a product of the sixties—a time of socially sensitive reflection. Attending high school in a one-school town deep within east Texas, I don't remember most of what I read in class, but I do recall experiences that directed my reflection. Outside class, I wrote poems, stories, and editorials about oppression in the African-American community. The first light of my own personal oppression came from reading such books as Simone de Beauvoir's *The Second Sex* (de Beauvoir, 1952). I was so impressed with her experiential/existential framework for reflecting upon life as a woman that I not only took her words into my own life, I gave the book to my mother. Both my mother and de Beauvoir convinced me that I could move beyond the second class status assigned to women with enough determination, struggle, and support. My sense of the path to equality, at that point, was to reject association with "women's work" and take up concerns that were more associated with "men's territory." Therefore home economics, as a course of study, was out—and mathematics was in. Without much practice at acknowledging the validity of my own experience, I felt I had to reject things associated with women in favor of more publicly valued experiences. Determining which of the many possible experiences I wanted for *myself* in the many different ways I see myself—including woman—was not yet part of my way of being.

However, taking the first steps in action on my feminist path, with my mom at my side, I marched into the school counselor's office to protest his barring me from advanced mathematics because "girls never need that level of math." Neither of our arguments—not even mine based on my emerging feminist consciousness—could sway him. I was doomed instead to some home-economics classes where (for lack of purposeful intent) I failed sewing. While I viewed my action to fail as protest, what I didn't notice was my unwitting compliance with a framework for constructing or reflecting on my own life that devalued it. In other words, to join the boys (and be seen as valuable as they were), I thought I had to reject interests and skills that publicly had less merit. Even though I married, enjoyed the company of two unique and special children, and came to enjoy sewing for my family, the gravitational pull toward publicly valued standards led me blindly through college math, statistics, objectively based research, and a PhD before my feminist consciousness came of age. I did come to enjoy mathematical thinking and the privilege that came with it, and had an opportunity to return to a high school reunion and tell the counselor that I *did* need advanced levels of mathematics in my work—and other women would as well. Regardless of my mathematical competence, however, I also longed for a way to reclaim the early poetic voice in my work, for nurturing in professional relationships, and for the full circle of possibilities I could claim as a woman in academia. I began to critique and revise my own reflective frame.

The changes haven't been easy. On my worst days, I wish that my life had been such that I would have been content to close my eyes to the struggle for urban literacy education. I've had to learn how to risk bringing my personal and holistic ways of understanding the world back into my writing and research—while, at the same time, hoping that my changing voices will be received and heard in the traditional academic press which tends to be impersonal and particularistic. I've come to understand that my immersion into the linear world of mathematics, statistics, and experimental research so highly valued in education, while ensuring me the safety of survival in a slow-to-change academic climate, was not fully my own choice. When I rebelled against the traditional mode of publish or perish, I was told to "Relax. There'll be a time and a place for your own voice. Joining the positivist club is simply a temporary passage to the other side of tenure." But I had seen too many of my colleagues never recover their own voices, and become marginalized even after tenure because of different ways of viewing the world (see Ford-Slack, 1993). And even if I believed that, it was too late. Because I had come to see the world in other terms, it felt intellectually dishonest to "join the club." The only choice that seemed to be immediately available was to trust that I could follow my own path and still survive. As I came to know the full range of possibilities from remembering other times of risk and survival throughout my life, I discovered the choices within those possibilities. I began to let go of the pursuit of the narrow social and epistemic framework that directed my actions and embark on another as yet undefined. I began to fight the tendency NOT to notice when my private values and reflections become suppressed in favor of more publicly valued ways of knowing. I began to clarify the issues, stances, and activities that were personally meaningful in my life. I began to understand my academic work from feminist perspectives.

As I've mentioned before, I knew the hard work of articulating and valuing both public and private reflections with my female undergraduate students in the South. When I took a position as a graduate-level teacher–educator at a research university on the West Coast, I assumed that my teacher–students would be very worldly, California progressive, broadly reflective, and continuously critical. I found them to *be* reflective and critical of the world, but—in the graduate academic world—often not willing to fully embrace either the problem or the potential of teaching as "women's work." Critical of their own limited opportunities, many were simply moving up within a linear system that often devalued them. Seeking administrative positions or other more powerful posts traditionally assigned to males, they could then become valued and better paid. They were following the same compliant reflective path that *I* had traveled.

As a feminist educator, I wanted to encourage both male and female teachers to see the range of possibilities and articulate the value of both administrative opportunities external to the classroom *and* alternative opportunities within it. I wanted to prepare them to reflect on the structural constraints of schooling that often limited possibilities for critical thinking, analytic discourse, and alternative modes of knowing (see Weiler, 1988). I wanted them to join with other like-minded teachers to create the space to articulate and expand notions of their own power, their own values, their own dreams and intuitions that too often were devalued in the educational system. Three legs of my journey were reported in chapter 11: changes in my research procedures; observing teachers' research; and changing my course work for teachers. This chapter looks at course work to emancipate future teacher–educators' frameworks for reflection, so that they might carry on this work with their own students.

RE-WRITING "REALITY": A NEW STORY FOR TEACHER–EDUCATORS

In designing a new course for potential and practicing teacher–educators to survey "research on teacher education," I wanted to apply the liberating principles of sustained conversation and ongoing research or critique as a feminist pedagogy while we read and discussed the literature on teacher preparation. I hoped to create a pedagogical atmosphere that would facilitate the articulation and broadening of socialized and epistemic frames for learning to teach. To do so, I wanted to reject standard evaluation schemes where the course leader judged the learning of the others, and to adopt a model of self-evaluation. Therefore, I thought it best to involve teacher-education doctoral students from the outset. To better understand the process of developing the course and the occasions for learning within it, one member of the class, Theodora Maestre, and I agreed to listen to tape-recorded transcriptions of the classes, review course papers, and write to each other about the important issues and processes that would emerge.

As we were planning for the new semester-long course, Thea and I realized that, although we would recommend a wide set of readings about research on teacher education, our pedagogical handling of those readings would involve a departure from more traditional views of the text as curriculum. We would not give text the authority over our own personal senses of authority. Our reading would be more aligned with a view of curriculum that Janet Miller expresses.

> [There are limitations to] the dominant conception of curriculum as course of study, as product, as text to be covered, and ends to be achieved and measured. I know that these conceptions are part of what constitute working definitions of curriculum especially for teachers and administrators in schools. However, . . . my work is aligned with those who view curriculum as also defined within students' and teachers' biographical, historical, and social situations that they bring to the classroom as well as within the relational classroom experiences that they share with texts, with education structures, and with one another. (Miller, 1990, p. 11)

To critique the existing literature on teacher education from biographical, social, political, and relational stances, Thea and I polled potential members of this course, then pulled together a body of readings around topics that had personal meaning for them: historical, contextual, and structural analyses of teacher education; an examination of reflection, knowledge, and power; a feminist critique of teaching and teacher education; contextual issues in learning from experience, including socialization, apprenticeship, and divergent experience; questions about the "knowledge base" in teaching; and a critical analysis of the national reform efforts. We chose some of the readings written by the teachers in our conversational group.

The 16 of us in the semester-long class—either teacher–educators or were preparing to be—found the readings to have some common personal meanings because of our related life experiences. All of us were women. All but one class member had school teaching experience.[1] At the same time, the readings meant different things to all of us because of our varied life experiences. Thea and I asked teachers with expertise or interest in the various topical areas to research, structure, and lead the class in critical conversation around the topics. Therefore, we all became coteachers in the course. We also encouraged the teachers to reflect on the readings from their personal experiences: to integrate self and text. We found that task, new to many of us, to be difficult but important. Thea wrote to me:

> The [teachers' personal] tie-in to the articles was being made more implicitly by everyone, than explicitly. . . . I think in some ways the whole course itself might be about making that connection between the personal and collective knowledge more explicit.

To facilitate such a connection, we asked the teachers to articulate their own teaching autobiographies in an attempt to situate teaching as "women's work." They took turns at the beginning of each class telling some of their own learning-to-teach stories. Pat Gallagher, a practicing teacher–educator taking this class as part of her doctoral work, reflected on the nature of our course, contrasting it with her usual experience in university course work:

> A "course" usually implies a predetermined path with obstacles chosen to exercise the student's capacity in a desirable direction. It implies further a competition to see who can meet the challenges with the most ease. This belief was made acutely apparent to me during a university course in which the male professor said that in graduate school the hurdles were kept in a fog so that the students don't know how high they are. As a result students stretch and strain so that when they are asked to demonstrate their knowledge in a formal examination they will likely clear the hurdles with ease. Contrast that model with the [current] course in which we made a collective effort to know ourselves and to teach each other.
>
> In Sam's course I began to see how my biography—my self—had formed my conceptions and reflections. It mattered, in my work with teachers: that I had gone to a high school for girls and a college for women; that I had not been formally "trained" as a teacher; that I grew up among immigrants and first generation Americans; that I had lived in the west, the northwest, the midwest, the northeast of the United States as well as in England; that I had married a foreigner and lived between two cultures; that I am the mother of three sons. These elements of my biography have shaped the teacher and teacher–educator I have become.

In addition to giving voice to our lives and forming connections among them, I wanted to construct a feminist critique of education by examining our personal experiences in relationship to an article on teaching as a stimulus for our conversation. Susan Laird (1988) had argued that the gender-neutral proposals of major reform papers neither acknowledged nor examined critically the traditional conception of school teaching as "woman's true profession." She analyzed the contradictory and ambiguous theses represented in the slogan.

> To take "woman's true profession" seriously at last and begin this immense critical project of reconceptualization, I urge the importance of philosophical inquiry concerning the meaning of feminist pedagogy, its implicit challenge to the dominant and so-called gender-neutral concept of teaching that the Holmes Group and the Carnegie Forum do not challenge, and the as yet unimagined practical possibilities it may suggest for actually educating—not simply training—schoolteachers. (Laird, 1988, p. 463)

Thea recalled how this process involved our whole selves in reflection, not just our minds.

> [In addition to] reading Susan Laird's article exploring layers within the meaning of the term "feminist," each person created a visual collage in response to the prompt "What is 'woman's true profession'?" The discussion that followed was personal, passionate, reflective, analytical: engaging at many levels. The inclusion of seemingly paradoxical meanings became evident in class responses. We could respond as whole human beings, with our visions, shadows, and contradictions.

In contrast to the meaning we might have assigned their engagement in the task, most teachers in our class had a hard time relating to the problematic thesis of teaching as a "woman's profession" as presented in the article. Because we consciously made a space for the teachers to talk about both how the text did *not* relate to their experiences, as well as the ways that it *did*, we learned that private reflections are not always compliant with the "liberating" framework I had established. For example, these teachers' personal experiences as women in the teaching profession, for the most part, were positive enough that they did not see such a strong need for feminist pedagogy. Most teaching members of our group, for example, were working mothers who appreciated the convenient schedule of teaching for raising a family. Most felt they had been treated as professionals while teaching school and did not experience the moral and political alienation as "women" expressed by Laird. One African-American teacher in our group could not connect with the problematic depiction of

teaching as a woman's issue, nor with Laird's understanding of the term
"feminist."

> I worked with the ministry of women's affairs in Grenada and we
> made strong statements about the rights of women in the society, but
> we didn't identify ourselves as feminists because we didn't see our-
> selves as separate from men. A major struggle for me now is the prob-
> lem of young black boys in the schools. That's a major concern. The
> boys are being destroyed. There are no black men. They are identified
> as an endangered species. We start losing them in the fourth grade.

Another member of our group, currently comfortable with quantita-
tive analyses in her doctoral work, took exception to what she perceived as
a good/bad perspective in the Laird article. "I had some problems with this
article because she made me feel really split. She used 'good' words that
were kind of feminine: nurturing, peaceful, that kind of thing. And then the
bad side: logical, analytic, reason before love, ambition, accomplishment."
Karen Teel, who was attending this class at the same time she and I
were meeting with our conversational group, replied in words that resonated with her earlier comments in this book on the topic:

> After reading Laird's article, I found I did not relate to it at all, in
> terms of the theses that underlie the whole thing—like that [teaching
> is] demeaning because it's woman's work. I just didn't resonate with
> that at all. I guess as a teacher, I never thought of myself as a woman.
> I thought of myself as a human being who had a real interest in kids
> and learning. I always felt respected and treated very professionally by
> men and women. The only [feminist issue] I can connect to is the pay
> difference. I don't think differential pay for "men's jobs" and
> "women's jobs" is right at all.

Broadening Our Reflections

Though their experiences did not allow all class members to identify with
a feminist critique of education, the same conversational process supported a broadening of reflective ways of framing the issue. Thea, for
example, reflected on the conversation in reference to her own daughter as
she wrote to me. Her comments go beyond the commonly experienced
issue of low pay for teaching professionals, to a critical analysis of how we
might broaden our socialized frames for reflecting on this issue.

> I certainly related personally to [the conversation]. My daughter has
> just taken a job in a preschool. She is good, sensitive, organized, nur-

turing and so on . . . and is getting low pay (and is happy to be working at all!) I'm glad for her, that she has a job, wouldn't invalidate where she is, and yet I hold the vision of preschool teachers being paid what they deserve. I think that the recognition of this contradiction will be one of the ways of gaining some sort of power of consciousness perhaps. . . . However, if we have not experienced the lack of respect, but have felt a strong sense of self and so on, [teaching as a "woman's profession"] may not seem problematic. The issue I think is that we need to hold both the truths of our own efficacy along with the visions of what can be. And this is the difficult part. Acknowledging our light and dark, our shadows and vision, and so on.

Thea's daughter experience a "maxim" of our society: the closer one's work is to children, the less valuable that work (and the worker) become. The more distant from children (e.g., administration, teacher–educator), the more prestige the work (and the worker) earn.

Two teachers in our group *did* recall devaluing experiences as schoolteachers in inner-city schools that helped them resonate more with the arguments made. One talked about the top–down evaluation of teachers in her school by those with more power. Another spoke of a form of censorship imposed on her development of students' writing. For some other teachers, the historical casting of teaching as a "woman's profession" brought up anger and frustration as well as celebrations. One brought a visual display of the article as a "nine patch quilt and nine issues which were interesting." One patch depicted a teacher with a bag over her head. Another showed pictures of girls in elementary classrooms. "That's really an issue for me. I always worry about the girls in my class. I had myself videotaped once and realized that I wasn't asking the girls higher-level thinking questions."

Broadening My Reflections

In each issue presented for discussion, we found similar variations in teachers' experiences and in their willingness to problematically position teaching as a "woman's profession." The fact that I clearly wanted them to broaden their reflections in that direction, however, *did* become problematic. One teacher wrote to me:

I just feel real uncomfortable. I'm not sure that our different perspectives are really accepted by you and some voices over here. And I want to be accepted where I am now and not pushed to be over there. I sort of get this hidden message like, "We [women] have come a long way and this is where it's at."

I heard that critique and others, and though I did not drop my valuing of examining the issues in teacher education from feminist standpoints, I did acknowledge the variations in those standpoints. I still had a commitment to an attitude for social equity in education—which seemed to involve not just the cognitive knowledge, but personal acknowledgment of social inequities as well. However, the teachers convinced me that we might also need to reflect more broadly than just on our own experiences to develop such attitudes. In each class session, for example, there was an expression of disappointment by at least one class member that we did not discuss the articles more thoroughly to gain the author's perspective, and that I didn't give the class an overview of my own perspectives on the issue at the outset. In my eagerness to have teachers create and critique their own knowledge, I had intentionally not promoted discussion of externally authored perspectives on the issues before they could articulate their own. However, the teachers taught me that such a stringent position was not helpful.

Inviting teacher–educators from outside our group to join our conversation was one way we promoted a balanced conversation. For example, the group and I found particularly refreshing Anna Richert's guest presentation about using case methods for reflection (see more of her perspectives in Richert, 1992). That she valued the opportunity to get out of the "mire of one's own experience," and reflect on the issues in an abstracted sense helped us achieve the balance between personal and external authority that we needed. Rather than relying primarily on our own autobiographical experiences, Anna gave us another means of making better connections with the literature on teacher education—including the Laird article.

Since there were no men in the class to talk about their experiences, experiments with these ideas outside class became still another means to understanding the issue of teaching from gendered perspectives. The teacher who earlier complained that I devalued her perspective, for example, performed an experiment to reflect on her current position. She invited a group of male teacher–educators to dinner to discuss their perspectives on male/female differences within their current groups of students. Surprised to learn that they did not expect any serious work from their women students, she came back to class to tell us that: "I thought I had put the 'feminist issue' to rest long ago. I guess I've got more work to do."

In Thea's extended conversations outside the class, participants reported a need to pull out of their own experience and look at issues from external theoretical perspectives, and to talk together extensively about them—a process our conversational group endorsed for our learning.

Some members of the class formed a separate study group to discuss the course readings in more depth.

In short, changes in my reflective framework in the course led me to reconstruct a better balance between autobiographical reflections and externally authored reflections. Eventually many class members came to understand and even internalize part of the personal, complex, critical, and action-oriented position on teaching—though most still would never define it as "feminist." For example, the balance of one's own and others' experiences was reflected in Pat's discussion with Thea on what she was coming to understand as a "critical perspective." Though Pat didn't adopt MY framing of a "feminist perspective," her choice of framing for her work as a teacher–educator clearly reflected a similar social attitude. In the conversation, she talked about what she was learning from some of the course readings in terms of her evolving personal position on teacher education.

> PAT: As I understand [Ken] Zeichner's (Zeichner and Gore, 1990)
> perspective that . . . as opposed to getting people ready to
> enter a system that is somewhat static and perhaps the best possi-
> ble approach could be . . . to ask questions why are we doing
> what we're doing. What is it all about? What is the institution for?
> What is my part in it? How is who I am reflected in what I do,
> think, believe, feel, act. How is my discourse reflective of who I
> am of my own social class of . . . you know, the activities that I
> conduct in the classroom, to what extent am I working to really
> assist my students and help them assist children to become critical
> thinkers, you know, and what are the consequences of that?
> THEA: Is a vision important to a critical perspective?
> PAT: Yes, it seems to be what Maxine Greene (1979) talks about in
> naming the obstacles to claiming teaching as personal reality. No
> obstacles appear unless there is a vision of what's beyond them.

Pat later reflected positively upon the influence of the liberating experience of this "course" in a presentation to AACTE (the American Association of Colleges of Teacher–Educators) (Hollingsworth, Gallagher, Maestre, Richert, & Sockett, 1992).

What began as a seminar to explore the research in teacher education became a collective effort to know ourselves and to teach each other, even as we ourselves were in the process of guiding novice teachers in their learning to teach children. Although SCS 289B [Research in Teacher Education] ended on May 1, 1990, the "course" continues in the work of us who are here today and in the lives and work of the other participants.

To have the opportunity to come together with others whose life work is to enhance the development of teachers and engage in the construction of knowledge was transforming and emancipatory. Letting go of my conceptions of the "official" occupational role of teacher–educator, I was able to move from a notion of myself as intermediary between the knowledge base and the novice teacher to an appreciation for the power of biography and the function of the self in teaching and learning to teach . . . (see Gallagher, 1992).

A feature of the "course" that distinguished it from others is that the effects on the individual participants could only be known through time. Traditional means of evaluating student learning did not apply. Transformed practices evolved. We did not learn about teacher education in such a way as to produce a single project, paper, or document reflective of our understanding of the literature we encountered. However, we did generate the beginnings of what has come to be a continuing investigation into our own practices.

I have incorporated opportunities for students to "tell their stories" so that we may better understand each other. In the course I now teach, *The Teaching of Reading-Language Arts and Social Studies,* I begin by asking the students to consider the question, "What does it mean to be literate?" In the course of two sessions the students come to see that their responses are very much determined by who they are and where they have been. . . . I have found myself increasingly attuned to the still, small voices under the academic discourse; the awakenings of self-discovery and emerging truths.

It appears that many of us [from the teacher education course] are weaving questions about equity, gender, biography, politics into our work with prospective teachers. We have formed alliances beyond the course, the school, the university, and are currently engaged in some exciting collective work on the development and use of cases in teacher education.

As Pat noted, the experience did not end with the course. She and Thea also joined with a group of 10 teacher–educators from four different colleges and universities in Northern California to form the "Teacher Education Research Group." Thea told the audience at AACTE:

We read each other's papers, conducted mock orals for each other, and continued to read research articles of interest. Out of this group grew an idea for a larger meeting. We planned an event which focused on a topic of mutual interest: Teacher Stories and Cases. We held our first meeting at Mills College and called it "Collaborative Conversation." We invited teacher–educators and teacher education researchers from around the San Francisco Bay Area. Since that time, our group has grown to about 40, and we're preparing for our third meeting at Far West Regional Laboratories. The evolution of this group can be linked to the ideas inherent in feminist pedagogy.*

CONCLUDING THOUGHTS ON "THE WAYS IT COULD BE"

In listening to the report of these experiences at AACTE, over 2 years after the course had officially ended, Anna Richert suggested that the evidence of lasting transformation in these teacher–educator's reflective frames rested in: (1) *expressed feelings* of transformation, including confidence that continued to grow beyond the course boundaries; (2) a realization of the importance of self in epistemological development; (3) a realization of the importance of "others" to clarify and construct knowledge; (4) the generation of an inquiry stance that continued to be transformative after the course ended and resulted in new critical themes and a view of the knowledge of teaching as problematic; (5) and, finally, a spirit of community and lasting alliance to support both personal and professional growth (Richert, 1991). What I've learned from Anna, Thea, Pat, and, indeed, from all our collectives stories up to this point has changed my own framework for constructing a feminist pedagogy. It currently reflects differently positioned experiences not only in terms of gender, but in relationship to race, class, sexuality, religion, and many other intersecting and colliding identities that may affect our opportunities to learn to teach.

Standing on their own merits, these storied examples have illuminated the processes of facilitating change in reflective frameworks for me. So I'll end this evolving narrative with some thoughts for educators who would like to construct pedagogies to enable teachers to become conscious and critical of their own values, of their own and others' research frameworks, and to develop social attitudes that can be transformed into action.

---

* Reviewing this passage, Thea clarified her statement: "'Feminist pedagogy' is meant to be read 'as we each interpret it through our experiences.' My own grounding also includes experiential learning, Jungian thought, the practice of yoga, and the narrations of 24 years or so being an elementary teacher."

Come Into Course Experiences as Learners as Well as Leaders

Without a sense of shared vulnerability, risking new ways of thinking, knowing, and acting might seem too risky for teacher–students. The stance I took as a learner, with the delights and surprises of learning, was well worth the risk. The example given in this chapter—how I learned to change my pedagogical approach to one with a more balanced format from the teachers—also helped me reach my instructional goal for the course.

Develop the Trust and Intimacy of Connected Conversation

Although the fits and starts of genuine conversation often played havoc on my "classroom management" and "lesson plan flow," this discourse style helped me become a learner, and encouraged the safety necessary for the difficult work of broadening socialized frameworks for teaching. It also provided opportunities for class members to understand the reflective biases that have evolved from teachers' own biographies. Through the conversation, as we've seen in Thea's analyses of the course, narratives of experience emerged, where full selves, not just disembodied minds, became involved in a relational process of learning.

Develop a Deep Appreciation for the Wisdom of Practice That Graduate Students Hold as Experienced Teachers

It is easy to forget sometimes, taking the privileged position of "university professor," just how tentative our own knowledge is—and that our students are actually adults with a wealth of experience and insight into the questions of how and what to teach others. The act of respecting another's experience is at once personal and caring—and politically powerful. Being valued and listened to for what one knows is a powerful catalyst for listening to others and learning from them. As one teacher said to me, "I didn't agree with you at first [about the feminist perspective on teaching]. I made that clear in class!! You listened to me and I felt respected by you. That prompted my respect for your experience in return. In the end, I understood what you meant . . . and, I sort of hate to admit it, but I think understanding it has changed my life."

Commit to Staying in the Question Rather Than Finding Principled Answers

At one point in the book, Leslie reminded me that you couldn't teach anyone something they didn't really want to know. The hardest thing about the change in my practice was to let go of answers—even newly constructed ones that slipped back into my thinking after I'd become aware of the need to give them up!! My training goes deep to draw conclusions in terms of categorical dualisms and significant results. I had to remind myself over and over that such practices, though comfortable in that they bring a sense of "closure"—actually impede the process of learning to teach in messy classroom environments where there are real people with complex and even contradictory lives. Keeping the question(s) alive, fresh, changeable, and finding processes to achieve desired outcomes, rather than principles, helps me stay (as much as possible) pedagogically honest.

Share the Responsibility for Teaching

To begin to construct different epistemological frameworks for learning, it seems important to see that not only questions, but also roles and positions are flexible and that knowledge itself is questionable. Allowing for variation in pedagogical and evaluative styles, although risky compared to the familiar safety of total control, demonstrates (for me as well as for teachers) that there are many pedagogical paths for reflection.

Eliminate Traditional Evaluative Schemes

The style of one authoritative leader judging the learning of others seems to be a very poor model for transformative learning. Teachers are among the best in the world at playing "guess the professor's knowledge and give it back as close as possible in order to get a good evaluative mark" game. Making evaluation problematic—and an issue for consideration in the group was probably the most powerful feature of my pedagogy that freed teachers to question and learn—and to challenge me when my pedagogy was too limiting for them.

Maintain a Balance of Experiential and External Reflection

An important lesson for me in this chapter was one that had resurfaced from chapter 11 with preservice teachers: How to meet their need for external direction and still create a pedagogical atmosphere for self-direction and knowledge construction. After finding a variety of ways to do so that met the spirit of my quest for transformative learning, I now find that I should encourage the connective transformation of self (personal interpretation of experience) and text (standard or externally authored interpretation of experience) by viewing *all* knowledge as personally interesting, tentative, and open to critique. Although more difficult to critique if the knowledge comes from an external "authority," I learned that it was important to do so, particularly for teachers with years of experience in deferring to external authority.[2]

The stories across this book have illustrated conversations, reflections, and research on teaching differently and problematically. They suggest that the construction of feminist pedagogies is personal, complex, and multifaceted. Though often ignored as an important issue in discussions of teacher preparation or teachers' reflective stances, these narratives point out the need for greater attention to the social and political positioning of teaching, if teachers are to become emancipated to develop their full reflective potential as educators. Perhaps they also point to new directions for teachers and teacher–educators who want to construct pedagogies for urban classrooms. And ultimately, my hope is that the stories will also help transform the lives of children and their opportunities to learn multiple literacies in urban schools. In other words, I do not envision this chapter as an ending, but a beginning.

Our friend and colleague, Jean Clandinin, joins our sustained conversation with an "afterword" to follow.

ENDNOTES

[1] For clarity in this chapter, however, I'll refer to all class members as teachers.

[2] I can only hope this new "understanding" doesn't become my new answer for teacher preparation course work. I'll have to reread this chapter regularly to remind myself—or telephone Jennifer.

Afterword

D. JEAN CLANDININ

When Sam Hollingsworth, on behalf of this group of authors, asked me to write an afterword for their book, I was surprised and honored, but also thoughtful about how I might undertake the task. And I was thoughtful for many reasons. The first had to do with the task. What meaning does an afterword have in a book? A foreword sets the tone for the book, gives the sense of someone's reading of the book, and establishes for others the way that one reader read the book. It is a kind of readers' guide. An afterword seems to me to say more about engaging the readers of the book with my questions and my wonders about the book, that is, about my next questions. It suggests that in the ending of the book there is a beginning that leads forward into the next conversation.

An afterword seemed appropriate to the meaning I was making of this book for this is a book that acknowledges our lives are always works in progress. It is a book that acknowledges that learning to teach, teacher education, and teacher research are not activities that we "do" and then set aside in the form of codified knowledge. This is a book about living our lives as teachers, about engaging with children's lives, with their parents' lives, with other teachers' lives, and with university researchers' lives. The book speaks of knowledge embodied in each of us as persons living out our lives in schools. It speaks of knowledge as relational, as personal, as practical, as constructed, as reconstructed, and as open to other interpretations. It is a book that begs us to ask questions about our lives, about our knowing, about our practices. There are no answers to any of these questions in this book, but much that invites us to reflect on our lives.

That knowledge is relational, personal, practical, and embodied in authors as persons, is not the only thing talked about in the book. The book shows us how these authors hold such knowledge. We see how this group of authors came to tell their stories in a demonstration of their own process as they turn back on their words and stories in conversations. For readers accustomed to dipping in and out of books looking for the authors' main points and prescriptions, this will be frustrating, for even as I read chapters and made sense of what I read, the authors turned back on those chapters in other conversations to show me their process of coming to know.

This book is no mere valorization of teacher talk. The questions that are struggled with in these pages are ones that concern all of us in teacher education and in education. What does it mean to know? What does it mean to have a feminist perspective? How do we know what we know? Is it important to pay attention to our language? Does it matter if we use the language of class? This is thoughtful conversation about what it means to teach and to learn, to live educated lives in which these are the important questions. The book demonstrated for me that knowledge is not a "thing" that can be applied to my teaching, to my life. As I read the pages I felt validated that these were questions worth asking about my teaching, that it was important that I ask them about my own teaching, and that it was in my asking the question that I could come to know my teaching in more thoughtful ways.

I am currently part of a group that is also struggling to make sense of teacher research, teacher education, teaching. We are trying to sort through similar issues in our practice. We too struggle with trying to transform our practices and to learn about what kind of spaces we need in order to engage in these transformations of our knowing and of our practices. We have begun to write of needing spaces where we feel safe, feel that we are valued as persons, and feel that our ideas are going to be heard and responded to from an ethic of caring. I feel a resonance with these authors as they share their stories and conversations. They also speak of transformations of their lived and told stories and how their transformations came about as they engaged intensely with each other in conversation about practice. Some of our questions resonated with theirs. We are trying to figure out how the professional knowledge landscapes on which we work shape our lived and told stories. We are struggling with notions of competing and conflicting stories as ways to transform the professional knowledge landscapes of our schools and universities. If we each tell and retell our stories in community and conversation with each other, if we try to imagine new stories to be lived and told, perhaps our competing stories can lead to change and transformed practices.

Many times I felt like a participant in the conversations as I read the pages. For example, Karen leads the group in a conversation about what it would mean for her if she were to live and tell a story of herself as feminist. She was trying not to come up with a singular view of what this might mean, but to figure out a more informed way to tell her story. The group offers Karen an alternative story, what we might call a competing story. We have a window into how Karen struggles with how she might retell her own story from the thoughtful response of her colleagues. There are other examples of this group's attempts to nurture competing stories that are shared with us in these collaborative conversations. The telling of competing stories is encouraged for it is only in these competing stories that we begin to see new imaginative possibilities for transforming each of our practices. In teacher education this book shows us we have lived too long with singular visions and prescribed right answers.

As I read these pages I realized that what was important here was how the richness of these chapters resonated with me and helped me to see that I could learn from this process, so richly demonstrated. Telling and retelling my own stories could be enriched through reading their stories. What do I learn from hearing the stories of these teachers? I think about Leslie struggling to teach Aaron and I hear my own stories of struggling to figure out how to make connections with children. As I read Mary's account of teacher research I think of my friends Annie Davies, Pat Hogan, and Cheryl Craig and their work as teacher researchers. I know that I now think of my own teaching more from a teacher research perspective as a result of my conversations with Pat, Annie, and Cheryl, and from reading the stories of Mary and Leslie. As I read these stories, I wanted to take them to share with other teachers and to use them to think more carefully about my own teaching.

I felt a sense of the difficulty of teaching as I read Jennifer's story and Lisa's story. Even with the support and strength of this community, they moved out of the classroom to pursue teaching in other spaces. Perhaps our classrooms are not places where any of us can sustain our lives. What does that suggest for schooling? I am reminded again of the power of the "sacred" story of the hierarchy, of knowledge, of theory and practice that shapes the lives of all of us in teaching and teacher education, and, of course, shapes the lives of children.[1] The need for transformation in the sacred story that sets our moral horizons seems particularly urgent. When Jennifer urges us to consider how teachers living and telling competing stories of research in teaching will challenge the story told in teacher education, teaching, and research, I sense the promise for transformation. Jennifer says "And I think that our teaching does that. And our research does that, but we can't do it alone. We have to educate teachers differently; and teacher–educators differently." In these words I sense the power this book will have for teachers, student teachers, and teacher-educators to challenge the sacred story, to shift our moral horizons, and to allow for many stories of knowledge.

ENDNOTE

[1]The teacher–authors in this book engaged in long conversation after reading Jean's metaphor for teaching stories. They felt honored that she had read their simple stories in such universal terms. Jennifer was also confused about the word "competing." Leslie tried to help: "I interpret 'competing' as a story that intends to reach the same place as the 'sacred' story, but uses a different means." Anthony added: "I thought the terms referred to different stories, running side by side, with different processes. Like our stories, running parallel to "the knowledge base," they can intersect or inform each other, but if they conflict, the stories cross and run incompatible courses." Leslie added: "I think of our stories as those with heart and spirit. Perhaps they're the unseen 'sacred stores'." Jennifer concluded the conversation on the topic: "Yeah. I see what you mean. But I think I'll have a long talk about it with Jean, myself, at AERA.

REFERENCES

Ahlquist, R. (1989, April). *Developing our diverse voices: Critical pedagogy for a multicultural classroom*. Paper presented at the Annual Conference of the American Educational Research Association, San Francisco.

America the Violent. (August 22, 1993). *Time, 142* (8), 65–68.

Anderson, R. C., & Pearson, P. D. (1984). A schema-theoretic view of basic processes in reading comprehension. In P. D. Pearson (Ed.), *Handbook of teaching research* (pp. 829–864). New York: Longman.

Anderson, L. W., & Sosniak, L. A. (in press). *Bloom's taxonomy of educational objectives*. Chicago: National Society for the Study of Education.

Anyon, J. (1991). Intersections of gender and class: Accommodation and resistance by working-class and affluent females to contradictory sex-role ideologies. In S. Walker and L. Barton (Eds.), *Gender, class, and education* (pp. 19–37). London: Falmer Press.

Apple, M. W. (1985). Teaching and "women's work": A comparative historical and ideological analysis. *Teachers College Record, 86* (3), 461–481.

Arendt, H. (1974). *The human condition*. Chicago: University of Chicago Press.

Au, K. H. (1980). Participation structures in a reading lesson with Hawaiian children. *Anthropology and Education Quarterly, 11* (2), 91–115.

Au, K. H., & Jordan, C. (1981). Teaching reading to Hawaiian children: Finding a culturally appropriate solution. In H. T. Trueba, G. P. Guthrie, & K. H. Au (Eds.), *Culture and the bilingual classroom* (pp. 139–152). Rowley, MA: Newbury House.

Beams, B. (1986). *Teaching Gracie to read*. Unpublished class report, University of Texas, Austin.

Belenky, M. F., Clinchy, B. M., Goldberger, N. R., & Tarule, J. M. (1986). *Women's ways of knowing: The development of self, voice, and mind*. New York: Basic Books.

Bernstein, B. (1977). *Class, codes, and control. Volume I: Theoretical studies towards a sociology of language*. London: Routledge & Kegan Paul.

Berscheid, E. (1985). Interpersonal modes of knowing. In Elliot Eisner (Ed.), *Learning and teaching the ways of knowing*. Eighty-fourth Yearbook of the National Society for the Study of Education, Part II, pp. 60–76. Chicago, IL: University of Chicago Press.

Beyer, L. (1988). *Knowing and acting: Inquiry, ideology, and educational studies*. London: Falmer Press.

Bloome, D. (1989). Beyond access: An ethnographic study of reading and writing in a seventh grade classroom. In D. Bloome (Ed.), *Classrooms and literacy*. Norwood, NJ: Ablex.

Bradley, L., & Bryant, P. E. (1981). Categorizing sounds and learning to read—a causal connection. *Nature, 30* (3), 419–421.

Bransford, J. D. (1979). *Human cognition: Learning, understanding and remembering.* Belmont, CA: Wadsworth.

Brittan, A., & Maynard, M. (1984). *Sexism, racism, and oppression.* Oxford: Basil Blackwell.

Brophy, J. E., & Good, T. L. (1986). Teacher behavior and student achievement. In M. C. Wittrock (Ed.), *Handbook of research on teaching* (pp. 328–325). New York: Macmillan.

Buber, M. (1966). In Maurice Friedman (Ed.), *The knowledge of man.* London: George Allen and Unwin.

California State Department of Education (1987). *California English language arts framework.* Sacramento: State of California.

Cantrell, M. (1988). *A reading course examined.* Unpublished master's thesis. University of California, Berkeley.

Clandinin, D. J., & Connelly, F. M. (in press). The promise of collaborative research in the political context. In H. Socket & S. Hollingsworth (Eds.), *Teacher research and educational reform* (pp. 86–102) Chicago: National Society for the Study of Education.

Clandinin, D. J., Davies, A., Hogan, P., & Kennard, B. (1993). *Learning to teach, teaching to learn: Stories of collaboration in teacher education.* New York: Teachers College Press.

Clark, C. M., & Peterson, P. L. (1986). Teachers' thought processes. In M. Wittrock (Ed.) *Handbook of research on teaching. Part 2: Research on Teaching and Teachers* (3rd ed, pp. 255–296). New York: MacMillan.

Cochran-Smith, M., & Lytle, S. (1990). Research on teaching and teacher research: The issues that divide. *Educational Researcher, 19,* 2–11.

Coles, R. (1989). *The call of stories: Teaching and the moral imagination.* Boston: Houghton Mifflin.

Collins, J., & Michaels, S. (1981). The importance of conversational discourse strategies in the acquisition of literacy. *Proceedings of the Sixth Annual Meeting of the Berkeley Linguistics Society.* Berkeley, CA: Berkeley Linguistic Society.

Collins, M., & Tamarkin, C. (1982). *Marva Collin's way.* Chicago: J. P. Tarcher.

Connelly, F. M., & Clandinin, D. J. (1986). On narrative method: Personal philosophy and narrative unities in the story of teaching. *Journal of Research in Science Teaching, 23* (4), 293–310.

Connelly, F. M., & Clandinin, D J. (1990). Stories of experience and narrative inquiry. *Educational Researcher, 19* (4), 2–13.

Cook-Gumperz, J., & Gumperz, J., & Simon, H. (1981). *School-home ethnography project.* Final report to the National Institute of Education. Washington, DC: U.S. Dept. of Education.

Cuban, L. (1990). Reforming again, and again, and again. *Educational Researcher, 39* (3), 4–12.

de Beauvoir, S. (1952). *The second sex.* New York: Bantam.

Delpit, L. J. (1986). Skills and other dilemmas of a progressive Black educator. *Harvard Educational Review, 56* (4), 379–385.

Delpit, L. (1988). The silenced dialogue: Power and pedagogy in educating other people's children. *Harvard Educational Review, 58,* 280–298.

Dewey, J. (1897/1962). My pedagogic creed. Cited in J. Bruner, *On knowing: Essays for the left hand*. Cambridge: Harvard University Press.

Donovan, J. (1988). *Feminist theory: The intellectual traditions of American feminism*. New York: Continuum.

Doyle, D. P. (1990). Teacher choice: Does it have a future? In W. L. Boyd, & H. J. Walberg (Eds.), *Choice in education: Potential and problems* (pp. 95–120). Berkeley, CA: McCutchan.

Doyle, W. (1983). Academic work. *Review of Educational Research, 53* (2), 159–199.

Doyle, W., & Carter, K. (1984). Academic tasks in classrooms. *Curriculum Inquiry, 14* (2), 129–149.

Doyle, W., & Carter, K. (1987). Choosing the means of instruction. In V. R. Koehler (Ed.), *Educator's handbook: A research perspective*. New York: Longman.

Drake, S. (1992). *Developing an integrated curriculum using the story model*. Toronto, Ontario, The Ontario Institute for Studies in Education Press.

Duffy, G., & Roehler, L. (1989). The tension between information-giving and mediation: Perspectives on instructional explanation and teacher change. In J. Brophy (Ed.), *Advances in research on teaching* (Vol. 1, pp. 1–34). New York: JAI Press.

Dybdahl, M. (1990, December). *Watching Mike and A.J.: A case study of this Filipino pair's responses to literature*. Paper presented at the Annual Meeting of the National Reading Conference, Miami.

Dybdahl, M., & Hollingsworth, S. (1989, March). *Literature and literacy: Supporting new teachers and culturally diverse learners (a conversation between Mary and Sam)*. Paper presented to the California Reading Association, San Jose.

Ekwall, E.E. (1979). *Ekwall reading inventory*. Boston: Allyn and Bacon.

Ellsworth, E. (1989). Why doesn't this feel empowering? Working through the repressive myths of critical pedagogy. *Harvard Educational Review, 59* (3), 297–324.

Feiman-Nemser, S. & Buchmann, M. (1985). The pitfalls of experience in teacher preparation. *Teachers College Record, 87* (1), 54–65.

Ferguson, A. (1989). A feminist aspect theory of the self. In A. Garry and M. Pearsall, *Women, knowledge and reality: Explorations in feminist philosophy*. Boston: Unwin Hyman.

Fine, M. (1990). *Framing dropouts*. Albany: State University of New York Press.

Flax, J. (1990). *Thinking fragments: Psychoanalysis, feminism, and postmodernism in the contemporary west*. Berkeley: University of California Press.

Ford-Slack, P.J. (1993, April). *The vampire chronicles: Academia and the politics of gender*. Readers theatre presented at the Annual Meeting of the American Educational Research Association, Atlanta.

Foucault, M. (1980). *Power/knowledge: Selected interviews and other writings: 1972–1977*. Trans. C. Gordon, L. Marshall, J. Mephan, and K. Soper. New York: Pantheon.

Freire, P. (1988). *Pedagogy of the oppressed*. New York: Continuum.

Gallagher, P. (1992, April). *Toward a habit of inquiry: Teacher questions and the "sensing of difficulty."* Paper presented at the Annual Meeting of the American Educational Research Association, San Francisco.

Gallego, M. & Hollingsworth, S. (1992). Multiple literacies: Teachers' evolving perceptions. *Language Arts, 69* (3), 206–213.

Gilligan, C. (1982). *In a different voice: Psychological theory and women's development.* Cambridge, MA: Harvard University Press.

Gilman, C. P. (1988). The home (1903). In J. Donovan (Ed.), *Feminist theory: The intellectual traditions of American feminism.* New York: Continuum.

Gilmore, P. (1987). Sulking, stepping and tracking: The effects of attitude assignment on access to literacy. In D. Bloome (Ed.), *Literacy and schooling.* Norwood, NJ: Ablex.

Giroux, H. A. (1988). *Teachers as intellectuals.* Granby, MA: Bergin & Garvey.

Gitlin, A., Bringhurst, K., Burns, M., Cooley, V., Myers, B., Price, K., Russell, R., & Tiess, P. (1992). *Teachers' voices for school change: An introduction to educative research.* New York: Teachers College Press.

Glaser, B. G., & Strauss, A. L. (1967). *The discovery of grounded theory: Strategies for qualitative research.* New York: Aldine De Gruyter.

Glesne, C. E. (1991). Yet another role? The teacher as researcher. *Action in Teacher Education, 13* (1), p. 11.

Goldberg, N. (1990). *Wild mind: Living the writer's life.* New York: Bantam.

Gough, P. B., & Hillinger, M. L. (1980). Learning to read as an unnatural act. *Bulletin of the Orgton Society, 30*, 93–113.

Gramsci, A. (1971). *Selections from the prison notebooks of Antonio Gramsci.* Q. Hoare (Ed.) and G. Smith (Trans.). New York: International Publishers.

Gray, J. (1988). *The Bay Area Writing Project and the National Writing Project.* Berkeley: University of California.

Greene, M. (1979). Teaching as personal reality. In A. Liebermann & L. Miller (Eds.), *New perspectives for staff development.* New York: Teachers College Press.

Greene, M. (1988). *The dialectic of freedom.* New York: Teachers College Press.

Grossman, P. L. (1990). *The making of a teacher: Teacher knowledge and teacher education.* New York: Teachers College Press.

Gumperz, J., & Tannen, D. (1979). Individual and social differences in language use. In C. Filmore (Ed.), *Individual differences in language ability and language behavior.* New York: Academic Press.

Guszak, J. F. (1985). *Diagnostic reading instruction in the elementary school* (3rd ed.). New York: Harper & Row.

Harding, S. (1987). *Feminism and methodology.* Bloomington, IN: Indiana University Press.

Harding, S. (1990). Whose science: Whose knowledge? Thinking from women's lives. Ithaca, NY: Cornell University Press.

Harste, J. C. (1990). The future of whole language. *Elementary School Journal, 90*, 243–249.

Hartsock, N. (1987). The feminist standpoint: Developing the ground for a specifically feminist historical materialism (pp. 157–180). In S. Harding (Ed.), *Feminism and methodology: Social science issues.* Bloomington, IN: Indiana University Press.

Heath, S. B. (1983). *Ways with words: Language, life and work in communities and classrooms.* Cambridge, England: Cambridge University Press.

Helle, A. P. (1991). Reading women's autobiographies: A map of reconstructed knowing. In C. Witherell and N. Noddings (Eds.), *Stories lives tell: Narrative and dialogue in education* (pp. 48–66). New York: Teachers College Press.

Herbst, J. (1989). *And sadly teach: Teacher education and professionalization in American culture.* Madison, WI: University of Wisconsin.

Hilliard, A. G. (1974). A helping experience in African education: Implications for cross-cultural work in the U.S. *Journal of Non-White Concerns in Personnel and Guidance, 2,* 733–735.

Hirschman, A. O. (1970). *Exit, voice and loyalty: Response to decline in firms, organizations and states.* Cambridge, MA: Harvard University Press.

Hollingsworth, S. (1988). Making field-based programs work: A three-level approach to reading education. *Journal of Teacher Education, 39* (4), 28–37.

Hollingsworth, S. (1989a). Learning to teach reading: Suggestions for preservice and inservice educators. *Reading Teacher, 42,* 698–702.

Hollingsworth, S. (1989b). Prior beliefs and cognitive change in learning to teach. *American Educational Research Journal, 26* (2), 160–189.

Hollingsworth, S. (1989c). *The role of personal theory in culturally-diverse classrooms: Smartenin' up the standard culture of school.* Paper presented to Phi Delta Kappa, University of San Francisco.

Hollingsworth, S. (1992). Learning to teach literacy through collaborative conversation: A feminist approach. *American Educational Research Journal, 29* (2), 373–404.

Hollingsworth, S., & Dybdahl, M. (1991). *Learning to teach literature: Structuring conversations to free children's responses to text* (Research Rep. No. 201). Michigan State University, Institute for Research on Teaching, Center for the Learning and Teaching of Elementary Subjects, East Lansing, MI.

Hollingsworth, S., Dybdahl, M., & Minarik, L. (1993). By chart and chance and passion: Learning to teach through relational knowing. *Curriculum Inquiry, 23* (1), 5–36.

Hollingsworth, S., Gallagher, P., Maestre, T., Richert, A., & Sockett, H. (1992, February). *Educating teacher educators: A feminist pedagogy.* Annual meeting of the American Association of Colleges of Teacher Educators, San Antonio.

Hollingsworth, S., & Minarik, L. (1991). *Choice, risk and teacher voice: Closing the distance between public perceptions and private realities of schooling.* (Research Rep. No.134). Michigan State University, Institute for Research on Teaching, Center for the Learning and Teaching of Elementary Subjects, East Lansing, MI.

Hollingsworth, S., Minarik, L., & Teel, K. (1990). *Learning to teach Aaron.* Paper presented at the Annual Conference of the International Reading Association, Atlanta. (Research Rep. No. 204.) Institute for Research on Teaching, Michigan State University, East Lansing, MI.

Hollingsworth, S., & Sockett, H. (1994). Teacher research and educational reform: An introduction. In S. Hollingsworth and H. Sockett (Eds.), *Teacher research and educational reform* (pp. 1–20). Chicago: National Society for the Study of Education.

Hollingsworth, S., and Teel, K. (1991). Learning to teach reading in secondary math and science. *Journal of Reading, 35* (3), 190–195.

Hollingsworth, S., Teel, K., & Minarik, L. (1992). Listening for Aaron: A teacher's story about modifying a literature-based approach to literacy to accommodate a young male's voice. *Journal of Teacher Education, 43* (2), 83–95.

Horney, K. (1937). *The neurotic personality of our time.* New York: Norton.

Horney, K. (1950). *Neurosis and human growth.* New York: Norton.

Jacobs, H. (1989). *Interdisciplinary curriculum: Design and implementation.* Alexandria, VA: Association for Supervision and Curriculum Development.

Jaggar, A. M. (1989). Love and knowledge: Emotion in feminist epistemology. In A. Garry & M. Pearsall, (Eds.), *Women, knowledge and reality: Explorations in feminist philosophy.* Boston: Unwin Hyman.

Jersild, A. T. (1955). *When teachers face themselves.* New York: Teachers' College Press.

Kennedy, M. M. (1989). *Means and ends in professional education.* (Report No. IP 89-3). East Lansing, MI: National Center for Research on Teacher Learning.

Kozol, J. (1991). *Savage inequalities: Children in America's schools.* New York: Crown.

Laberge, D., & Samuels, S. J. (1974). Toward a theory of automatic information processing in reading. *Cognitive Psychology, 6,* 293–323.

Laird, S. (1988). Reforming "Women's true profession": A case for "feminist pedagogy" in teacher education. *Harvard Educational Review, 58,* (4), 449–463.

Langer, J. A. (1987). A sociocognitive perspective on literacy. In J. A. Langer (Ed.), *Language, literacy and culture: Issues of society and schooling* (pp. 1–20). Norwood, NJ: Ablex.

Lather, P. (1991). *Getting smart: Feminist research and pedagogy with/in the post-modern.* New York: Routledge.

Leck, G. M. (1987). Review article—Feminist pedagogy, liberation theory, and the traditional schooling paradigm. *Educational Theory, 37* (3), 343–355.

Leinhardt, G., & Greeno, J. (April, 1983). *The cognitive skill of teaching.* Paper presented at the annual meeting of the American Educational Research Association, Montreal, Canada.

Lewis, M., & Simon R. (1986) A discourse not intended for her: Learning and teaching within patriarchy. *Harvard Educational Review, 56* (4), 457–472.

Lieberman, A., & Miller, L. (in press). Problems and possibilities of institutionalizing teacher research. In S. Hollingsworth and H. Sockett (Eds.), *Teacher research and educational reform.* National Society of Education Yearbook.

Liston, D. P., & Zeichner, K. M. (1991). *Teacher education and the social conditions of schooling.* New York: Routledge.

Little, J. W. (1990). The persistence of privacy: Autonomy and initiative in teachers' professional relations. *Teachers College Record, 91* (4), 509–536.

Lorde, A. (1984). *Sister outsider.* Freedom, CA: Crossing Press.

Lyons, N. (1990). Dilemmas of knowing: Ethical and epistemological dimensions of teachers' work and development. *Harvard Educational Review, 70* (2), 159–180.

Martin, J. R. (1981). The ideal of the educated person. *Educational Theory, 31* (2).

Mehan, H. (1974). Accomplishing classroom lessons. In A. V. Cicourel, K. H. Jennings, S. H. M. Jennings, K. C. W. Leither, R. McKay, J. Mehan, & D. Roth (Eds.) *Language use and school performance.* New York: Academic Press.

Middleton, S. (1993). *Educating feminists.* New York: Teachers College Press.

Miller, J. L. (1990). *Creating spaces and finding voices: Teachers collaborating for empowerment.* Albany: State University of New York Press.

Minarik, L. (1991). *Thinking about teaching: Sharing our perspectives* (pp. 1–2). Berkeley, CA: University of California.

Minarik, L. T. (1992, November). *Collaboration as a means of learning to teach.* Paper presented at the College of Teachers Autumn Forum, Vancouver, British Columbia.

Mishler, E. G. (1986). *Research interviewing: Context and narrative.* Cambridge, MA: Harvard University Press.

Mitchell, C., & Weiler, K. (1991). *Rewriting literacy: Culture and the discourse of the other.* Toronto, Ontario: The Ontario Institute for Studies in Education Press.

Murray, D. E. (1992). *Diversity as resource: Redefining cultural literacy.* Alexandria, VA: Teachers of English to Speakers of Other Languages.

Nemser, S. (1983). Learning to teach. In L. Shulman & G. Sykes (Eds.), *Handbook of teaching and policy.* New York: Longman.

Nespor, J., & Barylske, J. (1991). Narrative discourse and teacher knowledge. In *American Education Research Association Journal, 28* (4), pp. 805–823.

Nias, J. (1989). *Primary teachers talking: A study of teaching as work.* New York: Routledge.

Nielsen, J. Mc. (1990). *Feminist research methods: Exemplary readings in the social sciences.* Boulder, CO: Westview Press.

Noddings, N. (1984). *Caring: A feminine approach to ethics and moral education.* Berkeley, CA: University of California Press.

Noddings, N. (1986). Fidelity in teaching, teacher education, and research for teaching. *Harvard Educational Review, 56* (4), 496–509.

Noddings, N. (1992). *The challenge to care in schools.* New York: Teachers College Press.

Noddings, N., & Shore, Paul J. (1984). *Awakening the inner eye: Intuition in education.* New York: Teachers College Press.

Ogbu, J. (1979). Social stratification and the socialization of competence. *Anthropology and Education Quarterly, 10,* 3–20.

Paley, V. G. (1979). *White teacher.* Cambridge, MA: Harvard University Press.

Paley, V. G. (1990). *The boy who would be a helicopter: The uses of storytelling in the classroom.* Cambridge, MA: Harvard University Press.

Piaget, J. (1961, March). The stages of intellectual development of the child. *Bulletin of the Menninger School of Psychiatry,* 261–289.

Raffel, L. (1990, April). *Reflections on learning to teach: A beginning teacher's view.* Paper presented at the annual meeting of the American Educational Research Association, Boston.

Raphael, T., & Englert, C. S. (1990). Writing and reading: Partners in constructing meaning. *Reading-Teacher, 43* (6), 338–400.

Reinharz, S. (1992). *Feminist methods in social research.* Oxford, England: Oxford University Press.

Rich, A. (1985). Taking women students seriously. In M. Culley and C. Portuges (Eds.), *Gendered subjects: The dynamics of feminist teaching.* Boston: Routledge & Kegan Paul.

Richert, A. (1992). Using teacher cases to enhance reflection. In A. Liebermann (Ed.), *Staff Development* (2nd ed.). New York: Teachers College Press.

Rorty, (1979). *Philosophy and the mirror of nature.* Princeton: Princeton University Press.

Rose, M. (1989). *Lives on the boundary.* New York: The Free Press/Macmillan

Rosenshine, B. V. (1983). Teaching functions in instructional programs. *Elementary School Journal, 84* (4), 335–351.

Sadker, M. P., & Sadker, D. M. (1985, March), Sexism in the schoolroom of the 80's. *Psychology Today,* 54–57.

Schaef, A. W. (1981). *Women's reality: An emerging female system in a white male society.* San Francisco: Harper and Row.

Schon, Donald A. (1983). *The reflective practitioner: How professionals think in action.* New York: Basic Books.

Schultz, A. (1967). *The phenomenology of the social world* (G. Walsh & F. Lehnert, Trans.) Evanston, IL: Northwestern University Press.

Scollon, R., & Scollon, S. (1981). *Narrative, literacy and face in interethnic communication.* Norwood, NJ: Ablex.

Shulman, L. S. (1986). Those who understand: Knowledge growth in teaching. *Educational Researcher, 15* (2), 4–21.

Simon, R. I. (1992). *Teaching against the grain: Texts for a pedagogy of possibility.* Toronto, Ontario: Ontario Institute for Studies in Education Press.

Smith, D. (1990). *The conceptual practices of power: A feminist sociology of knowledge.* Toronto: University of Toronto Press.

Stanley, L. (1990). Feminist praxis: *Research, theory and epistemology in feminist sociology.* London: Routledge and Kegan Paul.

Teel, K. (1993). *Addressing "low achievement" among inner-city African-American middle school students: A teacher researcher's classroom study.* Unpublished dissertation. University of California, Berkeley.

Teel, K., & Minarik, L. (1990). *Learning to teach literacy to culturally-diverse children: A longitudinal collaborative study.* Paper presented at the annual meeting of the American Educational Research Association, Boston.

Tierney, R. (1991). Presidential address to National Reading Conference, Miami, FL.

Van Maanen, J. (1988). *Tales of the field: On writing ethnography.* Chicago: University of Chicago Press.

Van Maanen, J. (1990). *Researching lived experience: Human science for an actional sensitive pedagogy.* New York: SUNY Press.

Vygotsky, Lev (1978). *Thought and language.* Cambridge, MA: MIT Press.

Walmsley, S., & Walp, T. (1990). Toward an integrated language arts curriculum in elementary school: Philosophy, practice, and implications. *The Elementary School Journal,* 123–140.

Warner, S. A. (1963). *Teacher.* New York: Simon and Schuster.

Weiler, K. (1988). *Women teaching for change: Gender, class and power.* South Hadley, MA: Bergin & Garvey.

Westkott, M. (1979). Feminist criticism of the social sciences. *Harvard Educational Review, 49* (4), 422–430.

Wittrock, M. C. (1986). *Handbook of research on teaching* (3rd ed.). New York: Macmillan.

Zeichner, K. M. (in press). Personal renewal and social construction through teacher research. In S. Hollingsworth & H. Sockett (Eds.), *Teacher education and educational reform*. Chicago: National Society for the Study of Education.

Zeichner, K., & Gore, J. (1990). Teacher socialization. In W. R. Houston, M. Haberman, & J. Sikula (Eds.), *Handbook of research on teacher education* (pp. 329–348). New York: Macmillan.

Index

About the Authors

D. JEAN CLANDININ is an associate professor and director of the Centre for Research for Teacher Education and Development at the University of Alberta, Edmonton, Canada. Jean is a former teacher, counselor, and school psychologist. She has worked in educational research with teachers and teacher educators for the past 15 years. She is the author and coauthor of several books: With P. Michael Connelly she coauthored *Teachers as Curriculum Planners: Narratives of Experience* (Teachers College Press, 1988); and with Pat Hogan, Annie Davies, and Barbara Kennard, *Learning to Teach: Teaching to Learn. Stories of Collaboration in Teacher Education* (Teachers College Press, 1993). She is currently working on two new books with P. Michael Connelley entitled *Narrative and Education*, and *Teachers' Professional Knowledge Landscapes*. Jean is the 1993 winner of the American Educational Research Association Raymond B. Cattell Early Career Award.

ANTHONY CODY was born in 1958 and raised in Berkeley, California. He is the son of the founders of the well-known local bookstore, Cody's Books. He went through Berkeley Public Schools during the implementation of voluntary desegregation in the late '60s. He learned welding at a local community college and worked in foundries for 5 years. Anthony returned to the University of California, Berkeley, to earn his B.S. in environmental education and his secondary teaching credential. He recently spent a month in the Ecuadorian rain forest doing research and curriculum development with local teachers. His credentials include both life and physical science. Additionally, he has a language development specialist credential. He is bilingual (Spanish/English) and has taught at the same junior high school in Oakland, California since 1987. Mr. Cody is married and has two sons.

JENNIFER DAVIS-SMALLWOOD earned her undergraduate degree at the University of California at Santa Cruz. Upon completion of an economics major she entered the construction trades as a heavy equipment operator. After 8 years the ritualized racism and sexism of the trades had this mixed heritage (African-American, Native-American, and French-American) woman seeking out a more socially meaningful, and hopefully progressive, profession—teaching. After completing a credential program at the University of California, Berkeley, Jennifer taught 2 years at an inner-city school in Vallejo, California. Low pay and the need to interact with children in a less restrictive environment led her out of the classroom and back to construction in Berkeley, where she lives with her partner, Ruth. With rainy season time off, she is currently developing a farm program where children will feel safe to develop and use community, interdependent, and individual living skills.

MARY DYBDAHL is a third/fourth grade teacher in an inner city school in Vallejo, California. She came to teaching after 10 years in the electronic industry. She holds a masters degree in education from the University of California, Berkeley. In addition to her classroom work, Mary is involved in teacher research with a focus on assessment and teaching reading. She is also an activist in the teacher's union. Mary lives in Richmond, California with her partner and a house full of pets. When she's not absolutely exhausted she enjoys low-impact gardening and rock-n-roll.

PAT GALLAGHER taught French to 8-year-olds in Indiana, from whom she learned that teaching can be fun. She helped preschoolers in Maine who taught her that painting, playing, and singing are serious work. She taught first graders in New Hampshire who showed her the magic of learning to read. She taught British, East Indian, West Indian, and Maltese children in a primary school in London who showed her the power of family grouping and integrated curriculum in a multicultural classroom. And, for the past 20 years, Pat has worked with teachers-in-training who have taught her to listen, to challenge, and to tell stories. "They tell me it's my stories they remember when they're out there teaching on their own."

MARGARET GALLEGO is an assistant professor of education at Michigan State University. As director of La Clase Magica, a community-based literacy project, she is exploring the use of out-of-school contexts to inform in-school curricular change, literacy instruction, and educational reform. She has also co-taught social studies and English in an urban middle school in Michigan, studying the influence of gender on heterogeneous groups. Before joining the academy, she taught elementary school children in bilingual and English as a second language (ESL) classes in the southwest. Margaret Gallego holds a B.A. in bilingual elementary education, an M.Ed. in reading, and a Ph.D. in reading, language and culture—all from the University of Arizona When not interacting with community children or teaching, she and her husband Jeff are enjoying the wonders of their first year of parenthood with daughter Esmé Allison.

SANDRA HOLLINGSWORTH is an associate professor of education at Michigan State University. She recently joined the MSU staff from the University of California at Berkeley, where she directed this collaborative study of learning to teach urban literacy. Before that time, she held joint positions at a public school and a university in Texas where, as director of a literacy program for children of migrant farm workers, she led field-based literacy seminars for both preservice and inservice educators. Recently, Hollingsworth taught first-hour, 8th-grade world history, working with teachers at an inner-city middle school in Michigan as they integrated social studies curriculum with literacy processes and cultural awareness to increase students' success in school. Hollingsworth's current interests involve using principles of feminist pedagogy and narrative analysis to assist teachers who are researching their own instructional practices. She has spent part of the last 3 years in Asia teaching educators in international schools. "Sam" Hollingsworth holds a B.A. in history, an M.Ed. in reading from the University of Montana, and a Ph.D. in reading and teacher education from the University of Texas at Austin. She also takes a considerable amount of time out of her academic life for backpacking, folk dancing, blues guitar, and writing poetry.

THEODORA MAESTRE is a teacher in Oakland, California. She has taught grades 1 through 6 for over 20 years. She has also been a learning styles consultant with Bernice McCarthy's 4Mat System since 1985. In addition, she currently teaches a social studies curriculum course at St. Mary's College in Moraga, California. In her spare time, she likes to hike the regional park trails with her grandchildren, Elizabeth and Alex. With her friend Kathleen Jones, she has recently embarked on a project to hike around San Francisco Bay and would like to complete this goal, along with her doctoral dissertation at the University of California, Berkeley, by the end of the summer.

LESLIE TURNER MINARIK is currently teaching at Highland Elementary School, in Richmond, California, located in the San Francisco Bay area. Her class of 31 students has also been designated as "Sheltered English" (students for whom English is their second language) and "Full Inclusion" (a pilot program operated in conjunction with the Special Education Department at her site). Her undergraduate work was done at the University of California, Santa Barbara, and the University of Bordeaux, France. For 10 years she worked in sales administration for several Bay Area publishing companies. In 1987 she received her elementary teaching credential from the University of California, Berkeley. She is currently working on her language development credential. Leslie credits her most important teaching skills to the 7 years of support from the Learning To Teach Group, her husband, and an outstanding core group of teachers at her school with whom she has had the fortune to spend 6 years, including breakfasts, lunches, and dinners. She is married and has a daughter in the sixth grade.

LISA RAFFEL currently works at California Tomorrow, a nonprofit organization located in San Francisco. The organization is engaged in educational research, policy, and technical assistance work, in an effort to integrate racial, cultural, and linguistic diversity in California. With a team of colleagues from California Tomorrow, Lisa is finishing a 2-year research project and publication on restructuring and its relationship to issues of diversity and equity. Previously, Lisa worked as a teaching and program assistant in Peace Studies at Colgate University, and before that as a fourth and fifth grade teacher in Vallejo, California. She received her M.A.. in education, her multiple subject credential, and her B.A. in peace studies all from the University of California, Berkeley.

N. SUZANNE STANDERFORD has been a teacher, researcher and teacher–educator for the last 20 years. She has taught all grades in the elementary school and currently teachers undergraduate and graduate courses in literacy instruction at Northern Michigan University. She received her Ph.D. from Michigan State University in curriculum, teaching, and educational policy, focusing on teacher learning, literacy instruction, and policy as a means of improving instruction in the elementary schools. Dr. Standerford is also certified as an elementary administrator and a central office administrator for K–12 schools. Her current research interests involve alternative approaches to teacher education, which develop stronger voices in pre-service teacher candidates.

KAREN MANHEIM TEEL teaches seventh-grade World History at Portola Middle School in the West Contra Costa County School District in California, where she has been a teacher for 24 years. During the period from 1983 to 1985, Karen lived in Japan with her husband and three children and for part of that time taught English at a Japanese high school. Her experiences in Asia had a strong influence on her awareness of cultural diversity and led to her commitment to validate it in the classroom.

In the Spring, 1993, Karen received an Ed.D. degree from the University of California, Berkeley, where she had also received her B.A. and M.A. degrees and her teaching credential. Currently, Karen is a visiting scholar at U.C. Berkeley and is continuing with her classroom research. Her interests are teacher research, teacher education, and achievement motivation, especially among "low-achieving," inner-city African-American students.